Heal my heart and make it clean
Open up my eyes to the things unseen
Show me how to love like You have loved me

Break my heart from what breaks Yours
Everything I am for Your Kingdom's cause
As I walk from nothing to eternity

Hosanna, Hosanna
Hosanna in the highest
Hosanna, Hosanna
Hosanna in the highest

(*Hosanna*, Hillsong United[1])

All That is Seen and Unseen

A Journey Through the Book of Revelation

DR. LEE ANN B. MARINO, PH.D., D.MIN., D.D.

All That is Seen and Unseen
A Journey Through the Book of Revelation

DR. LEE ANN B. MARINO, PH.D., D.MIN., D.D.

Published by:
Righteous Pen Publications
(An imprint of The Righteous Pen Publications Group)
www.righteouspenpublications.com

Unless otherwise noted, Scriptures taken from the Holy Bible, New International Version ®, NIV® (1984), Copyright © 1973, 1978, 1984, 2011 by Biblica, Inc.™ Used by permission of Zondervan. All rights reserved worldwide.

All passages marked NLT are taken from the Holy Bible, New Living Translation copyright © 1996, 2004, 2007 by the Tyndale House Foundation. Used by permission of Tyndale House Publishers, Inc., Carol Stream, Illinois 60188. All rights reserved.

All passages marked NASB are taken from *The New American Standard Bible®,* Copyright © 1960, 1962, 1963, 1968, 1971, 1972, 1973, 1975, 1977, 1995 by The Lockman Foundation. Used by permission.

All passages marked KJV are taken from the Holy Bible, Authorized King James Version, Public Domain.

All passages marked EXB are from The Expanded Bible. Copyright ©2011 by Thomas Nelson. Used by permission. All rights reserved.

All passages marked AMPC are taken from The Amplified® Bible Classic Edition, Copyright © 1954, 1958, 1962, 1964, 1965, 1987 by The Lockman Foundation. Used by permission." (www.Lockman.org)

Cover and interior photos are in the Public Domain.

Book Classification: Books > Religion & Spirituality > Christian Books & Bibles > Bible Study & Reference > Commentaries > New Testament > Revelation.

Copyright © 2015, 2022, 2025 by Dr. Lee Ann B. Marino.

ISBN: 1940197279
13-Digit: 978-1-940197-27-2

Printed in the United States of America.

Table of Contents

Acknowledgements

It is probably not a shock to others who do not write to learn that, as a writer, we find writing different books to be a different experience each time. Writing on Revelation was no different. With each new challenge, each new pursuit, it seems that the writing process is a little unique, each with its own understandings and perspectives. I am always so glad for the opportunity to write on each book of the Bible, and to present the unique words and thoughts God gives to me through this process.

I thank everyone for forbearing with me while I undertook the process to write this commentary on Revelation, as it was the longest book of the Bible I have sought to write about and it took extended time, study, and research to complete it, far exceeding commentaries I have done in the past. I am so appreciative to those who are covered by this ministry, those closest to me, and those who are friends, for enduring through this process and who encouraged me to do it even when it got hard, I got tired, and I decided I was never going to read the book of Revelation ever again (I have since changed my mind, but nonetheless).

Above all, I thank and acknowledge Jesus Christ, the Word made flesh, the *Logos*, for revealing Himself to me in my life and for revealing so much to me about the mystical experience as I studied the work of Revelation. In studying His revelation to us, I received His revelation to me. Forever and ever, long into eternity, I shall forever be grateful for that.

Preface

Unlike other commentaries I have written to this point, the book of Revelation is not an uncommonly referenced book of the Bible in Christianity today. If anything, it is used so often, it is the official "go-to" reference for any eschatological reference that cannot be clearly or easily explained elsewhere in the Scriptures. When someone wants to proclaim anything unclear, anything questionable, or anything a bit muddled, Revelation is their book to run to. Riddled with imagery and terminology unfamiliar to believers today, it seems anyone can make the book of Revelation say whatever they want it to say if they try hard enough.

I've heard people argue about Revelation for years, to the point where the arguments became rather ugly. Thus, me being me, I avoided teaching, writing, and preaching on Revelation for a good part of my ministry. I do not desire to join the verse-by-verse debate of the book, arguing over its contents with other individuals. The point of Revelation always seems to get lost as people use it to prove themselves right instead of reading it and examining it on its own merit.

To date, the only pulpit commentary I have ever heard on the book of Revelation has been on television shows, watching the preachers preoccupied with the end times huff, puff, and bluster over its contents. As most average pulpit preachers today do not have a lot of theological training behind them, most take their cues from more popular preachers, recycling much eschatological teaching, without any consideration if what is spoken is true, or not. Most television "end times" preachers move so fast, speak with such vigor, and get so "into things" that it is hard to follow their exact precepts as they teach on these matters. Watching them claim what they teach is correct on matters and events that have not yet even happened is entertaining, to say the least, and almost dangerous, to say the worst. Analyzing commentary that is highly symbolic that has yet to come to pass within their claims ventures into dangerous territory, as evident in the way they casually make parts of the symbolism literal and other parts of it...mean whatever they want it to mean.

In this commentary, I strive to see Revelation in a symbolic understanding and from a mystical perspective, seeing it as an unveiling of all things relating to salvation history. Within the book of Revelation, we see the whole of salvation history, from eternity past to eternity future. It is the testimony of the Alpha and Omega, the one who was there in the beginning, and the one Who will be there in the end; the one Who, in His very existence, is both the beginning and the end, the promise of eternity, the promise of life that is one and the same, united with Him. It is a message to the churches of Asia and the church of all time, an unveiling of all things seen and unseen, of all promises wrought and all promises to come. It is much, much more than a writing meant to plug in current headlines and support vague and strange opinions based on the traditions of men.

Revelation is literally that: a revelation of something hidden, something covered up that has been uncovered in bits and pieces, in a way that would have been readily understood by believers in the first century. As believers back then believed Jesus would return in their lifetimes, nobody thought to write a commentary on the symbolism for subsequent generations. Just like believers today, nobody's foresight was beyond its own generation, considering that an interpretation may be necessary beyond what was seen and heard in that time.

Even though the symbolism might be a challenge to us today, the concept of Revelation (and all the apocalypses written in the early church, whether canonical or not) remains the same: Jesus wants to unveil salvation history to us, its purposes and points; things that have come, things that are to come, and things that will forever be. Revelation is a word to all of us: to leaders, to laity, to believers. It is a call to look at the church, to look at the world, and to be people knowledgeable about prophecy, understanding its cyclical nature, as history repeats itself and provides prominent clues about where we shall find ourselves when the end meets the beginning, once again.

From this commentary, I pray that this journey into the Kingdom: past, present, future, and eternal shall bring forth revelation on the prophetic nature of God's church. We are not here to call forth cars and houses out of the sky, but to make an eternal, spiritual impact on the world. Just as the various churches in the first century were losing their perspective, so too God wants us to gain our perspective in a world – and church – lost and blinded by idolatry, materialism and vanity.

The Scroll and

5 Then I saw i
sealed[t] with

break the seals an

scroll or even loo

scroll or look insi

dah, the Root of D

[6]Then I saw a L
by the four living cr
its[a] of God sent out
on the throne.[1] [1]An
before the Lamb. Eac

JESUS
IS ALWAYS
ABLE TO
OVERCOME

G

Introduction

About the Book of Revelation

What does God desire to unveil to His saints about the nature of the church, past, present, and future? Though often used in many different contexts, the book of Revelation is a message, a literal revelation about things God desires the church to know as it continues its mission into eternity. It is a book about authority, the shifting of paradigms, and the choices that each believer makes to align with God's Kingdom or align with the world. Within the book of Revelation, there are several things of which we should take note:

- Christ is the Head of the church because He is the Head of all things; the Alpha and Omega, present from the beginning to the end.

- The presence of the Kingdom of God in salvation history: past, present, and future.

- The structure of authority within the church on earth and the authority structure in heaven – and the way that the two overlap into the eternal nature of the Kingdom.

- The balance of encouragement and discipline present in the churches addressed in Revelation.

- Clear visions of heaven brought forth to echo authority and the impact of the message as from heaven.

- The imagery present in both sealing and multitudes; censers, trumpets, scrolls, angels (messengers), and witnesses.

- The relevance of the Two Witnesses, the woman, the dragon, beasts, plagues, and the waters.

- Why the time for the harvest is essential and how the believers of the Kingdom play a part in that harvest.

- The purpose – and role – of God's wrath upon the earth.

- Babylon and the "prostitute" on the beast, and why Babylon and a prostitute come up before the time of fall and victory.

- The thousand years, judgment, and the new heavens, New Jerusalem, and new earth.

- The lifting of the veil between heaven and earth which shall occur at the end of time as we understand it.

- Our ultimate message and encouragement in Revelation: to see and understand, repent where needed, and continue in the things that are right, just, and purposed.

Position in the Bible

The Book of Revelation is the last book of the New Testament and, subsequently, the last book accepted in the Biblical canon. It was included, excluded, included, and excluded again, with a long history of controversy over its inclusion. It is classified as an "apocalypse," which is a book whereby something long hidden or concealed has been revealed. Revelation is the only full apocalypse accepted into the New Testament canon. It is preceded by the book of Jude.

Length

The Book of Revelation is twenty-two chapters long. Even in Bibles that sometimes number verses differently, Revelation remains a 22-chapter book, and the content is the same.

Author

Tradition cites the writer, John, of Revelation to be the Apostle John, who was also the author of the Gospel of John, 1 John, 2 John, and 3 John. Often confused with John the Baptist, the Apostle John was referred to in the Gospels as "the disciple whom Jesus loved" (John 20:2 and John 21:24). His name means "God has been gracious." There is debate, however, as to whether the John of Revelation is John the Apostle. While there are obvious parallels between Revelation and the other works, Revelation is written in a different grammatical style than the other books. This does not discount the Apostle John as the author, but it does raise questions about authorship among scholars.

About the author

The Apostle John was one of the original twelve apostles of the Lamb who became a prominent apostle of the New Covenant. Tradition tells us he was the brother of James (also an original apostle) and was the son of Zebedee and Salome. He was believed to be the last of the original twelve to die, somewhere around the age of ninety-four in the year 100. John's identification as "the disciple whom Jesus loved" indicates the Apostle John had a special and unique relationship with Christ, one who had a true revelation of Jesus as the Word made flesh, full of grace and truth, walking among us (John 1). If, as some scholars debate, Revelation was written by another individual named John, we have no knowledge about him or his life, whatsoever.

Time written

The book of Revelation was written between 90 and 100 AD, usually cited somewhere around 94 AD.

Who is Revelation for?

Revelation is a book for all believers, one that calls for discernment and careful attention to understanding and interpretation. It was God's will that, through the unveiling of spiritual things, believers had the opportunity to learn in greater detail about all that was, is, and is to come. Revelation is a book about spiritual life; about decision-making and choices, things that believers face in their churches as well as in their everyday lives; and about the ultimate spiritual realities to be discovered and the results of such knowledge and purpose in the bigger (*karios*) view of time.

Revelation calls us to be aware, as all the things within its pages happen not just in the past or future, but happen every day; happen in unique ways; and we can be a part of and aware of them because we have the Spirit of God to reveal these sacred and powerful truths to us.

History

The book of Revelation appears to have been written during a time that was after an empire-wide persecution under the Emperor Domitian. Much of the imagery present in Revelation probably alludes to Rome and different symbolisms of the Roman government, but that does not mean that is the only way to understand the context of Revelation's symbols. The tone of post-persecution is echoed in the letters to the seven churches, which are now dealing with the realities of regular church life: standing out from the world, meeting the needs of the congregants and maintaining the finances of the church, the temptations of a pagan culture, and the lures of money and power and control. Revelation was given in this time to prove that what was unseen to the naked eye sill made a difference in spiritual things, and that just because things look a certain way on the surface doesn't mean that that's the way they really are from a spiritual perspective.

Revelation has a long and controversial history. There are currently two hundred and thirty different manuscripts of its contents. It was not included in the Bible canon until 419 and was of debate because it was a central text of the Montanists, a Christian sect known for its emphasis on prophecy and female leadership that was later denounced as heresy by threatened leaders. Martin Luther felt it was neither "apostolic nor prophetic" and John Calvin refused to write commentary on it. To this very day, it is never read in the cyclical readings of the Divine Liturgy in the Orthodox Church, and scholars of all denominations and backgrounds disagree about its contents.

There are four main ways Revelation is understood:

- Historicist – The book reflects different eras of church and secular history, overlapping.

- Preterist – The entire contents of Revelation occurred in the first century, and the book's events are now closed.

- Futurist – The entire book of Revelation details future events, and they will be detailed by specific occurrences yet to happen.
- Idealist – The book of Revelation, beyond being symbolic, is an allegory of sorts, representing the struggle between good and evil.

In this work, I will not seek to present any of these theories, although points of this commentary may tap into each of them. More than presenting a common viewpoint, I desire to let Revelation be a revelation of that which is hidden, unveiling itself to us from a mystical perspective, that we may hear its words in history, in our time today, and for all time.

Context

Revelation appears to have three main components, all of which overlap. The first portion of Revelation is composed of letters: those sent to the seven churches in Asia, who are cited as being the recipients of the entire contents of Revelation. The second portion of Revelation is apocalyptic, which relates to the unveiling of spiritual matters occurring in heaven and coinciding with matters on earth. The third portion of Revelation is prophetic, relating to things that shall come. Revelation is also unique in that it is highly repetitive, repeating phrases, using numbers to illustrate different points and concepts of perfection, and giving insight into the spiritual urgency to align with the Kingdom of God rather than that of the world (typified by Babylon).

Through imagery that we find confounding today, the book of Revelation reveals to us salvation history: past, present, and future. In it, we can gain a powerful perspective of time, purpose, and the positioning of God's Kingdom, from eternity past to eternity future. It is impossible to read Revelation and not see the Kingdom of God as a part of God's plan throughout the ages and even into the future, all throughout time.

Chapter One

THE *LOGOS* REVEALS HIMSELF
(REVELATION CHAPTER 1)

<u>Key verses</u>

- **Verses 1-3:** *The Revelation of Jesus Christ, which God gave Him to show His servants what must soon take place. He made it known by sending His angel to His servant John, who testifies to everything he saw – that is, the Word of God and the testimony of Jesus Christ. Blessed is the one who reads the words of this prophecy, and blessed are those who hear it and take to heart what is written in it, because the time is near.*

- **Verses 5-7:** *And from Jesus Christ, Who is the faithful witness, the firstborn from the dead, and the ruler of the kings of the earth. To Him Who loves us and has freed us from our sins by His blood, and has made us to be a Kingdom of priests to serve His God and Father – to Him be glory and power forever and ever! Amen. Look, He is coming with the clouds, and every eye will see Him, even those who pierced Him; and all the peoples of the earth will mourn because of Him. So shall it be! Amen.*

- **Verse 8:** *"I am the Alpha and the Omega," says the Lord God, "Who is, and Who was, and Who is to come, the Almighty."*

- **Verse 11:** *Which said: "Write on a scroll what you see and send it to the seven churches: to Ephesus,*

Smyrna, Pergamum, Thyatira, Sardis, Philadelphia and Laodicea."

- Verses 13-16: *And among the lampstands was someone "like a son of man," dressed in a robe reaching down to His feet and with a golden sash around His chest. His head and hair were white like wool, as white as snow, and His eyes were like blazing fire. His feet were like bronze glowing in a furnace, and His voice was like the sound of rushing waters. In His right hand held seven stars, and out of His mouth came a sharp double-edged sword. His face was like the sun shining in all its brilliance.*

- Verses 19-20: *"Write, therefore, what you have seen, what is now and what will take place later. The mystery of the seven stars that you saw in my right hand and of the seven golden lampstands is this: the seven stars are the angels of the seven churches, and the seven lampstands are the seven churches."*

Words and phrases to know

- Revelation: From the Greek word *apokalupsis* which means "a laying bear, making naked; a disclosure of truth, instruction; manifestation, appearance"[1]

- Servants: From the Greek word *doulos* which means "a slave, bondman, man of servile condition; a servant, attendant."[2]

- Angel: From the Greek word *aggelos* which means "a messenger, envoy, one who is sent, an angel, a messenger from God."[3]

- John: From the Greek word *Ioannes* which means "John = "Jehovah is a gracious giver;" John the Baptist was the son of Zacharias and Elisabeth, the forerunner of Christ. By order of Herod Antipas he was cast into prison and afterwards beheaded; John the apostle, the writer of the Fourth Gospel, son of Zebedee and Salome, brother of James the elder. He is that disciple who (without mention by name) is spoken of in the Fourth Gospel as especially dear to Jesus and according to the traditional opinion is the author of the book of Revelation; John surnamed Mark, the companion of Barnabas and Paul. Acts 12:12; John a certain man, a member of the Sanhedrin Acts 5:6."[4]

- Word: From the Greek word *logos* which means "of speech; its use as respect to the MIND alone; In John, denotes the essential Word of God, Jesus Christ, the personal wisdom and power in union with God, his minister in creation and government of the universe, the cause of all the world's life both physical and ethical, which for the procurement of man's salvation put on human nature in the person of Jesus the Messiah, the second person in the Godhead, and shone forth conspicuously from His words and deeds."[5]

- Testimony: From the Greek word *marturia* which means "a testifying; what one testifies, testimony, i.e. before a judge."[6]

- Blessed: From the Greek word *makarios* which means "blessed, happy."[7]

- Reads: From the Greek word *anaginosko* which means "to distinguish between, to recognise, to know accurately, to acknowledge; to read."[8]

- Prophecy: From the Greek word *propheteia* which means "prophecy."[9]

- Hear: From the Greek word *akouo* which means "to be endowed with the faculty of hearing, not deaf; to hear; to hear something."[10]

- Take to heart: From the Greek word *tereo* which means "to attend to carefully, take care of."[11]

- Written: From the Greek word *grapho* which means "to write, with reference to the form of the letters; to write, with reference to the contents of the writing; to fill with writing; to draw up in writing, compose."[12]

- Time is near: From two Greek words: *kairos* which means "due measure; a measure of time, a larger or smaller portion of time, hence: a fixed and definite time, the time when things are brought to crisis, the decisive epoch waited for; opportune or seasonable time; the right time; a limited period of time; to what time brings, the state of the times, the things and events of time;"[13] and *eggus* which means "near, of place and position; of time, of times imminent and soon to come pass."[14]

- Seven churches: From two Greek words: *hepta* which means "seven"[15] and *ekklesia* which means "a gathering of citizens called out from their homes into some public place, an assembly."[16]

- Spirits: From the Greek word *pneuma* which means "a movement of air (a gentle blast), of the wind, hence the wind itself; the spirit, i.e. the vital principal by which the body is animated; a spirit, i.e. a simple essence, devoid of all or at least all grosser matter, and possessed of the power of knowing, desiring, deciding, and acting; of God; the disposition or influence which fills and governs the soul of any one."[17]

- Faithful witness: From two Greek words: *pistos* which means "trusty, faithful; easily persuaded"[18] and *martus* which means "a witness."[19]

- Firstborn from the dead: From two Greek words: *prototokos* which means "the firstborn"[20] and *nekros* which means "properly: one that has breathed his last, lifeless, deceased, departed, one whose soul is in Hades; metaph. spiritually dead."[21]

- Kingdom: From the Greek word *basileus* which means "leader of the people, prince, commander, lord of the land, king."[22]

- Priests: From the Greek word *hiereus* which means "a priest, one who offers sacrifices and in general in busied with sacred rites; metaph. of Christians, because, purified by the blood of Christ and brought into close intercourse with God, they devote their life to him alone and to Christ."[23]

- Alpha: From the Greek letter *a* which means "first letter of Greek alphabet; Christ is the Alpha to indicate that He is the beginning and the end."[24]

- Omega: From the Greek letter *omega* which means "the last letter in the Greek alphabet; the last."[25]

- Voice: From the Greek word *phone* which means "a sound, a tone; a voice; speech."[26]

- Trumpet: From the Greek word *salpigx* which means "a trumpet."[27]

- See: From the Greek word *blepo* which means "to see, discern, of the bodily eye; metaph. to see with the mind's eye; in a geographical sense of places, mountains, buildings, etc. turning towards any quarter, as it were, facing it."[28]

- Book: From the Greek word *biblion* which means "a small book, a scroll, a written document; a sheet on which something has been written."[29]

- Golden lampstands: From two Greek words: *chruseos* which means "golden; made of gold; overlaid or covered with gold"[30] and *luchnia* which means "a (candlestick) lamp stand, candelabrum."[31]

- Sash: From the Greek word *zone* which means "a girdle, belt, serving not only to gird on flowing garments but also, since it was hollow, to carry money in."[32]

- Bronze: From the Greek word *chalkolibanon* which means "some metal like gold if not more precious."[33]

- Stars: From the Greek word *aster* which means "a star."[34]

- Double-edged sword: From two Greek words: *distomos* which means "having a double mouth as a river, used of the edge of the sword and of other weapons, so has the meaning of two-edged"[35] and *rhomphaia* which means "a large sword; properly a long Thracian javelin, also a kind of long sword wont to be worn on the right shoulder."[36]

- Sun: From the Greek word *helios* which means "the sun; the rays of the sun; the light of day."[37]

- First: From the Greek word *protos* which means "first in time or place; first in rank; first, at the first."[38]

- Last: From the Greek word *eschatos* which means "extreme; the last."[39]

- Keys: From the Greek word *kleis* which means "a key."[40]

- Death and Hades: From two Greek words: *thanatos* which means "the death of the body; metaph., the loss of that life which alone is worthy of the name; the miserable state of the wicked dead in hell; in the widest sense, death comprising all the miseries arising from sin, as well physical death as the loss of a life consecrated to God and blessed in him on earth, to be followed by wretchedness in hell"[41] and *hades* which means "name Hades or Pluto, the god of the lower regions; Orcus, the nether world, the realm of the dead; later use of this word: the grave, death, hell."[42]

- Mystery: From the Greek word *musterion* which means "hidden thing, secret, mystery; of God: the secret counsels which govern God in dealing with the righteous, which are hidden from ungodly and wicked men but plain to the godly; in rabbinic writings, it denotes the mystic or hidden sense: of an OT saying, of an image or form seen in a vision, of a dream."[43]

Revelation 1:1-3

The revelation of Jesus Christ, which God gave Him to show His servants what must soon take place. He made it known by sending His angel to His servant John, who testifies to everything he saw – that is, the Word of God and the testimony of Jesus Christ. Blessed is the one who reads the words of this prophecy, and blessed are those who hear it and take to heart what is written in it, because the time is near.

(Related Bible references: Daniel 2:28, Daniel 8:19, Amos 3:7, Luke 11:28, John 1:1-14, John 12:49, John 13:17, Acts 2:22, Galatians 1:12, 1 Timothy 4:13, James 1:22, Revelation 22:6-10)

The book of Revelation opens with a clear and distinct proclamation about its author and the source of the uncovering; that is of Jesus Christ. Many Bibles refer to it as the "Revelation of St. John the Divine" or "the Revelation of John," but both terms are clearly incorrect if we study just the first few verses of Revelation. The book of Revelation is not a revelation of John or a personal enlightenment, but a clear revelation from Jesus Christ, given to show forth to His servants. It is a Word, a *Logos* expression, from the *Logos* Himself, the one Who was, and is, and is to come, forever.

Within the Bible itself, the way in which the apocalypse is written seems different, strange, even foreign from other books included in the Biblical canon. Historically, the work of the "revelation" or "unveiling" of things mysterious or covered is not unique. The book of Revelation is not the only apocalyptic revelation received in the early centuries of Christianity, nor is it the only apocalyptic experience had in the church, period. From studying the various apocalypses (all of which can be accessed via Apocrypha studies and resources, shows the style and manner of revealing things formerly hidden) the mysterious things of the spiritual realm, all are manners of apocryphal revelation. To understand the nature of the book of Revelation, we must first ask the question: what is special, or relevant, about an apocalypse?

We must first understand the term "apocalypse" is now used in pop culture and sci-fi-eqsue features to refer to what is commonly called "the end of the world." An apocalypse has now been replaced with "the apocalypse," and the term has come to be associated with an alien invasion, great world war, battles with creatures from other worlds, and all sorts of outlandish, strange conflicts between groups of people. The fact about apocalypse is that it does not necessarily have anything to do with any such thing. The word "apocalypse" literally means "a laying bare, making naked; a disclosure of truth, instruction, concerning things before unknown, used of events by which things or states or persons hitherto withdrawn from view are made visible to all; manifestation, appearance."[44] In an ironic twist, the word "apocrypha" and "apocalypse" have the same origin: they both refer to something that is hidden, something that is kept from view. The difference is an "apocrypha" remains hidden (in the case of the Apocrypha, it is because the books were not considered to be canonical and were to remain from public view or acceptance) while an apocalypse is, within its own right, an uncovering of that which is once hidden. In other words, an apocalypse is an unveiled apocrypha. In the case of Revelation, the entire book is an unveiling of sorts. It reveals the mysteries of heaven and earth, of the church in salvation, and things both present, ongoing, eternal, and to come, forever and ever.

There is a certain style by which apocalypse comes forth, as we can see from common and accepted first-century apocalypses, such as the books of Enoch, the Apocalypses of Baruch, Ezra, Peter, Paul, and Thomas, and the poetic apocalypses:

- The recipient is typically a figure that has an established mystical characteristic or quality within the faith, either through authority (a Biblical apostle or prophet) or one who was noted for an excellent spiritual character (such as Enoch).

- The recipient testifies as to having a vision, usually exceedingly detailed in its descriptiveness.

- The vision typically depicts, or unveils, the workings of heaven, usually detailed in levels or realms of authority, structure, and purpose, all showing forth the grandeur of God in the process. Things commonly seen include ranks of angels, battles in the heavenly realms, actions of worship, martyrs or deceased individuals raised to life in the worship and praise of God, symbols of purification, and spiritual songs.

- The apocalypse is full of spiritual symbolism, typically readily understood by the people of its time, able to conceal the messages from outsiders who might perceive the message as threatening. They are, of sorts, written in code.

- There is a distinction made between those who are of God and those who choose to be enemies of God, manifest in a variety of ways.

- They contain an ultimate choice between God and the ways contrary to God, and the struggle between good and evil is clearly manifest within them.

- Most visually describe good and evil in terms of reward and punishment, heaven and hell, and a triumphant vindication of good over evil.

- Life is seen in the context of eternity, or *karios* time, rather than in the context of lifetime, or *chronos* time.

The specified contents, falling under these categories, however, take drastic turns:

- The book of 1 Enoch (Jewish Pseudepigrapha Apocrypha) covers mysteries relating to the creation of the world (including the fall of angels and the transmission of mysteries and secrets), the creation of the heavens, and the existence of *She'ol*, judgment, and ultimately, the Son of Man, all of which shall relate to a time when the dead shall rise.

- The book of 2 Enoch (Jewish Pseudepigrapha Apocrypha) details a vision of heaven and hell.

- The Apocalypse of Baruch (2 Baruch, Jewish Pseudepigrapha Apocrypha) details a long lament over Zion and a vengeance on those who overtook and destroyed Zion.

- The Apocalypse of Ezra (4 Ezra, Jewish Pseudepigrapha Apocrypha) is about the defeat and destruction of God's people, that they might come to a place where they are saved by the Son of Man.

- The Apocalypse of Peter (Christian Apocrypha) is a dramatic rendering of judgment, visualizing punishment for sin in the eternal torment of hell.

- The Apocalypse of Paul (Christian Apocrypha) depicts the apostle's vision of being "caught up" into the third heaven, mentioned in 2 Corinthians 12, along with a depiction of torture for sin.

- The Apocalypse of Thomas (Christian Apocrypha) depicts the entire course of the "end times" occurring within a seven-day period, to parallel the creation of the world as also having taken place in a seven-day period. The last day represents the eternal "Sabbath rest," which shall come after Christ returns.

- Various poetic and musical literature (the Sibylline Oracles, Christian Sibyllines) detail in careful execution salvation history, detailing both the first and second comings of Christ, and the essential change of salvation within God's people.

If we seek to see apocalypse like this, it changes the way in which we understand Revelation in a way that helps us understand its flow and purpose better. Revelation should help us be better able to understand spiritual experience in the revelatory experience, now and within our own lives. The essence of Revelation is walking in, seeing, and experiencing the mystical realm of faith via sensory perception in a way that transcends the material world. It is seeing, hearing, tasting, smelling, and touching the spiritual in an up close and personal way, having an experience with the divine that cannot be understood by science, that is doubted by those who have never experienced it, and that changes the one who perceives it.

There is no doubt that part of Revelation's controversy is its sensual perceptiveness. The visionary is more than just someone who sees things, but one who takes part in a total experience. As I have discussed in my commentary on the Song of Solomon, human nature has branded all sensuality to be evil, without properly understanding that sensual perception is a part of human experience and is part of the way in which we come to an experience of God and spiritual things. The exercise of spiritual gifts, given by God; the exercise of the prophetic, also given by God, are all for the benefit of the believer, there because human nature demands we do not just believe in God, but we experience Him. Within every human heart is the yearning, the restlessness that seeks to understand, to find something deeper than what we can see in this life. It is why being drawn into things such as drug or alcohol addiction is a form of witchcraft: the vision, the sensory experience one has in such, is counterfeit. It mirrors what one may experience, but it doesn't lead one to an understanding of God because it does it without Him. The manipulation of one's senses into a spiritual frenzy does not equate to divine revelation.

That is why understanding the realm of the apocalypse is so important for anyone who seeks God in a deeper way or claims revelation by Him. While "revelation" can come in many forms and God can make things known to His servants via any means of spiritual gifts He desires, mystical revelation requires a discernment on the part of the recipient and the part of the hearers. Anyone can claim to have had a supernatural, spiritual experience in the mystical realm, but that does not mean someone had a genuine encounter. Revelation is a book for the mystics and for those who seek to understand mysticism. It is very rare today to find a genuine individual we would classify as a "mystic," but receiving an apocalypse – especially with the graphic depictions we find of the experience – we can see that John had more than just a vision, more than just a nominal experience with the supernatural. A mystic does not just see something in a visual sense but is one who experiences what they see. Being a mystic involves more than having a few supernatural experiences or walking in a spiritual gift. Everything a mystic encounters, they perceive by their senses, able to come back and explain in detail exactly what it was like.

The mystical, therefore, is a sensual realm of spiritual understanding; it is sensual in its perception of things by the senses in real time, and yet outside of time; and gives us a context for the spiritual in a way we can understand this side of heaven. Not every believer is a mystic; not every apostle or prophet is a mystic. Seeing something in a prophetic sense alone or perceiving something by the Spirit does not make one a mystic. As a part of the functions of the church (as a mystic is not an office of the Ephesians 4:11 ministry nor an appointment but is a part of a grouping of general gifts that relate to specific calling in certain areas), the mystic delves into the rarity of spiritual experience that many fear to go or handle, only to come back and reveal the mysteries they themselves are privileged to experience.

The Apostle John was one such individual who had the mystical experience of transcending vision and experiencing the mysterious. He wasn't special or unique in the sense of being rich or grand, beyond his extraordinary faith and his extraordinary understanding of Who Jesus was.

If we are going to understand the Revelation, we must understand Jesus as the *Logos* in mystical revelation. The mystic's purpose is to unveil the *Logos*, Jesus Christ, the ultimate mystery existing from the beginning, before the foundations of the world. To mention the "Word of God" (*Logos* of God) and the testimony of Jesus Christ is to speak of the same thing, in two different terminologies. The Word of God, the *Logos*, refers to Jesus' prophetic purpose: in time and space, as the Alpha and Omega, beginning and end. The revelation of the *Logos*, first established by the Apostle John in the Gospel of John, reflects an understanding of Jesus beyond His earthly work and ministry.

The term *Logos*, often translated as "Word," is actually a difficult word to translate into any language aside from its original Greek. Originally used as a philosophical term found throughout Greek philosophy, *Logos* was used to indicate an origin, especially as pertains to a word, a speech, or a reason. Over time, it became used to indicate order and knowledge and was intimately associated with the creation and set order of the universe. The term *Logos* embodied far more than the concept of a spoken word (which is *rhema*), and it embodies more than just the concept of speech. *Logos* literally embodies everything God desires for humanity to know or have, His every thought, wish, perception, order, and establishment – in that one uttered concept. *Logos* is used to indicate the very foundational essence of God, His mind, His purpose, His creation, His order, and His will.

Why is the *Logos* understanding of Jesus so essential to understanding the mystical realm? Because in the *Logos*, we see an unveiling of the very foundation and nature of Jesus. Jesus, the Word made flesh, Emmanuel, God with us, is the literal embodiment of everything God wants us, as people, to know and receive about Him. Jesus as the Word is of the same substance and essence as the Father. We see His divinity at work beyond His humanity, His position of order and authority in eternity, and the things that we can rely upon because He is Who He says He is. The Word of Christ is sure; and testimony of Him reflects His eternal nature, in the *Logos*, as the testimony speaks of the *Logos*, through foundational Word.

Thus, blessed is the One Who receives this *Logos*, this eternal foundational Word, in all His forms: in the form of divine utterance, whereby His presence is made real, yet again, through the Spirit that rests upon us and comes forth in Jesus' Name; and in the individual of Christ, accepting and seeing His sovereignty as Lord of all heaven and earth. It is a blessing to receive this into our lives, seeing heaven and the mysteries of the world open before us, as the time for these things has been set up, established, and near to us as if we could reach out and touch it.

Revelation serves to make us aware of spiritual things around us, the times in which we live, and the things that are so close, but we do not see. We are called herein to pay attention, be alert, and realize everything around us is connected to the spiritual realm. In Revelation, we see the significance of God in everything, and God over everything, even perhaps the things that seem most difficult, chaotic, or disordered when viewed this side of heaven. God wants us to see our lives in the picture of eternity. As we do so, we see God revealed in cycles, seeing our experiences as a smaller version of eternity. Revelation helps us to gain the insight with which to do just that.

Revelation 1:4-8

John, To the seven churches in the province of Asia: Grace and peace to you from Him Who is, and Who was, and Who is to come, and from the seven spirits before His throne, and from Jesus Christ, Who is the faithful witness, the firstborn from the dead, and the ruler of the Kings of the earth.

To Him Who loves us and has freed us from our sins by His blood, and has made us to be a Kingdom and priests to serve His God and Father – to Him be glory and power for ever and ever! Amen.

Look, He is coming with the clouds, and every eye will see Him, even those who pierced Him, and all the peoples of the earth will mourn because of Him. So shall it be! Amen.

"I am the Alpha and the Omega," says the Lord God, "Who is, and Who was, and Who is to come, the Almighty."

(Related Bible references: Exodus 3:14, Exodus 6:3, Exodus 15:18, Exodus 19:6, Psalm 89:27-37, Psalm 145:13, Isaiah 48:12, Daniel 7:13, Matthew 16:13-20, Matthew 24:30, Matthew 26:64, Mark 13:26, Luke 17:20-21, Luke 22:29, John 8:54-58, Acts 1:11, Ephesians 1:18, Colossians 1:18, 1 Timothy 6:15-16, 1 Thessalonians 4:17, Hebrews 9:14, 1 Peter 1:18-19, 1 Peter 2:5, 2 Peter 1:11, 1 John 1:7, Revelation 11:15).

The book of Revelation was not a message written to the

entire world, something to be circulated among new Christians or non-believers. It was never meant to be an evangelistic tool, but one to provide essential information to individuals who were already a part of the Kingdom. Specifically, Revelation was addressed to seven churches in the province of Asia. While we commonly associate the letters that list their good and bad points with those churches, the entirety of Revelation's content was circulated in addition to the specific addresses to each one of those churches. That means the whole of Revelation was a revelation to each one of them, a word in due season, something that would aspire them to be better believers and stronger in their faith.

The spread of the church had clearly gone beyond the immediate experience in Jerusalem 60 years earlier, starting with the first Pentecost. Now we can see a letter to seven churches in the Roman province of Asia. These were not the only churches in this region, but the fact that there were seven of them addressed in this letter needs to call us to attention. It is not possible to understand Revelation without an understanding of how the ancients viewed numbers, associating numbers with different meanings. Seven was associated with perfection as the "God number," to reflecting all perfect in the spiritual realm. The church, therefore, represents the perfection of God, as He is the originator of our church, the community that is His Body. It is not that we, as members of the church, have obtained perfection. We can see from the writings and words to the churches that they themselves were also far from perfection. The perfection of the church seals God's plan for humanity, proving His involvement with humankind from eternity past to eternity future. Jesus promised that, despite the trials and problems the church would encounter, the church would remain forever (Matthew 16:13-20). History has tried to take these words any number of ways, but what Jesus was trying to tell us was that the establishment of the church was not only a signpost of perfection, but a part of the journey to perfection. Even though we may not see such perfection within ourselves this side of heaven, the church is our connection to our spiritual lives; our connection to Christ, as He has bought us with His own blood; it livens our connection to God, and to one another.

So many of us run from the buildings that are identified as "church" due to our own experiences with the non-perfected individuals who operate them. Revelation teaches us that "church" is far more than just cute, white churches on corners. The church is more than just the local group of individuals who come together in that cute, white church on the corner. The church is as much at the throne of God, praising Him in a great host, as it is among people down here who devote every action unto Him. We are the church here, as well; we are the church when we reach out to others; we are the church when we praise and worship Him; when we gather; when we sit in our solitude with the Lord. God has set us up in something better than any Kingdom the world can offer: while a king in a secular government cannot be everywhere, at all times, He is with us, everywhere; we can know His presence, touch His grace, and embrace His will for us. Even in our darkest or loneliest times, we know there are others in this world who also call upon His Name and embrace His salvation. We can see this perfection, a system established to be without spot or wrinkle, working for us, with us, within us, around us, and among us: established with His leadership, His spiritual gifts given to us, and His eternal presence, connecting us past, present, and future (Luke 17:20-21).

Once again, we see reference to Jesus, tied in relationship with the church. This is no accident, and a key point that the Apostle John desired for us to see in writing the Revelation. Jesus Christ is the faithful witness, the One on Whose testimony, account, and reference we can always rely. Being a faithful witness indicates He has not just been our witness once, but He has been it repeatedly, over and over, in a way and manner we can trust. Revelation tells us, "The testimony of Jesus is the spirit of prophecy," which, as we discussed earlier, relates to His nature as the *Logos*. It also relates to His position as "faithful witness." He is made faithful as prophecy of Him has repeatedly come true throughout the ages. Every time a *Logos* word is released, Jesus is there, verifying Himself within that literal word. We make Jesus true, faithful, eternal, and reliable every time we walk in a prophetic gift, every time prophecy is spoken, every time we point to the true apostolic and prophetic nature of His Church, His Body. He made Himself faithful and true again when He rose from the dead, fulfilling prophecy, and taking authority granted to Him as the Ruler of this world. The Kingdoms of this world are passing away, but the Kingdom of God shall exist forever, just as it always has (Psalm 145:13, 2 Peter 1:11). Jesus bought us by His blood, establishing and placing us into His Kingdom, where we can forever serve God.

We know, as Christians, that Jesus shall return. The vision in Revelation is about this time, but it is not just reserved for that time. Jesus is in authority right now, just as much as He will be in times to come. This authority is now recognized by believers, even though we cannot see it with our eyes at this time. When the revelation of Christ's sovereign rule is made manifest, it shall not bring joy to everyone. People who have rejected Him or who see His rule as a threat to their own power will find themselves grieving over what was lost, and what will never be again. Humility is key to Christianity because we forever accept Christ's rule in our lives. Accepting Christ now is an eternal process, something that prepares us not just for better living now, but for the various things to come that will change our lives at what we call the "Second Coming."

By its very nature, the Second Coming is a movement of authority. At the Second Coming, that which is invisible shall become fully visible. The Kingdoms of this world shall align with the Kingdom of Christ, the work and promise the church has acknowledged and called to relevance since its inception at Pentecost in 33 AD. Now, we make Jesus' presence known in each and every way, whenever we worship Him, herald His gifts alive in us, and as we acknowledge Him.

Revelation makes yet another *Logos* statement when it echoes the Lord as "Alpha and Omega." The words of

Genesis, which echo the founding of all Holy Scripture, starts with the English words, "In the beginning." The Hebrew term for this is *"B'reshit"* which literally means, "When God began to create."[45] This tells us that Genesis is not even the very "beginning" of everything, and the fact that the first word of Genesis starts with the second letter of the alphabet points us to the fact that before the beginning as we understand it, God was there. The One, however, that the Word points us to, of all places, in Revelation, is the "Alpha" – Christ – Who was in the beginning and will be in the end. Not only was Christ at the beginning, He is also the end – the Omega, the last letter of the Greek alphabet. The beginning and the ending are one, as in each beginning there is an ending and, in each ending, there is a new beginning. This reveals to us the nature of prophetic cycle, which does not operate by modern understandings of a timeline, but by cyclical understanding in the time of eternity. To understand Revelation, to understand the Kingdom, to properly understand anything spiritual, we must have this eternal mindset, understanding prophecy to flow onward and forever, one season of development, understanding, and ultimately, life, flowing into the other. In Kingdom understanding, "time" as we seek it out does not exist. Jesus' eternal nature as the *Logos* is prevalent nowhere more so than in Revelation, because it reveals Him as present in each and every spiritual, prophetic, and purposed moment forever and ever (Exodus 15:18, John 8:54-58, Revelation 11:15). To understand prophecy, eternity, and revelation, we must clearly understand the thread running through it all: the Logos.

Revelation 1:9-16

I, John, your brother and companion in the suffering and Kingdom and patient endurance that are ours in Jesus, was on the island of Patmos because of the Word of God and the testimony of Jesus. On the Lord's Day I was in the Spirit, and I heard behind me a loud voice like a trumpet, which said: "Write on a scroll what you see and send it to the seven churches: to Ephesus, Smyrna, Pergamum, Thyatria, Sardis, Philadelphia and Laodicea."

I turned around to see the voice that was speaking to me. And when I turned I saw seven golden lampstands, and among the lampstands was someone "like a son of man," dressed in a robe reaching down to his feet and with a golden sash around His chest. His head and hair were white like wool, as white as snow, and His eyes were like blazing fire. His feet were like bronze glowing in a furnace, and His voice was like the sound of rushing waters. In His right hand He held seven stars, and out of His mouth came a sharp double-edged sword. His face was like the sun shining in all its brilliance.

(Related Bible references: Genesis 22:17, Genesis 26:4, Exodus 26:15-18, Exodus 27:2, Exodus 32:13, Exodus 36:21-22, Numbers 21:9, Judges 3:16, 1 Kings 7:15, 1 Kings 7:48-50, 1 Chronicles 28:13-15, 2 Chronicles 4:7, 2 Chronicles 4:20, Psalm 149:6, Proverbs 5:4, Proverbs 16:31, Proverbs 20:29, Ezekiel 1:24, Ezekiel 43:2, Daniel 7:9-13, Daniel 7:22, Daniel 8:15-17, Habakkuk 2:2, Malachi 4:2, Matthew 10:22, Matthew 17:2, Matthew 24:9, Mark 16:17, John 8:12, John 14:26, Acts 2:3, Acts 15:22, Acts 16:14, Romans 8:17, 1 Corinthians 1:8, 1 Corinthians 3:13, 1 Corinthians 4:1, 1 Corinthians 13:12, 2 Corinthians 8:22-24, Galatians 2:2, Ephesians 1:1, Ephesians 2:11-22, Ephesians 4:11-16, Colossians 4:16, 2 Timothy 2:12, Hebrews 1:7, Hebrews 4:12, Hebrews 4:15, Hebrews 10:33, Hebrews 11:12, Hebrews 13:7, Hebrews 12:23, Hebrews 12:29, Hebrews 13:17, Hebrews 13:24, Revelation 1:16, Revelation 2:12)

John continues in his direct discourse to the churches by speaking on his suffering. "Suffering" is not a word that we often discuss in our church today, but it has historically been a mark of the church, especially among those who received the most mystical revelation. In the Old Testament, the word "prophecy" literally meant, by extension, "burden."[46] It is never an easy task to accept the revelation of God and report it to others. There remains a severe shadow of doubt surrounding every aspect of the spiritual, even sometimes among those who claim to believe. Having the responsibility to see such incredible things now concealed from plain sight and make them real through testimony is an incredible and monumental task, complete with strain, offense, and isolation. People do not accept it, people do not understand it, and the mystic has received a piece of eternity that changes how they view reality for themselves. Knowing so much more than meets the eye is hiding from plain view causes a mystic to have a different level of spiritual insight that sees God – and often the enemy, too – at work, all around them. This poises the mystic to be the perfect recipient of the message and the perfect herald to stand in a position of authority and relay this message.

Perhaps the most important poise of authority within Revelation is the way in which authority is deposed, both in heaven and on earth. Today we are deeply confused about authority, associating it with consistent negativity. The concept of authority has been tainted to be associated with excessive legalism and abuse, and the answer many have to this association is to abandon any concept of authority that might exist. The Bible does not encourage us to do this (Acts 15:22, Ephesians 4:11-16, Galatians 2:2, Hebrews 13:7, Hebrews 13:17, Hebrews 13:24); it encourages us to follow discernment with leadership, and to follow good leaders. The Scriptures have given us a complete model of things to look for in solid leadership (Matthew 20:25-28, John 13:4, Acts 2:42, Acts 17:11, 1 Peter 5:1-4) and to honor such (Hebrews 13:7). In echoing the leadership authority present throughout the New Testament, Revelation affirms and upholds the office of the apostle, in a way that is quite different from how many understand it.

Today we are confused about apostles and their exact role in the edification of the church. Many perceive the role of the apostle to be akin to that of a pastor, with the apostle somehow being a "big pastor." Still, there are those who confuse the apostle with a bishop, and those who inexplicably link the apostle and prophet into the same work. It's no wonder that, with such confusion, people are confused about just what an apostle does and where an apostle has territory. Many believe apostles are limited to authority immediately over ministries or churches they found themselves, and others still believe apostles only have a local authority. In contrast, Revelation upholds and affirms the following:

- There is no specific indication that the Apostle John founded the seven churches of Revelation to whom Revelation was addressed. In fact, we know that the church at Ephesus was founded by the Apostle Paul, who was deceased at the time of this writing. There is no indication that John directly covered any of these churches, or that he had a personal relationship with them of any sort. Revelation was a revelation, which means what was written therein came from Christ, not from personal knowledge.

  It is worth saying, however, that he must have been of some knowledge and some relationship (even if it wasn't direct leadership) to have the authority to write such revelation and it be accepted. He might not have been their apostle, but he was recognized as being someone's leader.

- The authority of the Apostle John was not in question in connection with acceptance of the letter, even though these may not have been "his" churches.

- The universal authority of the apostle shines through heavily in Revelation, proving the apostle to have authority beyond just the churches they may establish themselves. The apostle has authority everywhere in the world, anywhere they are received. They do not have to be the personal apostle of that group or church to have a word, a revelation, or an instruction received.

- In fact, the "angels" of the churches are most likely a reference to the apostles over those seven churches (2 Corinthians 8:22-24), therefore proving the Apostle John not to be the direct leader over any of those churches (while connected indirectly to only

Pergamum via a bishopric ordination), and those apostles, probably not being the founders of those churches.

- The apostolic nature of "being sent" is the reason for the analogy between the apostle and the angels. Both apostles and angels are sent by God with a special message.

- When apostles are deceased, other apostles are called to step up and take over as apostles of those ministries. Just because someone once had an apostle during a founding or during the planting of a church does not mean that the work of the apostle ends there. Churches need apostles and leaders need the guidance of the apostle throughout their ministry.

- The teaching role of the apostle is most poignant in Revelation, because the words of the Apostle John bring both correction and praise, insight, and address the core of the Christian walk and Christian purpose. These are things apostles should be doing. Rather than aimlessly starting churches here and there or trying to generate numbers, apostles should be about building up the church, structuring it, guiding it, disciplining it, and encouraging it, all together building it up to exactly where it needs to be.

Thus, the authority entrusted to the Apostle John remained with these churches, whether they liked the words they received, or not. They were the words of the apostle, received from Christ, delivered to them. People argue over whether "the Lord's Day" is a reference to Saturday or Sunday, but I do not believe which day of the week it was matters. It was the Lord's Day in that it was a day in which the Lord revealed Himself clearly and without question, revealing His reign. In heaven, every day is the "Lord's Day."

We should pray that this would be recognized on earth, just as it is in heaven. The voice that came to John was loud, blasting, attention-grabbing. He could not deny what he heard, nor what he was about to see. Along with that voice, we find a description of both atmosphere and the person of Jesus:

- Seven golden lampstands: We have already discussed the significance of the number seven as representative of the perfection of God. Gold also represents the perfection of heaven, of things beyond the natural realm and of a preciousness beyond value. Ancient lampstands were crafted out of a singular piece of whatever metal they were made from, consisting of a single base and a single stand, branching out into (in this case) seven different candle holders. The lampstands were hammered out of fine metal, worked and wrought by their designers. The fact that one piece of metal is hammered into seven holders for a candle reminds us of the fact that in God's perfection, He is still one – and from the one that He is comes forth the perfection and purpose we seek. This perfection emanates through His church, proving that the church is also one when we are in Him (1 Kings 7:48-50, 1 Chronicles 28:13-15, 2 Chronicles 4:7, 2 Chronicles 4:20).

- Son of Man: The term "Son of Man" echoes Daniel's prophecy (Daniel 7:13-14, Daniel 8:15-17). This is the cornerstone of the incarnation, which, as Madeline L'Engle put it, "There is nothing so secular that it cannot be sacred, and that is one of the deepest messages of the Incarnation."[47] The whole concept of the Word being made flesh, dwelling among us, the incorruptible putting on corruption, is truly more than I believe the human mind can fathom. We have a God Who loved us so much, He became one of us so we could better find Him. Rather than guessing as pagans do, we can find our God for ourselves. "Son of

Man" reminds us that He was divine in His nature and also human in His flesh while on earth, a High Priest Who understands what we go through, our temptations, and our issues (Hebrews 4:15). Bringing this up in Revelation brings us back to the *Logos*, and reminds us that in delivering this Word, He understands all manner of what we face.

- Robe reaching to His feet: Revelation is unique because it contains symbolism familiar to those in the major cross-cultures common in the day of its writing: Jewish, Greek, Persian, Syrian, Hellenistic (which is an extension of Greek), and Roman. The description of Jesus' robe would have been easily understood and visualized by people from any culture represented in Revelation's era. Wearing a robe signified authority, and signified wealth and prestige as fabric was considered expensive. Shorter garments signified labor-intensive work for poorer classes. Robes were also worn by priests among the ancient Hebrews, thus the nature of Jesus as our High Priest is also seen in such garments.

- Golden sash around His chest: Wearing a golden sash indicated a garment was so long, it had to be held closer to the body or somehow "hiked up" to keep from tripping on it. This relates to the nature of the garment, and the amount of fabric, which would have been associated with wealth, prestige, and ruling authority.

- Head and hair white like wool, white as snow: This also reiterates Daniel's prophecy, paralleling Jesus as the Ancient of Days (Daniel 7:9-13, Daniel 7:22). White signifies purity, as does wool. It also signifies age (paralleling Him to be the most Ancient of Days), associating Him with great wisdom (Proverbs 16:31, Proverbs 20:29).

- Eyes like blazing fire: We know that fire is a symbol for the presence of the Holy Ghost (Acts 2:3, 1 Corinthians 3:13, Hebrews 1:7, Hebrews 12:29) and that He comes in the Name of Jesus (Mark 16:17, John 14:26). This shows for the Spirit of God alive and present in Christ, visible with the intensity of His gaze and the power present in His visual contact. By looking into the eyes of Jesus, it is clear Who He is.

- Feet bronze, glowing in a furnace: Bronze was a common metal in ancient times, but with the advance of more modern metals and instruments, we don't always identify the relevance of bronze because we don't hear about it much. As an alloy metal (fused using heat), bronze made copper much stronger than it would be on its own. It was commonly used in tools and weaponry. It had a heavy, punitive association. In the Old Testament temple, bronze represented the judgment of God (Exodus 26:15-18, Exodus 27:2, Exodus 36:21-22, Numbers 21:9, 1 Kings 7:15). As bronze was used through weapons to stomp out opposition and leave only those on the "right side" behind, the imagery of using bronze in this manner signifies the judgment of Christ. We also see mention of the work of the Holy Ghost here, as well, as furnaces are heated through fire.

- Voice was the sound of rushing waters: Water was an element commonly understood by agrarian societies. It was also highly prized, especially in desert regions, such as those found throughout the ancient Middle East. Rushing water, waterfalls, and waves could all be considered to "roar," as in they get the attention of the people around them. You cannot deny a "rushing" or "roaring" water when it is within your proximity. This reference parallels Ezekiel's visions (Ezekiel 1:24, Ezekiel 43:2).

- Seven stars: Echoing the reference to seven as the number of perfection or completion, stars represent to us types and shadows of truth, and the way in which we see through a glass dimly (1 Corinthians 13:12) this side of heaven. We learn in this passage that the seven stars represent the "angels of churches," which refers to the seven apostles of the seven churches of Revelation (compared to the seven classical planets). The apostle is girded with the revelation of Christ and is sent to reveal the mysteries of God (1 Corinthians 4:1), bringing with them the pieces and points of truth as they go. As a result of the sent-ones, we find fulfillment in the prophecy made to Abraham that his descendants shall be numerous as the stars (Genesis 22:17, Genesis 26:4, Exodus 32:13, Hebrews 11:12), for through the work of the apostle, the world has the opportunity to become a part of the completion and perfection of God through His church (Ephesians 2:11-22, Hebrews 12:23).

- Double-edged sword coming out of His mouth: There are exactly six references in the New International Version of the Bible to the "double-edged sword" or "two-edged sword" (Judges 3:16, Psalm 149:6, Proverbs 5:4, Hebrews 4:12, Revelation 1:16, and Revelation 2:12). A two-edged sword was sharpened on both sides, enabling the one who uses it to work faster and more effectively when it strikes an enemy. Once again, we see reference here to the work of Jesus in judgment, but there is another reference at hand, one which many do not consider. Hebrews 4:12 tells us, *For the Word of God is living and active. Sharper than any double-edged sword, it penetrates even to dividing soul and spirit, joints and marrow; it judges the thoughts and attitudes of the heart.* The word "Word" is actually the word *Logos*, and not the word for "Scripture," which is how many commonly misinterpret it. This represents the power of prophecy, and the way in which it brings forth judgment and repentance, in its perfect completion and purpose.

- Sun shining in brilliance: Brilliance gives a visual component to the attention-grabbing nature of our Lord's appearance. The sound of rushing waters gives the audio component, hair like wool gives both a visual and a tactile sense of identity, and brilliance indicates He is so bright, it is impossible not to notice Him. These two parallels see how deeply sensory perception plays in a mystical experience. Jesus was just not seen off in a distance, as in a dream, but was real and thunderous, causing notice and attention. Jesus saying He is the light of the world (John 8:12) gives us an idea and an automatic comparison between Him and the sun (Malachi 4:2). It is not that He is physically the sun, but He is brilliant enough, striking enough, and enough of a force to drive out darkness that He is, indeed, brilliant to our sight. I am reminded of the promise of Malachi 4:2:

But for you who fear My Name, the Sun of Righteousness will rise with healing in His wings. And you will go free, leaping with joy like calves let out to pasture. (NLT)

The descriptiveness of this passage lets us know two very important things about that which is unseen, and the role of the mystic in the revelation of the unseen. The first thing it teaches us is the incredible, unfathomable, commanding presence of Jesus, while reminding us that He is still perceivable by the senses. He is not so distant, nor so detached, that we cannot recognize Him when we see, hear, or feel Him. The spiritual realm can be perceived by our senses, as the spiritual realm is not some paranormal, distant, ethereal understanding that we cannot know is before us and around us. The second thing we need to realize is that the mystic's perceptions of the spiritual realm are beyond real. The true mystic is not making things up, imagining things, or spinning tales of clever fantasies. Mystics see, hear, taste, smell, and touch their experiences. They are as real as any one of us sitting, talking, or speaking with another. To the mystic, the spiritual realm as real and visible as the natural realm, and the two are frequently intertwined. The mystic has not just seen Jesus; they have experienced Him.

<u>Revelation 1:17-20</u>

When I saw Him, I fell at His feet as though dead. Then He placed His right hand on me and said: "Do not be afraid. I am the First and the Last. I am the Living One; I was dead, and behold I am alive for ever and ever! And I hold the keys of death and Hades.

"Write, therefore, what you have seen, what is now and what will take place later. The mystery of the seven stars that you saw in my right hand and of the seven golden lampstands is this: the seven stars are the angels of the seven churches, and the seven lampstands are the seven churches."

(Related Bible references: Matthew 16:18, John 5:21, John 6:40, Luke 24:5, Acts 26:23, Romans 6:9, Colossians 1:18, Hebrews 3:1, Hebrews 4:16, Hebrews 7:24)

Most of us have heard the expression, "I was frightened to death!" This was clearly the case of the Apostle John in this vision. What he saw, what he encountered, what he perceived by all his senses was so overwhelming, it became frightening. Seeing that which is not seen with the natural eye sounds awesome and inspiring to those who have not experienced it, but there is a reason the mystic tends to be a serious, reserved, often isolated person. Having such a profound revelation of the seen and the unseen – and the way in which the two are related – changes an outlook.

Jesus, however, tells John not to be afraid. There is nothing for us to fear in recognizing the supernatural when it stands before us. We need not fear coming before the

Throne if we are found in Him (Hebrews 4:16). He is the Living One; the one from Whom all life comes forth, Who once was dead, but now is with us forever. Revelation describes Him as holding the keys of death and Hades, but in essence, what this is telling us is He has the authority and rule over life. Jesus has the authority to speak, call, bring forth, and resurrect life. Keys symbolize authority in the spiritual realm (Matthew 16:18), thus the authority has been given unto Him over all life.

It is clear the authority of Jesus, repeated first through keys, and then by speaking of His right hand and what it contains. The Apostle John is also given a direct command by Jesus, thus showing the authority over John and, by extension, the apostolic office. Even though the apostle may hold great authority in the church, the Chief Apostle, Jesus Christ, is still over every apostle (Hebrews 3:1). He is there to guide, to direct, and to instruct us within His authority, as we are commanded to love and follow Him.

John is commanded to write what he sees in his mystical experience. He is not told to speak it, to record an audio series, to create a series of preaching messages on it, but to write it, because that is what will preserve it. The mystical revelation is most convincing in written form, right down to this day. Writing gives an instructional quality to every mystical encounter, taking it beyond experience to practical instruction. It is in this that we discover the essence of mysticism. Anyone can sound dramatic and exciting, claiming any experience they so desire via testimony. Writing mysticism takes the drama out of it, making it something that becomes practical and useful for spiritual realization and teaching. Jesus makes it clear that John is to write about what is now and what will take place later. In other words, Revelation is eternal. It is about what is, and about what is to be uncovered. He also ends chapter 1 by uncovering symbolism discussed earlier: the mystery of the seven stars and seven golden lampstands are the seven messengers (apostles) of the seven churches of Revelation, which are represented by the seven golden lampstands.

What is so notable about these seven churches that their admonishments, praises, and corrections have been recorded for all of history? The next chapters will reveal in detail the reasons why we are still talking about the churches of Ephesus, Smyrna, Pergamum, Thyatira, Sardis, Philadelphia, and Laodicea – and what we need to learn from them.

The Scroll and

5 Then I saw
sealed[t] with
break the seals ar
scroll or even loo
scroll or look insi
dah, the Root of D

[6]Then I saw a l
by the four living cr
its[u] of God sent out
on the throne.[v] [7]An
before the Lamb, [w]
[prayers][x] of the saint

JESUS IS ALWAYS ABLE TO OVERCOME

G

Chapter Two

EPHESUS, SMYRNA, PERGAMUM, AND THYATIRA (REVELATION CHAPTER 2)

Key verses

- Verses 4-5: *Yet I hold this against you: You have forsaken your first love. Remember the height from which you have fallen! Repent and do the things you did at first. If you do not repent, I will come to you and remove your lampstand from its place.*

- Verses 9-10: *I know your afflictions and your poverty – yet you are rich! I know the slander of those who say they are Jews and are not, but are a synagogue of Satan. Do not be afraid of what you are about to suffer. I tell you, the devil will put some of you in prison to test you, and you will suffer persecution for ten days. Be faithful, even to the point of death, and I will give you the crown of life.*

- Verses 14-16: *Nevertheless, I have a few things against you: You have people there who hold to the teaching of Balaam, who taught Balak to entice the Israelites to sin by eating food sacrificed to idols and by committing sexual immorality. Likewise you also have those who hold to the teaching of the Nicolaitans. Repent therefore! Otherwise I will soon come to you and will fight against them with the sword of my mouth.*

- Verses 20-23: *Nevertheless, I have this against you: You tolerate that woman Jezebel, who calls herself a prophetess. By her teaching she misleads my servants into sexual immorality and the eating of food sacrificed to idols. I have given her time to repent of her immorality, but she is unwilling. So I will cast her on a bed of suffering, and I will make those who commit adultery with her suffer intensely, unless they repent of her ways. I will strike her children dead. Then all the churches will know that I am He Who searches hearts and minds, and I will repay each of you according to your deeds.*

- Verse 29: *He who has an ear, let him hear what the Spirit says to the churches.*

<u>Words and phrases to know</u>

- Ephesus: From the Greek word *Ephesinos* which means "a native or inhabitant of Ephesus."[1]

- Perseverance: From the Greek word *hupomone* which means "steadfastness, constancy, endurance; a patient, steadfast waiting for; a patient enduring, sustaining, perseverance."[2]

- Wicked: From the Greek word *kakos* which means "of a bad nature; of a mode of thinking, feeling, acting; troublesome, injurious, pernicious, destructive, baneful."[3]

- Forsaken: From the Greek word *aphiemi* which means "to send away; to permit, allow, not to hinder, to give up a thing to a person; to leave, go way from one."[4]

- Love: From the Greek word *agape* which means "brotherly love, affection, good will, love, benevolence; love feasts."[5]

- Repent: From the Greek word *metanoeo* which means "to change one's mind, i.e. to repent; to change one's mind for better, heartily to amend with abhorrence of one's past sins."[6]

- Nicolaitans: From the Greek word *Nikolaites* which means "Nicolaitans = "destruction of people;" a sect mentioned in Rev. 2:6,15, who were charged with holding the error of Balaam, casting a stumbling block before the church of God by upholding the liberty of eating things sacrificed to idols as well as committing fornication."[7]

- Tree of life: From two Greek words: *xulon* which means "wood; a tree"[8] and *zoe* which means "life; life of the absolute fullness of life, both essential and ethical, which belongs to God, and through him both to the hypostatic "logos" and to Christ in whom the "logos" put on human nature; life real and genuine, a life active and vigorous, devoted to God, blessed, in the portion even in this world of those who put their trust in Christ, but after the resurrection to be consummated by new accessions (among them a more perfect body), and to last for ever."[9]

- Paradise: From the Greek word *paradeisos* which means "among the Persians a grand enclosure or preserve, hunting ground, park, shady and well watered, in which wild animals, were kept for the hunt; it was enclosed by walls and furnished with towers for the hunters; a garden, pleasure ground; the part of Hades which was thought by the later Jews to be the abode of the souls of pious until the resurrection: but some understand this to be a heavenly paradise; the upper regions of the heavens. According to the early church Fathers, the paradise in which our first parents dwelt before the fall still exists, neither on the earth or in the heavens, but above and beyond the world."[10]

- Smyrna: From the Greek word *Smurnaios* which means "of or belonging to Smyrna, an inhabitant of Smyrna."[11]

- Afflictions: From the Greek word *thlipsis* which means "a pressing, pressing together, pressure; metaph. oppression, affliction, tribulation, distress, straits."[12]

- Poverty: From the Greek word *ptocheia* which means "beggary; in the NT poverty."[13]

- Jews: From the Greek word *Ioudaios* which means "Jewish, belonging to the Jewish race; Jewish as respects to birth, race, religion."[14]

- Synagogue of Satan: From two Greek words: *sunagoge* which means "a bringing together, gathering (as of fruits), a contracting; in the NT, an assembling together of men, an assembly of men; a synagogue; an assembly of Jews formally gathered together to offer prayers and listen to the reading and expositions of the scriptures; assemblies of that sort were held every sabbath and feast day, afterwards also on the second and fifth days of every week; name transferred to an assembly of Christians formally gathered together for religious purposes; the buildings where those solemn Jewish assemblies are held. Synagogues seem to date their origin from the Babylonian exile. In the times of Jesus and the apostles every town, not only in Palestine, but also among the Gentiles if it contained a considerable number of Jewish inhabitants, had at least one synagogue, the larger towns several or even many. These were also used for trials and inflicting punishment"[15] and *Satanas* which means "adversary (one who opposes another in purpose or act), the name given to: the prince of evil spirits, the inveterate adversary of God and Christ; he incites apostasy from God and to sin; circumventing men by his wiles; the worshippers of idols are said to be under his control; by his demons he is able to take possession of men and inflict them with diseases; by God's assistance he is overcome; on Christ's return from heaven he will be bound with chains for a thousand years, but when the thousand years are finished he will walk the earth in yet greater power, but shortly after will be given over to eternal punishment; a Satan-like man."[16]

- Suffer: From the Greek word *pascho* which means "to be affected or have been affected, to feel, have a sensible experience, to undergo."[17]

- Prison: From the Greek word *phulake* which means "guard, watch; a watching, keeping watch; to keep watch; persons keeping watch, a guard, sentinels; of the place where captives are kept, a prison; of the time (of night) during which guard was kept, a watch i.e. a period of time during which part of the guard was on duty, and at the end of which others relieved them. As the earlier Greeks divided the night commonly into three parts, so, previous to the exile, the Israelites also had three watches in a night; subsequently, however, after they became subject to the Romans, they adopted the Roman custom of dividing the night into four watches."[18]

- Test: From the Greek word *peirazo* which means: "to try whether a thing can be done; to try, make trial of, test: for the purpose of ascertaining his quantity, or what he thinks, or how he will behave himself."[19]

- Crown: From the Greek word *stephanos* which means "a crown."[20]

- Pergamum: From the Greek word *Pergamos* which means "Pergamos = "height or elevation;" a city of

Mysia Minor, in Asia Minor, the seat of the dynasties of Attalus and Eumenes, famous for its temple of Aesculapius and the invention and manufacture of parchment. The river Selinus flowed through it and the Cetius ran past it. It was the birthplace of the physician Galen, and had a great royal library. It had a Christian church."[21]

- Antipas: From the Greek word *Antipas* which means "Antipas = "like the father;" a Christian of Pergamos who suffered martyrdom."[22]

- Teaching of Balaam: From two Greek words: *didache* which means "teaching; the act of teaching, instruction"[23] and *Balaam* which means "Balaam meaning "perhaps;" A native of Pethor a city in Mesopotamia, endued by Jehovah with prophetic power. He was hired by Balak to curse the Israelites; and influenced by the love of reward, he wished to gratify Balak; but he was compelled by Jehovah's power to bless them. Hence later the Jews saw him as a most abandoned deceiver."[24]

- Balak: From the Greek word *Balak* which means "Balak = "a devastator or spoiler;" a king of Moab."[25]

- Idols: From the Greek word *eidolothuton* which means "sacrificed to idols, the flesh left over from the heathen sacrifices."[26]

- Sexual immorality: From the Greek word *porneuo* which means "to prostitute one's body to the lust of another; to give one's self to unlawful sexual intercourse; metaph. to be given to idolatry, to worship idols."[27]

- Overcomes: From the Greek word *nikao* which means "to conquer."[28]

- Hidden manna: From two Greek words: *krupto* which means "to hide, conceal, to be hid; escape notice; metaph. to conceal (that it may not become known)"[29] and *manna* which means "manna = "what is it;" the food that nourished the Israelites for forty years in the wilderness; of the manna was kept in the ark of the covenant; symbolically, that which is kept in the heavenly temple for the food of angels and the blessed."[30]

- White stone: From two Greek words: *leukos* which means "light, bright, brilliant"[31] and *psephos* which means "a small worn smooth stone, a pebble; a vote (on account of the use of pebbles in voting)."[32]

- Name: From the Greek word *onoma* which means "name: univ. of proper names; the name is used for everything which the name covers, everything the thought or feeling of which is aroused in the mind by mentioning, hearing, remembering, the name, i.e. for one's rank, authority, interests, pleasure, command, excellences, deeds etc.; persons reckoned up by name; the cause or reason named: on this account, because he suffers as a Christian, for this reason."[33]

- Thyatira: From the Greek word *Thuateira* which means "Thyatira = "odour of affliction;" a colony of Macedonia Greeks, situated between Sardis and Pergamos on the river Lycus; its inhabitants gained their living by traffic and the art of dyeing in purple."[34]

- Tolerate: From the Greek word *eao* which means "to allow, permit, let; to allow one to do as he wishes, not to restrain, to let alone; to give up, let go, leave."[35]

- Jezebel: From the Greek word *Iezabel* which means "Jezebel = "chaste;" wife of Ahab, an impious and cruel queen who protected idolatry and persecuted the prophets; the symbolic name of a woman who pretended to be a prophetess, and who, addicted to antinomianism, claimed Christian liberty of eating things sacrificed to idols."[36]

- Misleads: From the Greek word *planao* which means "to cause to stray, to lead astray, lead aside from the right way."[37]

- Hold Fast: From the Greek word *krateo* which means "to have power, be powerful; to get possession of; to hold."[38]

- Authority: From the Greek word *exousia* which means "power of choice, liberty of doing as one pleases; physical and mental power; the power of authority (influence) and of right (privilege); the power of rule or government (the power of him whose will and commands must be submitted to by others and obeyed)."[39]

- Morning star: From two Greek words: *proinos* which means "pertaining to the morning"[40] and *aster* which means "a star."[41]

Revelation 2:1-7

"To the angel of the church in Ephesus write:
These are the words of Him Who holds the seven stars in His right hand and walks among the seven golden lampstands: I know your deeds, your hard work and your perseverance. I know that you cannot tolerate wicked men, that you have tested those who claim to be apostles, but are not, and have found them false. You have persevered and have endured hardships for My Name, and have not grown weary.
Yet I hold this against you: You have forsaken your first love. Remember the height from which you have fallen! Repent and do the things you did at first. If you do

not repent, I will come to you and remove your lampstand from its place. But you have this in your favor: You hate the practices of the Nicolaitans, which I also hate.

He who has an ear, let him hear what the Spirit says to the churches. To him who overcomes, I will give the right to eat from the tree of life, which is in the paradise of God.

(Related Bible references: Genesis 3:1-24, Psalm 139:21, Malachi 1:10, Matthew 7:15-20, Matthew 11:15, Luke 21:19, John 2:25, Acts 3:21, Acts 19:1, Acts 20:30, Acts 26:20, Romans 2:7, Romans 5:12-21, Romans 16:17, 2 Corinthians 11:13, Galatians 6:9, Ephesians 1:1, 2 Timothy 4:1-5, Titus 3:9, 2 Peter 2:1-3)

Revelation 2 gets right down to business, dispensing with many formalities that were reserved for chapter 1. From its first words, Revelation 2 segues into the section of Revelation that is devoted to specific letters "to the seven churches in the province of Asia:" Ephesus, Smyrna, Pergamum, Thyatira, Sardis, Philadelphia, and Laodicea.

The major question history has tried to answer as pertains to these churches: why these seven churches? Clearly, by this time in church history, they were not the only churches in existence. Revelation could just have easily been written to the churches of Rome, or the churches of Jerusalem, or other churches in the province of Asia, or to the churches of another region, rather than these seven churches of Asia. So why these churches?

In an attempt to try and explain the relevance of these churches, history has done a poor disservice to the basic facts about these churches and their locations. Each one of these churches was on a "route," so to speak, by which a courier could easily deliver the letter to each one of them. It was perfect for contact, sharing information, and making sure a message got around. Beyond that, I believe these seven churches were selected for several reasons:

- They were a survey of the issues the whole church was facing in multiple areas: All of us can read the seven churches and identify with the issues and challenges they faced, the rebellions present, the disobediences, and the praises of each church. No matter where in the world someone is or what era of history they were a believer, everyone can read about those churches and see the same issues affecting believers throughout time. These churches, whether we want to believe it or not, are a reflection of all churches, throughout all time.

- The issues of the churches give a realistic view of church and the problems of local churches: People like to sanitize the church, pretending that it doesn't face the same issues that the rest of the world faces. The human element of Christianity is often where many lack, and often where many get lost. When leaders in church bring up issues of lack of support, false prophets running off with half the congregation, lack of finances, division within the local group, maintaining membership, and maintaining the focus on Christ rather than everything else, people want to pretend those matters do not exist. Revelation's seven churches prove that God not only knows, but cares about the issues that churches face, no matter their size or location. It also acknowledges that the church as a whole should be concerned about the issues local churches and groups of congregations face and about helping leaders to resolve the issues that exist.

- They show the complication of what happens when we fall in love with all the wrong things: The seven churches of Revelation each dealt with enchantment unto idolatry. Whether it was falling away from the first works, following false prophetesses, embracing false teaching, idolatry, relying on money to save them, or ignoring their spiritual responsibilities, these churches show us that it's easy to fall in love with the wrong things. They also show us it can happen to any church, to anyone if they do not remain consistent in proper spiritual pursuits.

- The balance between right and wrong action: Very few churches do all things right or all things wrong. The temptation always exists to over-emphasize the extremes of right or wrong that someone does without finding the balance in the middle. The churches of Revelation received praise for the things they did right, and correction for the things they did wrong. This helps us to keep perspective for church discipline as well as overall analysis and judgment on church systems and situations.

- In recognizing the balance, we see that the environments we come from are also the very thing that helps us to do both what we do right and what we do wrong: Every single one of these churches existed in a culture that did not, according to popular understanding, support its belief systems. Their cultures were often largely influenced by pagan belief, and there weren't clear parameters as to where religion ended and culture or work started. The ancient churches understood the principles of common, interwoven threads. They knew how to serve, how to do right, how to take care of other people, and how to have faith because they had grown up in social atmospheres that taught them the interconnectedness of things. They knew how to connect actions with doing right and this led to praise for doing right. This interconnectedness, however, is also what led them astray, time and time again. Not seeing the need to exclusively interconnect Christian theology and theory into their belief systems, it caused them to be led into a place where they interconnected pagan and Christian principles. That is why what Jesus seems to mention to these churches seems contradictory to us today. In modern society, we are so used to dividing things up, we fail to look at the whole of things and see things from the perspective of interconnectedness. Jesus' messages to the churches do not seem contradictory if we see it from this viewpoint. He was looking at them as a whole, or entire churches. He was viewing them through the lens of the entire thread, rather than breaking things apart and making judgments based on one singular issue. How many of us are guilty of this very same thing today, not recognizing that certain principles, attributes, and underlying concepts should be guiding our lives, our faith, and our movements? Instead of seeing underlying principles, we are quick to decide someone is going to hell for this singular issue or that one, when, even in the face of all these problems, Jesus never declared as such to these churches. Where we come from influences us in both positive and negative ways. The church has the unique perspective to fit into every culture worldwide, if it will only model itself on the foundation of principles rather than trying to fix the entire world from a religious understanding.

- The church is multi-faceted: It's easy to stereotype the church as being a singular, neat, white-skinned entity rather than a real, living Body that is forever changing, growing, and developing. The church is more than just one ethnic group, one type of people, one income bracket, and one circumstance. It is important to keep in mind that, no matter what you see on a regular basis in a local church, that the church is more than just what you see in your immediate congregation.

- By its very founding nature, the local church is designed to be an urban entity: This is not to say that churches cannot exist in rural or suburban areas. We are, however, in modern times, upholding the suburban and rural churches, as if they are the model or exalted purpose for the church. Every church addressed in the New Testament falls into the category of an "urban church," one in a municipality locale that was noted for trade routes, travel, business, and interaction. There are two reasons why the church has, in its nature, an urban feel: the first is because cities are where people are, and they are important centers to carry essential messages all over the world quickly. The second is because urban centers are seats for what we now classify as "urban issues," including poverty, "throw away" people (orphans, widows, etc.), diversity in spiritual belief, and a need for hope and truth.

It's clear from the above points that these churches in Revelation are important entities. They aren't just individual churches; they are the church. They are the very embodiment of every single one of us, working the good with the bad, embracing things we shouldn't, walking away from things we need to run back toward, facing life, facing changes, facing hostile atmospheres and challenges. The seven churches of Revelation need to cause each of us to step back and examine our own selves and our own interactions with the church.

Some have attempted to explain the churches of Revelation as "eras" or points in church history, dividing up church history into different dispensations of issues and activity within their work. While I can see how this teaching evolved, I disagree with it. I believe these seven churches have existed at all points within the history of the church, revealing important truths to us. To marginalize any one of these churches as one specific era and ignore the rest is to ignore the bigger message present in these churches.

Perhaps most important for us today is to realize Revelation was not intended to make us so deep that we start ignoring regular realities of church life. Overall, that is one of the most important reasons why these seven churches are specifically addressed in the discourse of Revelation. God is not so distant that He is unaware of the issues we are facing, here and now. The point of having a revelation, of going deeper in the Lord, is to make us more available and more relevant in our here and now. The

Apostle John saw things many will never be blessed to see within their lifetimes, but he still came back from that revelation with the assignment to do the work of the apostle while down here. Knowing what is seen and unseen is to know the Kingdom and is here to advance that Kingdom with all that we do. As with all things Revelation, Jesus' will for each one of these churches was completion: obtaining a center of perfection in which they were able to present a wholeness or completion of faith in their local communities. The motive wasn't to be critical or judgmental, but to aid the churches in their process to offer the wholeness of faith, complete, with nothing lacking. When we look at correction in this light, we understand how important the role of correction is in church understanding and development.

Ephesus was the third largest city in Asia Minor, located on the coast of Ionia (today it would be located in the nation of Turkey). It was specifically set apart for the temple of Diana (Artemis), and the chief shrine to this goddess (considered one of the Seven Wonders of the Ancient World) was in Ephesus. History considers the Apostle Paul to be the founder of the church here (evident in his letter to them), and many believe the Apostle John lived in Ephesus for a period. This made it an early center for the Christian church and an important aspect of church history. For this reason, the fact that it literally means "desirable" is important, because it was a desirable area to many people. It was also, obviously, desirable for the Lord's work.

The specific message to Ephesus began with Jesus affirming Himself as the author of the message. He affirms Himself as the Lord of the church, having the authority to bring forth the necessary message. He began by commending them for the things they were doing right. The church at Ephesus was notable for their good works and perseverance. They knew how to do things and do them well. They were also a discerning church, evident in that they knew how to discern a true leader from a false one. Even in the late first century, false leaders were still prominent, and it was required for the church to know who was true from who was not. They were also a church that had persevered many hardships on behalf of being believers and did not grow weary.

With such a glowing recommendation, it would be hard to imagine that Jesus had anything to say about the church at Ephesus that was contrary. We all know how hard it is to get people interested in doing the spiritual works, how frustrating it is to watch people follow false leaders without discernment or spiritual insight, and how easily people give up. But Jesus wasn't done with the church at Ephesus. Despite the good they were doing, there were some very important things they were not doing.

The first issue Jesus addresses with Ephesus is the issue they had forsaken their first love. Given all the works they were doing, many might not consider the severity of this issue. Some believe that as long as they do the "works," it doesn't matter why they are doing them, how they are doing them, or their intentions of them behind-the-scenes. I grew up in a church that espoused this sort of theory. The women of the church believed works were more essential than faith or motives. They were doing, doing, doing, but often did so with a sour attitude and angry disposition. They did it, but they didn't want to do it. Their actions didn't come from a place of love or faith. They were quick and frequent to look down on others who didn't do as many things as they did, regardless of the reason. As long as they kept doing things, that was all that was relevant. Jesus' words to the church at Ephesus completely dispels the notion that works are above intentions. It's obvious that both are important, and both are relevant in the assessment of a work as either complete or incomplete.

Forsaking their first love was a serious issue. It meant they had lost their love and zeal for the Lord and, by extension, for His work of ministry, and for one another. If we don't love the Lord before all things, we open the door for idols to invade our churches (not to mention our lives). They were going through the motions, doing what they had done out of obligation rather than love, and without any depth of meaning. Their works were not leading anyone to anything or reflecting anything greater. Jesus even went on to tell them to remember the height from which they had fallen! They clearly had been in a different place at one time but had fallen from that place. The question many ask is how did they wind up so far from where they started?

It's hard to say exactly what happened. None of us were there, and we don't know how they handled the pressures of the world around them. Based on experience, however, I believe that their intense gift of discernment might have had something to do with it. Very few people are honest about the difficulties in spiritual gifts today, and even less teach on those difficulties one will encounter when they walk powerfully in them. We do not have spiritual gifts for our self-esteem, to make us feel good, or to make church a source of entertainment. The spiritual gifts that we have are often difficult to execute, especially in churches that don't want to hear anything but encouragement. Discernment is a particularly difficult gift to have, as it changes how one views the operation and the people within the church. Recognizing so many leaders as false, seeing spirits on people and operating in people's lives, and having to discern such things unto difficult situations (removing people from the church, refusing to follow a false leader, etc.). If one doesn't keep a healthy balance to what they are seeing or experiencing – making sure to seek God, to have the right base and good support in one's faith, and to have plenty of time to worship God and celebrate with other believers – it's easy to start to believe that the entire church is suspect.

The answer for Ephesus was to repent. This was no laughing matter! They weren't told to think about their actions and then do better, but to literally repent! Turn around, change directions, and go in a different way from their current course. Turning away from Jesus and from the love needed to operate within the work of faith was considered serious enough to demand a repentance. As we know, the word "repent" means "to change direction," to "turn around." The church at Ephesus needed to turn itself around, change the course it was taking away from the things of God and get itself back on track. It was so serious, in fact, that if they did not turn back toward God and return to where they needed to be, He would come and "remove their lampstand from its place." This is parallel to what the Prophet Malachi spoke of when he talked about shutting the doors and putting out the temple fires (Malachi 1:10). God would – and will – shut down every false house of worship that bears His Name. Every time someone turns from their first love and does not return to it, that church becomes an empty place. Turning back diverts this, refusing to return snuffs out the church, just like a candle on a lampstand.

They were told they had one thing in their favor: they hated the practices of the Nicolaitans, which Jesus also is described to hate. The major question to readers now is just who were the Nicolaitans and why were they so important that they were mentioned here in Revelation? Truth be told, we don't really know exactly who they were or what it was specifically that they believed. There is a lot of speculation about what they believed, who they were, and what their worship was like, but it remains exactly that: speculation. What we do know is that they were a group founded by a deacon named Nicholas. The agreement ends there. Some believe they were a group of hedonists, some believe they were a group that made distinctions between the laity and the clergy, thus adhering to a non-Biblical hierarchy, and still others believe that they would eat food that was offered to idols. It is my own belief that it doesn't specifically matter what they believed, what matters is that they did not adhere to the truth Christ taught. This should make us cautious of groups that do not teach what is true, even if they seem to have started from a reputable source. Remaining in truth means we examine teaching and not just judge by the associations of its source. We are cautioned repeatedly not to fall into false teaching (Matthew 7:15-20, Acts 20:30, Romans 16:17, 2 Timothy 4:1-5, Titus 3:9, 2 Peter 2:1-3), and that is, perhaps, the strongest point of the church at Ephesus. Their strength, however, had led them to a place where they had lost hope, faith, and perspective on why they did what they were called to do. God calls us to a completion here: yes, have discernment, but do not fall away from the love of Christ and faith that we are first called to when we are in our works of ministry.

The letter to the church at Ephesus ends the same way all the letters end: calling those who have an ear to hear to listen to what the Spirit is saying. This is just as much for us now as it was for them in the first century, as it is for people of times in between. The Spirit is speaking. The Spirit speaks through the prophets; He speaks through the mystics; He speaks through the leaders; He speaks through His revelation. We need to be attuned enough with the Spirit to hear exactly what He is saying in every time: to hear the call to completion and perfection, in every age. That call has not and will not change. The words then segue into speaking about "he who overcomes." What does it mean to overcome? It means that we can deal with and conquer the issues we face, and to defeat the work of the enemy in our lives. The reward mentioned in this letter is the right to eat from the tree of life in the paradise of God. We understand the paradise of God to be a reference to heaven, but it is also a reference to the "new heavens and new earth," by which both shall be transformed and the veil between the two will be lifted. Scholars disagree about the imagery of the tree of life, and whether it is a reference to a real tree or a metaphor for something else. I believe it is an imagery of the life cycle, readily and easily understood by believers to recognize the continuity of it in the context of an agrarian society. Trees return, year after year, with proper care and tending. The use of the tree symbolizes the choice of life – that we choose to eat of its fruits, to tend to it, to receive from it – and the fact that life is something eternal and never-ending. From this natural representation, we find a spiritual lesson. It represents the ultimate victory of humanity, returning from its fallen state, as Adam and Eve ate of the tree of the knowledge of good and evil (Genesis 3:1-24), thus leading them into the fall of sin and death. Eating of the tree of life represents an eternal victory, overcoming the state of Adam's sin and entering the restoration of all things (Acts 3:21, Romans 5:12-21).

Revelation 2:8-11

"To the angel of the church in Smyrna write:

These are the words of Him Who is the First and the Last, Who died and came to life again. I know your afflictions and your poverty – yet you are rich! I know the slander of those who say they are Jews and are not, but are a synagogue of Satan. Do not be afraid of what you are about to suffer. I tell you, the devil will put some of you in prison to test you, and you will suffer persecution for ten days. Be faithful, even to the point of death, and I will give you the crown of life.

He who has an ear, let him hear what the Spirit says to the churches. He who overcomes will not be hurt at all by the second death.

(Related Bible references: Esther 2:12, Psalm 45:8, Song of Solomon 1:13, Matthew 7:15, Acts 19:10, Acts 20:29, Romans 14:9, 1 Timothy 6:18, James 1:12, James 2:5, 1 John 5:5)

The second church, the church in Smyrna, is one of only two churches to receive praise without strong words of correction. I believe Smyrna received praise without correction because their circumstances were such that whatever needed purging would be purged. Leaders should never underestimate the value of circumstances to train churches, leaders, ministries, and people, all on their own. There are leaders who need to just step back and allow the circumstances, whether they are trials, tribulations, or difficult circumstances, or not, to teach and grow the people in those situations. I don't question the church at Smyrna had its issues because all churches have their issues. I know, however, that God knew things we do not know about each of these churches, and He knew that what was in store for them would work some things out. It wasn't necessary to reiterate where they needed improvement, because circumstances would change them, from glory to glory and faith to faith.

Smyrna was a strategically located port city on the Aegean coast. The church at Smyrna was most likely founded during the Apostle Paul's third missionary journey (Acts 19:10). It was at least double the size of Ephesus, with heavy emphasis on Roman commercial development.

The word "Smyrna" is from a Greek word which means "myrrh."[42] Myrrh was an anointing perfumed oil placed on bodies as they were prepared for burial (Matthew 2:11, John 19:39). It was also used by women as a perfume and was considered of great value (Esther 2:12, Psalm 45:8, Song of Solomon 1:13). As we will learn, it is most relevant that the church at Smyrna had such a name reflecting its very nature.

Smyrna's church was, apparently, an urban church. They were what we would classify today as a "ghetto" church, one that is in the inner city, dealing with inner city issues, including poverty. From what we can see in the text, they were dealing with these issues, head on. Jesus does not put these believers down, not at all. He commends them as being poor but being rich! I believe this tells us something important about the church, and, specifically, about "ghetto" churches and those who operate, run, or are a part of them.

Today, we love the big, suburban church movements with arena-like churches in affluent neighborhoods. We scoff at poorer churches, struggling to survive. It is important that we stop buying the lie that suburban life, complete with everything we could ever want, equates to spiritual success. Just because people have things does not mean they have God. A church that has nothing materially – that can be run down, working in more outreaches than income – and helping people live and maintain under difficult to unbearable conditions – is exactly where God can move and where it all "can be at." The church at Smyrna had something the rich churches, the churches that were prosperous financially, the churches that "wanted for nothing" didn't have, couldn't touch, and couldn't fathom.

We need to pay more attention to the ministers that preach in the world's "undesirable" areas. We need to see who is moving and flowing in them, what they are saying, and what God is doing in these urban, inner-city, "ghetto" areas. We also need to see who is coming up in these churches and what God is going in these lives, the testimonies that shall come forth and shall come up as God continues to move through them. For this reason, I believe everyone should be somehow connected to an inner-city church, whether it is directly through covering or attendance, by visiting a few times per year, by fellowshipping, or participating in some way. If we want to learn what it means to be rich, even though we may be financially poor, the Lord clearly tells us in Revelation – look to the "ghetto."

Smyrna was about to undergo trial, from "those who claimed to be Jews, but were of the Synagogue of Satan." Historians and scholars have tripped over this passage time and time again, curious about what it is referring to. If we are to understand imagery properly, we know that Revelation contains Roman, Greek, Persian, Syrian and Jewish imagery – all wrapped up into one. This would have alluded to people who came from a Jewish background, but were not genuinely Jewish, and who have the appearance of belief on the outside (go to the right meeting place, hold to the exterior rituals, and observe the right day), but are frauds. We can apply this imagery to any wolf in sheep's clothing; to those who appear to go to the right church, are associated with the right names, who do the right things and hold to the right exteriors, but inwardly, they are ready to pounce and seize at any moment (Matthew 7:15, Acts 20:29). Smyrna had these coming, people who were ready to turn them over, who were ready to attack them and throw them into prison and persecute them. The Lord made it clear it would only last for a short period, but that those who are faithful would last, even unto the end. The Lord encourages us to endure through trials and periods of suffering, coming to a place where we understand and learn what is really important and what matters to God as we walk through our trials.

Smyrna was clearly fitting of its name, meaning

"myrrh." It brought forth something beautiful from the smell of trial and difficulty, which it walked through in many ways. It had something precious and costly within it, something money couldn't buy. No wonder they were told that he who overcomes shall never encounter the second death. These people who put their faith into action, who walked through their faith even when it wasn't easy, were those who would overcome unto eternal life. Overcoming reminds us that God does not force us to be saved, and while we do not save ourselves, we must allow ourselves to be transformed into His likeness and image as we walk through our journey of faith.

Revelation 2:12-17

"To the angel of the church in Pergamum write:
These are the words of Him Who has the sharp, double-edged sword. I know where you live – where Satan has his throne. Yet you remain true to My Name. You did not renounce your faith in Me, even in the days of Antipas, My faithful witness, who was put to death in your city – where Satan lives.
Nevertheless, I have a few things against you: You have people there who hold to the teaching of Balaam, who taught Balak to entice the Israelites to sin by eating food sacrificed to idols and by committing sexual immorality. Likewise you also have those who hold to the teaching of the Nicolaitans. Repent therefore! Otherwise, I will soon come to you and will fight against them with the sword of my mouth.
He who has an ear, let him hear what the Spirit says to the churches. To him who overcomes, I will give some of the hidden manna. I will also give him a white stone with a new name written on it, known only to him who receives it.

(Related Bible references: Exodus 16:15, Exodus 16:31, Exodus 16:33-34, Leviticus 19:14, Numbers 22:1-41, Numbers 25:1-18, Numbers 31:1-24, Psalm 78:24, Luke 12:8, John 6:51, Acts 15:9, Romans 14:13, Ephesians 5:5, 1 Timothy 3:3-8, Titus 1:7-11, 1 Peter 5:2, 2 Peter 2:15, Hebrews 9:4,

Pergamum (the northernmost city on our list), whose name means "height or elevation,"[43] was not just any city. It was a center for education and eventually a library, containing over 200,000 volumes.[44] This library was second only to the Library of Alexandria. It was also the seat of a great altar in tribute to Zeus, who was, according to Greek theology, the ruler of all things. Under the Attalid dynasty, it became a major cultural center of the ancient Greek world. What this tells us about the church at Pergamum is that it was surrounded by and deeply influenced by the pagan culture which engulfed it. This was not just any ancient city with a few pagans in it, but an important seat for worship within the Greek pagan understanding. It was as if Pergamum hosted the seat of one of the chiefest gods in paganism, thus drawing people to this grand altar to worship a false god on a regular basis.

The church at Pergamum had an awesome opportunity for evangelism. At the same time, they were the minority in a very high pagan culture, saturated by its effects and infiltrations. It is obvious from the words Jesus spoke to this church that some of the effects of their surroundings had sunk in, creating a mix of truth and error, Christian and pagan, that would have affected their witness. Jesus starts by affirming He has the sharp, double-edged sword, which we know is a sword with the ability to cut both ways with little effort. He can cut to the heart of a matter, to execute justice swiftly and cleanly. He also affirms that He knows where the church is, thus acknowledging the unique challenges of the church at Pergamum.

We can see that the church at Pergamum had not forsaken the Name of Jesus, even though they lived in such a pagan atmosphere. They did not renounce their faith, even in the days when a faithful individual named Antipas was put to death. According to church history, Antipas (sometimes called Antipas of Pergamum) was a bishop ordained by the Apostle John. There is a tradition that states he was martyred somewhere around 92 AD. While we know little of his life, what we do know about Antipas tells us a lot about the church at Pergamum and the kind of leadership it had. Antipas was established by the Apostle John as bishop of Pergamum during the Emperor Nero's reign, thus connecting them to his leadership (at least at one point in time, although it does not appear to at the time of Revelation as Antipas had died) and they were people who, we can trust, knew the truth of spiritual matters.

The reputation of the church at Pergamum wasn't all sunshine and roses, however. The church was apparently divided, having issues as some taught one thing and others taught something else. The first major thing Jesus seeks to deal with is the teaching of Balaam. Balaam was an Old Testament prophet hired by Balak, king of the Moabites, to curse the Israelites before they entered the Promised Land (Numbers 22:1-41, Numbers 25:1-18, Numbers 31:1-24). Balaam was a true prophet (according to the Scriptures) but was not an Israelite. He was offered a great amount of money to disobey God and speak against His people. Even though he refused to speak something to Israel that God did not say, he still sought to sabotage Israel as they entered the Promised Land. Balaam returned to Balak and let him know exactly how to get the Israelites to bring about cursing upon themselves: they could be enticed by prostitutes and eating food sacrificed to idols. Even though he didn't do directly what Balak asked of him, he was still enticed by the offer and found a way to bring the Israelites into transgression, leading a plague to fall upon them. Balaam let his spiritual gift and his office be easily swayed by financial profit or gain unto the end of sabotage.

Balak reveals the power of weaknesses, especially in spiritual matters. Financial profit is a temptation for many leaders. Cheating on God by engaging with idols (whether through food or sex) can be a general temptation for many. In his weakness, he led Israel into a weak spot.

Leaders in the New Testament are warned against this type of temptation in more than one place (1 Timothy 3:3-8, Titus 1:7-11, 1 Peter 5:2), thus revealing to us that it must have been an issue among first-century leaders. There will always be someone who desires to sabotage others, especially if the opportunity to sabotage takes on the form of introducing self-sabotage. We know that it is against our faith to cause others to stumble (Leviticus 19:14, Romans 14:13). It is essential leaders, especially those with influence (such as prophets) do not seek to sabotage, derail, or influence believers away from the things of God, because using their power to do so is evil. We also see the church at Pergamum corrected because it was teaching the doctrines of the Nicolaitans, which were mentioned earlier. These issues were so important to Jesus, to the continuation of the faith of this church, they were commanded to repent or He Himself would fight against those of this church who were in these matters with His own words, His own clear judgment rendered on these individuals.

The "hidden manna" referred to in Revelation 2:17 puzzles scholars. In a literal context, it can refer to the manna hidden in a pot and placed within the Ark of the Covenant (Exodus 16:33-34, Hebrews 9:4). Manna was a representative of the way in which God cared for the Israelites, even when they were unable to care for themselves. The hidden manna, thus, has a deeper spiritual understanding for us. It can represent all the ways God has taken care of the church and His people in the church; in ways we were unable to see or did not see at the time. It can, as a source of provision in the Old Testament, represent God's provision to us today, both spiritual and natural. It can represent the important, deeper spiritual truths that are far beyond the elementary things that we do not always learn, because people distort or hide them from us (or in this era, simply do not teach them). The hidden manna is our deeper spiritual food, which brings us into a new place and a new revelation of Him, a mystical sense, of understanding those things that are not seen with the naked eye.

The "white stone with a new name" is equally puzzling to scholars, and a little research reveals this one is of great debate. The mistake many make is to take the image of hidden manna and try to reconcile it with mention of the white stone, not realizing they are two different systems of reference. The hidden manna is uniquely Jewish, while the white stone is uniquely Greek. In ancient times, a stone or pebble was used as a source of admittance or entry into an event (kind of like a concert or ticket stub). Having proved that whoever had it had the right to be where they were. This obviously refers to the last day, to all things relating to the return of Christ and the new heavens and new earth, and that those who overcome would be able, by proof, to enter into the physical manifestation of eternal life. The term "white" does not necessarily mean the color white (although it can be used in that context) but can also refer to being brilliant or clear. It may refer to a precious stone, such as a diamond, or another precious stone of tremendous value or brilliance. Changing one's name was an ancient practice across various cultures, and signified changes in social, marital, spiritual, cultural, interest, or familial status. Just as Revelation talks about newness – new heavens and earth, new creatures, and a new song sung by the redeemed – a name change signifies this new status, one where sin and death no longer have any hold upon a person, and all of life is made new, with a permanent change in their life status. The way in which this change shall affect each person will be known only to them, for it will be something that no one can describe – or explain – what a change has taken place.

Revelation 2:18-29

"To the angel of the church in Thyatira write:

These are the words of the Son of God, Whose eyes are like blazing fire and whose feet are like burnished bronze. I know your deeds, your love and faith, your service and perseverance, and that you are now doing more than you did at first.

Nevertheless, I have this against you: You tolerate that woman Jezebel, who calls herself a prophetess. By her teaching she misleads my servants into sexual immorality and the eating of food sacrificed to idols. I have given her time to repent of her immorality, but she is unwilling. So I will cast her on a bed of suffering, and I will make those who commit adultery with her suffer intensely, unless they repent of her ways. I will strike her children dead. Then all the churches will know that I am He Who searches hearts and minds, and I will repay each of you according to your deeds. Now I say to the rest of you in Thyatira, to you who do not hold to her teaching and have not learned Satan's so-called deep secrets (I will not impose any other burden on you): Only hold on to what you have until I come.

To him who overcomes and does my will to the end, I will give authority over the nations – 'He will rule them with an iron scepter; He will dash them to pieces like pottery" – just as I have received authority from My Father. I will also give him the morning star. He who has an ear, let him hear what the Spirit says to the churches.

(Related Bible references: 1 Kings 16:29-33, 1 Kings 19:1-5, 1 Kings 21:1-29, 2 Kings 9:22, Psalm 2:8, Matthew 16:27, Matthew 19:28, Matthew 28:20, Luke 22:29, Acts 15:29, Acts 16:14, Romans 2:4-5, 1 Corinthians 4:5, Galatians 5:19, Philippians 3:16, Hebrews 6:10, James 2:20)

The last church to be mentioned in Revelation 2 is the church at Thyatira, which, as we can gather from what is said about it, had issues like that of Pergamum: being Christian in a largely pagan atmosphere, one that caused challenge and issue to their faith.

Thyatira was a wealthy Lydian community, so near to the ancient country of Mysia, some believed it was a part of that nation. Even though it was a wealthy city, it was not located on a trade route. It was known for artisan trade guilds, of which every artisan was required to belong, and each professional body owned property and was able to create great buildings, altars, and fixed items. Thyatira was also known for its fabric dyers' guild, known for its signature purple-red color, known as a sign of wealth and royalty. More significantly, Thyatira was a pagan seat, so much so that the artisan guilds were deeply interconnected with the religious beliefs of the community. There were several temples and honors to different pagan deities, specifically the sun god (Tyrimnos), a goddess associated with the sun god (Boreatene), and a Persian-influenced sibyl (Sambethe).[45]

It's obvious from historical research that Thyatira had issues separating the sacred and the secular. Everything was so intertwined: from politics, to work, to even religion, it was impossible to say one ended in one point and another began. This caused great solidarity, great work ethics, even great financial abundance. It did not create good spiritual discernment among the Christian church there. It also caused conflict for Christians there, uncertain of what to do, what to partake in, what line was "too far," and what was or was not acceptable. To say that the church at Thyatira was the "odor of affliction" (that being what the name Thyatira means) was certainly not due to financial difficulties. Quite the contrary, the church at Thyatira suffered from spiritual affliction; from the price of compromise that led the people far from where they needed to be in Christ and into such a serious state of spiritual question, it caused damage to the faith identity of the people. They were afflicted in conflict; by a culture that demanded more of them than they were faithfully allowed to give; and by constant concerns about where their faith was to begin in the face of economics and profit.

Jesus begins by lauding them for deeds, love, faith, service, and perseverance. They were doing more of these things than they did at first. They clearly showed their love for others, and their true heart for others, through their deeds. They understood love to be an attribute, an underlying principle that ran as a thread through all other things, that defined the exteriors of their faith. They excelled in this understanding due to, of all things, their cultural influences. The people at Thyatira didn't understand distinctions, such as separation of church and state, or a separation of the sacred from the secular. Everything was a part of one thing, flowing from that one concept. They knew how to do, how to be, how to give, how to serve, and how to persevere because of the environment they found themselves in. This led them to do good – to do more – and to be more than anyone would have ever expected or anticipated.

This common thread, however, is also what wound up leading them astray in certain areas. The church at Thyatira was following the woman "Jezebel," who was calling herself a "prophetess." Who was this woman, and why was she such an issue within the community?

If you're familiar with Old Testament history, Jezebel was a queen, reigning during the time of the Prophet Elijah. She was the wife of King Ahab. The story tells us she was the daughter of King Ethbaall I of Tyre, minding her own business in her pagan nation when King Ahab deliberately sought her out because she was an idolater. She set herself against the prophets of God (especially Elijah) and had Naboth, a citizen of Jezreel killed because he refused to sell his vineyard to Ahab (1 Kings 16:29-33, 1 Kings 19:1-5, 1 Kings 21:1-29).

By New Testament times, Jezebel was long dead. That tells us this woman must have been associated with her for some spiritual reason, but what?

The first option is that her name was actually Jezebel. It's not impossible, but it's unlikely.

The second option is that, much like Jezebel, the church at Thyatira sought this woman out as an idolater and brought her into the house of God. Through her idolatry, the church was led into sexual immorality (likely pagan sex rites) and was no longer following true theology, as they were following false gods (specifically Sambethe, a Persian deity adopted by Jewish idolaters, influencing the general Judean world with prophecies of national leaders).

That "prophetess Jezebel" was most likely a reference to is the female oracle who sat in the temple of Sambethe and spoke words on behalf of the sibyl to the people, the sibyl who was believed to be an oracle herself. She taught the people to eat food sacrificed to idols in connection with the pagan rites and rituals she would have been accustomed to and a part of as well as pagan sexual or fertility rites. By encouraging as such, she wasn't just encouraging people to eat the meat – because eating the meat in this particular culture would have been understood as participation along with the rites. Rather than following sound prophets, the people of the church at Thyatira were being influenced by this pagan oracle, engaging in rites to her gods and acting contrary to the works in which they excelled. The matters were so serious, Jesus states that she had been addressed, did not repent, and she would have to reap the consequences for her actions (suffering and the death of her spiritual offspring). Those who chose to follow in her ways would have to experience the consequences reserved for her, each choosing the results deserving of their deeds. Jesus explains that this is not without purpose, however. Because of the consequences, all the churches will know that Jesus knows all things, even those which were hidden. He searches hearts and minds, and it will be a call to the churches to conduct themselves in a complete way, transcending belief and action, and putting the two together, once and for all. Doing a few things right and a few things wrong shows a disunity. It is God's desire that the same concept of underlying principles would engage the church, without conflict of belief or action.

Those in the church who did not embrace the principles of the false prophetess were told to hold on to what they had until He comes again. They were not given the responsibility to fix the wrongdoers, to try and impose on others, but were simply told to hold fast and persevere, not succumbing to false teaching. Jesus' final words to the church at Thyatira were not just about overcoming but doing His will to the end. Those who do both will be given authority to rule, along with Christ. The authority He has received, He in turn will give to us, to rule and guide. We must remain faithful to rule with and receive Him in our lives. We must recognize the line between the social and the spiritual and find the proper balance as we go along in our lives. The Morning Star can represent Jesus Himself, it can represent the brightness of the eternal day, the "morning star" here representing the sun, or eternal brightness, the promise of eternity with no darkness. Surely, with such profound words, those of us with ears to hear, we should hear.

The Scroll and

5 Then I saw i
sealed[t] with
break the seals an
scroll or even loo
scroll or look insi
dah, the Root of D

[6]Then I saw a L
by the four living cr
its[u] of God sent out
on the throne.[v] [7]An
before the Lamb. Eac
[prayers][w] of the sain

JESUS IS ALWAYS ABLE TO OVERCOME

G

Chapter Three

Key verses

- Verses 1-3: *To the angel of the church in Sardis write: These are the words of Him Who holds the seven spirits of God and the seven stars. I know your deeds; you have a reputation of being alive, but you are dead. Wake up! Strengthen what remains and is about to die, for I have not found your deeds complete in the sight of my God. Remember, therefore, what you have received and heard; obey it, and repent. But if you do not wake up, I will come like a thief, and you will not know at what time I will come to you.*

- Verses 8-10: *I know your deeds. See, I have placed before you an open door that no one can shut. I know that you have little strength, yet you have kept My Word and have not denied My Name. I will make those who are of the synagogue of Satan, who claim to be Jews though they are not, but are liars – I will make them come and fall down at your feet and acknowledge that I have loved you. Since you have kept my command to endure patiently, I will also keep you from the hour of trial that is going to come upon the whole world to test those who live on the earth.*

- Verses 15-18: *I know your deeds, that you are neither cold nor hot. I wish you were either one or the other! So, because you are lukewarm – neither hot nor cold – I am about to spit you out of my mouth. You say, 'I am rich; I have acquired wealth and do not need a thing.' But you do not realize that you are wretched, pitiful, poor, blind and naked. I counsel you to buy from me gold refined in the fire, so you can become rich; and white clothes to wear, so you can cover your shameful nakedness; and salve to put on your eyes, so you can see.*

- Verse 20: *Here I am! I stand at the door and knock. If anyone hears My voice and opens the door, I will come in and eat with him, and he with Me.*

Words and phrases to know

- Sardis: From the Greek word *Sardeis* which means "Sardis = "red ones;" a luxurious city in Asia Minor, the capital of Lydia."[1]

- Alive: From the Greek word *zao* which means "to live, breathe, be among the living (not lifeless, not dead); to enjoy real life; to live i.e. pass life, in the manner of the living and acting; living water, having vital power in itself and exerting the same upon the soul; metaph. to be in full vigour."[2]

- Strengthen: From the Greek word *sterizo* which means "to make stable, place firmly, set fast, fix; to strengthen, make firm; to render constant, confirm, one's mind."[3]

- Complete: From the Greek word *pleroo* which means "to make full, to fill up, i.e. to fill to the full; to render full, i.e. to complete."[4]

- Soiled: From the Greek word *moluno* which means "to pollute, stain, contaminate, defile."[5]

- Book of life: From two Greek words: *biblos* which means "a written book, a roll, a scroll"[6] and *zoe* which means "life."[7]

- Philadelphia: From the Greek word *Philadelpheia* which means "Philadelphia = "brotherly love;" a city of Lydia in Asia Minor, situated near the eastern base of of Mount Tmolus, founded and named by the Pergamene king, Attalus II Philadelphus. After the death of Attalus III Philometor, 133 BC, it together with his entire kingdom came by his will under the jurisdiction of the Romans."[8]

- Holy: From the Greek word *hagios* which means "most holy thing, a saint."[9]

- Strength: From the Greek word *dunamis* which means "strength power, ability."[10]

- Hour of trial: From two Greek words: *hora* which means "a certain definite time or season fixed by natural law and returning with the revolving year; the daytime (bounded by the rising and setting of the sun), a day; a twelfth part of the day-time, an hour, (the twelve hours of the day are reckoned from the rising to the setting of the sun); any definite time, point of time, moment"[11] and *peirasmos* which means "an experiment, attempt, trial, proving."[12]

- Soon: From the Greek word *tachu* which means "quickly, speedily (without delay)."[13]

- Pillar: From the Greek word *stulos* which means "a pillar; a column; a prop or support."[14]

- Temple: From the Greek word *naos* which means "used of the temple at Jerusalem, but only of the sacred edifice (or sanctuary) itself, consisting of the

Holy place and the Holy of Holies (in classical Greek it is used of the sanctuary or cell of the temple, where the image of gold was placed which is distinguished from the whole enclosure)."[15]

- New Jersualem: From two Greek words: *kainos* which means "new"[16] and *Hierousalem* which means "Jerusalem = "set ye double peace;" denotes either the city itself or the inhabitants; "the Jerusalem that now is", with its present religious institutions, i.e. the Mosaic system, so designated from its primary external location; "Jerusalem that is above", that is existing in heaven, according to the pattern of which the earthly Jerusalem was supposed to be built; "the heavenly Jerusalem", that is the heavenly abode of God, Christ, the angels, saints of the Old and New Testament periods and those Christians that are alive at Christ's return; "the New Jerusalem", a splendid visible city to be let down from heaven after the renovation of the world, the future abode of the blessed."[17]

- Heaven: From the Greek word *ouranos* which means "the vaulted expanse of the sky with all things visible in it; the region above the sidereal heavens, the seat of order of things eternal and consummately perfect where God dwells and other heavenly beings."[18]

- Amen: From the Greek word *amen* which means "firm; verily, amen; at the end - so it is, so be it, may it be fulfilled. It was a custom, which passed over from the synagogues to the Christian assemblies, that when he who had read or discoursed, had offered up solemn prayer to God, the others responded Amen, and thus made the substance of what was uttered their own."[19]

- Laodicea: From the Greek word *Laodikeus* which means "a Laodicean, an inhabitant of Laodicea."[20]

- Cold: From the Greek word *psuchros* which means "cold, cool; metaph. cold i.e. sluggish, inert, in mind: of one destitute of warm Christian faith and the desire for holiness."[21]

- Hot: From the Greek word *zestos* which means "boiling hot, hot; metaph. of fervour of mind and zeal."[22]

- Lukewarm: From the Greek word *chliaros* which means "tepid, lukewarm; metaph. of the condition of the soul wretchedly fluctuating between a torpor and a fervour of love."[23]

- Rich: From the Greek word *plousios* which means "wealthy, abounding in material resources; metaph. abounding, abundantly supplied."[24]

- Wretched: From the Greek word *talaiporos* which means "enduring toils and troubles; afflicted, wretched."[25]

- Pitiful: From the Greek word *eleeinos* which means "to be pitied, miserable."[26]

- Poor: From the Greek word *ptochos* which means "reduced to beggary, begging, asking alms; destitute of wealth, influence, position, honour; lacking in anything."[27]

- Blind: From the Greek word *tuphlos* which means "blind; mentally blind."[28]

- Naked: From the Greek word *gumnos* which means "properly unclad, without clothing, the naked body; metaph. naked, i.e. open, lay bare."[29]

- Rebuke: From the Greek word *elegcho* which means "to convict, refute, confute; to find fault with, correct."[30]

- Discipline: From the Greek word *paideuo* which means "to train children; to chastise."[31]

- Door: From the Greek word *thura* which means "a door."[32]

- Knock: From the Greek word *krouo* which means "to knock: at the door."[33]

- Eat: From the Greek word *deipneo* which means "to sup."[34]

Revelation 3:1-6

"To the angel of the church in Sardis write:
These are the words of Him Who holds the seven spirits of God and the seven stars. I know your deeds; you have a reputation of being alive, but you are dead. Wake up! Strengthen what remains and is about to die, for I have not found your deeds complete in the sight of my God. Remember, therefore, what you have received and heard; obey it, and repent. But if you do not wake up, I will come like a thief, and you will not know at what time I will come to you.
Yet you have a few people in Sardis who have not soiled their clothes. They will walk with Me, dressed in white, for they are worthy. He who overcomes will, like them, be dressed in white. I will never blot out his name from the book of life, but will acknowledge his name

before My father and His angels. He who has an ear, let him hear what the Spirit says to the churches.

(Related Bible references: Exodus 38:26, Numbers 1:19-22, Numbers 1:44-47, Numbers 2:32-33, Numbers 3:22-42, Numbers 4:34-49, Matthew 24:42, Luke 12:39, Luke 21:36, James 2:26)

Revelation 3 continues and finishes the discourse to the seven churches. While chapter 2 contained praise and criticism, it would appear that the churches in Revelation 3 receive far more criticism than praise. In fact, two of the three churches mentioned in Revelation 3 do not receive any praise whatsoever, and the church at Philadelphia was encouraged to continue and to persevere (with minimum praise, but a call to endure, instead). The chapter immediately opens with words to the church at Sardis, and ends with words to the church at Laodicea.

Jesus reveals Himself to be the one Who holds the seven spirits of God and the seven stars, the seven stars we already have discussed. The term "seven spirits of God" can also be translated as "sevenfold Spirit," and is a reference to the seven spiritual gifting attributes mentioned in Isaiah 11:1-2: *Then a shoot will spring from the stem of Jesse, And a branch from His roots will bear fruit. The Spirit of the* LORD *will rest on Him, The spirit of wisdom and understanding, The spirit of counsel and strength, The spirit of knowledge and the fear of the* LORD. *(NASB)* Jesus was affirming His authority, as He fulfills prophecy; but they are also important to keep in mind as He addresses the final three churches that receive specific address in the book of Revelation. This seven-fold Spirit is:

- Spirit of the LORD: The phrase "Spirit of the LORD" is a reference to the Holy Spirit, also called the Holy Ghost, which expresses supremacy and emphasis that this is not just some random spirit, it is not a demonic spirit, but it is truly the essence, power, and experience of God from a spiritual perspective. We can trust it, rely on it, believe in it, and recognize His authority.

- Wisdom: Wisdom has been defined throughout history in many different ways, but it is often associated with the ability to figure out complicated situations in a just and fair way. We can understand wisdom to be a practical application of God's precepts in a way that changes life. If we walk in wisdom, we will come to a place of good judgment, the ability to foresee the results of future decisions, and a perspective only God can give us, especially when we can't always see the outcome of a circumstance. Walking in wisdom ensures we can see a situation as God would have us see it, so we are able to implement His characteristics of judgment, fairness, and practicality in everything we encounter. Wisdom gives us the personal 'check' in our personalities to make sure we allow God to work through us, rather than operating on ego or personal attitude.

- Understanding: Understanding is an important precept that we do not often think much about today or consider, especially when forming opinions or working with others. While we hear a lot about tolerance, tolerance eliminates the principle necessary to develop understanding all together. Understanding requires an emptying of oneself and personal perspectives, while tolerance does not, because tolerance puts up with whatever does not conform to its own opinions. If we are people of understanding, we are called to empty ourselves of our own perspectives, allowing God to enlighten and educate on vital matters. If we want to be people of compassion, we need to be people who understand the issues, problems, and challenges people face. Understanding comes from both study and revelation, knowing about current events and ways we can assist people in the things that challenge, bother, affect, and impact others.

- Counsel: Counsel is the ability to give advice in a given situation. If we understand counsel beyond the world's definition of it, it is about giving advice, practical word, and hope as we breathe life into the dying world. Counsel operates not on opinion or personal feelings, but on spiritual perspective to help and guide someone beyond the obvious, beyond the immediate, into the eternal.

- Strength: Strength is the ability to handle something that is somehow heavy or burdensome. With physical, emotional, and spiritual uses, strength relates to our endurance, flexibility, and purpose through tests and trials.

- Knowledge: Knowledge is the application of learning. It indicates we understand the things we have studied and know how to apply them to life and explain them to others. It is the result of visible discipline, of reaping the result of the learning process. Knowledge is acquired: it is not something that just happens. For a person to acquire knowledge, they must pursue learning through study and application.

- Fear of the Lord: Today we associate fear with negativity, but in its basic form, the term "fear" means to have a sense of reverence, awe, or reverential awe. For someone to have the "fear of the Lord" means they recognize Who God is, the power He has, and that they understand His sovereign position over both the universe and them personally as an individual. Fear of the Lord is to consider the position of oneself in humility next to the incredible being and power found in God, our Creator.

These different attributes relate to leadership authority and are components for good leadership. It's no wonder that we find them perfectly balanced in our Lord and Savior, and also that these are attributes spoken of in connection with leadership during His reign at the end of time. They are gifts, not just to Jesus, but to those who walk in His footsteps as leaders of His people. The churches of Asia were not just being prepared for things in their immediate, but also for things to come and things that would one day be even more relevant than they were back then. The three churches of Asia mentioned in Revelation 3 all represent circumstances and situations that relate to leadership exercises, either in a positive or negative way. Jesus establishes Himself as the Leader of all, and the One we need to seek as we go about our lives in ministry leadership.

Sardis, capital of Lydia, was an ancient city that was in what would be modern-day Turkey. It was one of the most important seats of the Persian Empire and was the seat of a proconsul in the Roman government. It was known for its military strength, its important roadway that led from the interior of the province to the coast of the Agean sea, and then its wide and fertile plain, perfect for agricultural endeavors. Its name means "red ones,"[35] which refers to both its luxurious style of life and the fertile plain it was known for.

The church at Sardis teaches us a little thing about reputations: they aren't always true. Today, people talk a lot about the reputations they have and focus on portraying a certain image...even if the image is a complete lie. The church at Sardis had a great reputation: they were a church that had a reputation for being alive. Everyone knew about them! They were the "alive" church, one that was known for being lively, vibrant, desirable, one everyone wanted to attend and connect to. They looked large, prosperous, healthy, and purposeful...but the truth was far from the reputation they had. They were a church that looked alive but was dead.

This kind of deception was not a laughing matter, nor was it something Jesus addressed lightly. It wasn't a situation where Jesus said, "Well, they mean well, I'm not going to be critical of them." He looked at the internals of their dynamics, while everyone else looked at what was going on with them on the surface. They were to strengthen that which remains by building upon essential principles and repenting from their actions. The inside, or interior life of their church, needed to match what it appeared to be on the surface. They were warned to repent and change their ways, or the Lord would come to them as a thief, taking what needed to be removed, even unto death, and the end of the church.

Many believe Jesus' words to Laodicea were the harshest He spoke to the churches, but I disagree. I believe the dishonesty, misleading nature, and deceptiveness in Sardis rendered Jesus' harshest rebuke, urging the church to get it together before it was too late. Recognizing the church to look alive but really was dead should cause us all, especially leaders, to examine the states of our church and make sure we are not just putting on a good display for onlookers. Being the church is about far more than just appearances. The church at Sardis reminds us how important it is to be real – be real as believers, be real as people, be real as the church – and not just a stodgy church, up for the perfect appearance. Christians are called to be real people, dealing with real issues in our real-life settings. Putting on airs or pretensions is not going to help people get real with God...it's going to further stereotypes that church people look a certain way but aren't really what they appear to be.

What does it mean to be "real?" What is a "real church" and what does it look like? We need to understand that zeal or enthusiasm can be had by anyone, regardless of doctrine. If we think an "alive" church is one that seems to have a lot of noise, excited people, or a lot of running around and confusion, we've been sucked into the same mindset that led people to think the church at Sardis was alive to begin with. Truly being real means that both the leadership and membership of the church can connect with those who come to them in need of the Lord on all levels. A real, living church recognizes the Holy Spirit is alive and active, developing the gifts and callings needed to help individuals as they develop their relationship with God. It's not about special-interest evangelism or only reaching out to one specific group of people, such as seekers or emergers. The true church is alive and active, bringing the experience of heaven to earth present in the Kingdom of God, no matter what the group may be singing, listening to, or if they have no music at all. It's not about comfortable atmospheres, but purposeful to become one, holy, and eternal church, connecting us both from eternity past to eternity future. This also means the church is living no matter what they are doing. Whether street evangelism, reaching out to the homeless or hurting, talking to a friend, performing the rites, rituals, and ordinances of the church, or simply sitting in His presence, the church continues to be alive through the constant ability to connect and live, rather than amuse and entertain.

The few people who did not "soil their clothes" (taint themselves by presenting one thing on the outside but being something else on the inside) in the church at Sardis would experience the ability to walk with Christ, in salvation, celebration, and authority. Those who do likewise and persevere to overcome will experience the same, along with their inclusion in the book of life. The book of life is an echo of Old Testament registers by which people were "counted" or included among a certain group for a certain purpose (Exodus 38:26, Numbers 1:19-22, Numbers 1:44-47, Numbers 2:32-33, Numbers 3:22-42, Numbers 4:34-49). To be included in such indicated salvation. What a wonderful thing to encounter, and to behold, as we are proclaimed in the presence of the Father and His angels!

Revelation 3:7-13

"To the angel of the church in Philadelphia write:

These are the words of Him Who is holy and true, Who holds the key of David. What He opens no one can shut, and what He shuts no one can open. I know your deeds. See, I have placed before you an open door that no one can shut. I know that you have little strength, yet you have kept My Word and have not denied My Name. I will make those who are of the synagogue of Satan, who claim to be Jews though they are not, but are liars – I will make them come and fall down at your feet and acknowledge that I have loved you. Since you have kept my command to endure patiently, I will also keep you from the hour of trial that is going to come upon the whole world to test those who live on the earth.

I am coming soon. Hold on to what you have, so that no one will take your crown. Him who overcomes I will make a pillar in the temple of My God. Never again will he leave it. I will write on him the Name of My God and the name of the city of My God, the new Jerusalem, which is coming down out of heaven from My God; and I will also write on him My new Name. He who has an ear, let him hear what the Spirit says to the churches.

(Related Bible references: 2 Chronicles 3:17, Psalm 90:4, Isaiah 22:22, Isaiah 60:14, Luke 1:32, John 6:69, 1 Corinthians 12:3, 2 Corinthians 2:12, Galatians 5:22-23, Ephesians 2:21, James 1:12, 1 Peter 2:5, 2 Peter 3:8, Revelation 13:15-18)

If you do an internet search on the sixth church, the church of Philadelphia, you will probably discover a universal praise for this church. There are those who speak of it in "golden" terms, as if it represents the most positive, glowing ideal for the church that could ever exist. It's almost universal to believe that the church at Philadelphia is the perfect church, the one we should model to be like and embrace. Jesus didn't criticize it, and many believe that means all they received was praise...but is this the truth?

In reading the words to the church at Philadelphia, it is true that they do not receive any correction. This, however, doesn't mean that they automatically received exclusive praise, either. In stark contrast to the churches that received both praise and criticism, the church at Philadelphia doesn't appear to receive either one. The church at Philadelphia is acknowledged for doing things right, but these acknowledgements aren't exceeding or fussed over. There is a completely different focus in the letter to the church at Philadelphia than praise or criticism, and it is one of endurance.

The focus of Jesus on the exclusive principle of endurance to the church at Philadelphia is unique among the letters. I highly doubt that this means there were no problems in the church; most likely, given the things they had and were to encounter, this is probably far from the truth. The word "Philadelphia" means "brotherly love," a title given to the city in honor of the love King Eumenes had for his brother, Attalus. The city itself was in the Kuzucay Valley, in the modern Turkish province of Manisa.[36] Philadelphia was known for wine produced from fertile grape fields and a series of volcanic cliffs found behind the city, called "inkwells." It was also known for its pagan temples, thus its reputation as "Little Athens."[37] In other words, the city of Philadelphia was still a pagan city, and the church at Philadelphia, surrounded by a largely pagan culture. We know there were one or two people, here and there, who still adapted to the culture that surrounded the church and the challenges that existed in that vicinity.

Jesus outright tells the city that they have little strength. They were probably small in number and long weary from the trials and tribulations they faced. The thing the church at Philadelphia had which the others mentioned prior did not is a resolve to do right in unity. The church in Philadelphia was not divided all over the place, despite the problems they might have had as people. They remained a constant force, as tired as they might have been. They didn't let the things that were going on break them up. This should immediately tell us that while we might not get everything right, unity is an essential and important precept in church living. The next essential points are to uphold His Name and keep His Word. In looking at Sardis, we discussed what it means to have a church that was alive and real, versus one that was dead. One point made was the essential nature of the activity of the Holy Spirit, moving and working in and through the believers. We know that no one can say "Jesus is Lord" except by the Spirit (1 Corinthians 12:3) and that the Spirit is what makes the church alive and active, vital and relevant from age to age.

To keep His Word means to keep and uphold prophecy, to understand and obey what is spoken to us by His Word, and to proclaim His Name throughout our lifetimes. No matter how tired the church at Philadelphia was, they stuck together and stuck out their adherence to the Gospel. It's important to keep going in God's direction, no matter how tired we are.

Those who appear one way, but are another, will come forth and fall down at the feet of Philadelphia's church, to acknowledge God has loved them. This is about far more than just revenge or vengeance on an enemy. There are many who desire people to come and repent before them because they think it will vindicate what happened to them. Jesus isn't saying this will be an action of, "Oh I am so sorry, we wronged you." He is saying that these false people will be forced to recognize that He loved the church of Philadelphia. Too often, we believe that we "go through" trials as some sort of punishment. People are quick to assume that God does not love, nor is with someone else, because they are having a difficult time. People assume God is only with someone if things are easy or good and take opposition as a sign of punishment. Clearly God was always with the church at Philadelphia, no matter how difficult their circumstances became. To acknowledge that God loved this church was a victory in proving that circumstances don't dictate the underlying principle of love that God has for each and every one of us. Our trials prove that God loves us in them, and what we learn from them shows us God loves us because He teaches us through them. God does not love our judgment of others and our unwillingness to stand with others through trials, and thus, the synagogue of Satan shall come to a place of humility as the love of God is not based on status.

The church at Philadelphia knew how to endure, and not just get through, but to endure patiently. They knew that patience is a fruit of the spirit (Galatians 5:22-23) that comes about by resting in God's timing rather than in one's own. Patience is a sign that we trust God beyond words, beyond theism and theology, and rest that He knows the end from the beginning, even if we don't like the way things seem or the length of time it takes to complete. Patience isn't about waiting; it is about living while God works things out for our good, and we trust Him completely in the meantime. Patience enabled the church at Philadelphia to avoid a period of trial to come upon the earth, and if we truly know how to endure with patience, we too will be able to be kept from massive and major trials by God's protective hand.

Jesus speaks of coming "soon." When we speak of something happening "soon" in English, we think that means it will happen any second. It is not untrue to expect that Jesus could return at any second, but it is clear from history that Jesus did not come back in the way we use the term "soon." Understanding immediacy in *karios* time is different from *chronos*, recognizing that the way in which God looks at timetables is radically different from the way we view them (Psalm 90:4, 2 Peter 3:8). Putting things into place, aligning matters, and watching the Lord return all happens in the blink of an eye to God, but seems to take an eternity to us. It is God's desire that, by coming to a deeper understanding of revelation, we might recognize the differences in God's timing and become more accustomed to His workings than ours. Those who wait things out to overcoming become pillars in the temple of God – they become a very foundation to its structure, to the way in which it is upheld, to the way in which it can stand. By upholding the Word to become overcomers, we shall become something so foundational that it cannot be removed without causing the entire building to collapse. Never again shall we leave it, but shall we uphold and enhance it, all the days to come. The Name of God and God's city shall be written upon such as these, a counter to the mark of the beast (Revelation 13:15-18), meant to signify not necessarily a literal writing, but to indicate they belong to God, and God to them. Even Jesus Himself shall receive a new name, which He shall also write upon us, for we shall be His eternal treasure.

Revelation 3:14-22

"To the angel of the church in Laodicea write:

These are the words of the Amen, the faithful and true witness, the ruler of God's creation. I know your deeds, that you are neither cold nor hot. I wish you were either one or the other! So, because you are lukewarm – neither hot nor cold – I am about to spit you out of my mouth. You say, 'I am rich; I have acquired wealth and do not need a thing.' But you do not realize that you are wretched, pitiful, poor, blind and naked. I counsel you to buy from Me gold refined in the fire, so you can become rich; and white clothes to wear, so you can cover your shameful nakedness; and salve to put on your eyes, so you can see.

Those whom I love I rebuke and discipline. So be earnest, and repent. Here I am! I stand at the door and knock. If anyone hears My voice and opens the door, I will come in and eat with him, and he with Me.

To him who overcomes, I will give the right to sit with Me on My throne, just as I overcame and sat down with My Father on His throne. He who has an ear, let him hear what the Spirit says to the churches."

(Related Bible references: Leviticus 27:30-32, Deuteronomy 4:6, Deuteronomy 8:5, Deuteronomy 14:22-28, Judges 9:36, Proverbs 3:12, Proverbs 8:22, Matthew 19:28, Luke 22:30, John 1:14, John 18:37, 1 Corinthians 4:8, 1 Corinthians 11:32, 2 Corinthians 1:20, 2 Corinthians 9:7, Colossians 1:15, Hebrews 3:6, Hebrews 8:5, Hebrews 10:1, Hebrews 10:12, Hebrews 12:6-11, James 1:17, James 5:9, 1 Peter 1:7)

The last church of Asia addressed in these letters is the church at Laodicea. Out of these seven churches, the church of Laodicea is the most written about, preached on, commented on, and discussed, especially in modern times. The church at Laodicea seems to be good fodder because of the language used to describe it and the way in which Jesus seems to have nothing particularly positive to say about it. People use the church at Laodicea to describe the church in modern times, to describe Christians that they do not feel are "zealous" enough in their faith, and as a general judgment to accuse people who disagree on political or social issues. The words from Jesus to the church at Laodicea, however, don't have the sting that people tend to use them for. Jesus' commentary to the church in this city wasn't about political or social opinions, it wasn't used as a comparison against any of the other churches (Jesus didn't compare Laodicea to Philadelphia or Ephesus or any of the others) or to somehow pit believers against each other. The letter was written for the church at Laodicea to look at itself and, recognizing what it was doing, turn itself around. If we look at this letter in this way (and, in essence, look at all the letters to the churches like this) we can see it as a call to examine ourselves, not everyone else.

Laodicea is from a word that means "A people judged; people's opinions." It indicates a place where the people had rule, or control over the area. The city itself was originally named Diospolis ("City of Jupiter"), then Rhoas, after King Antiochus II's wife. It was a city populated with Syrians and Jews, thus making it a little different in circumstance than the other churches spoken of in Revelation. The culture was not so much Greek as Syrian and Jewish (even though the worship of some Greek gods was common), making the challenges and difficulties they faced the same in their essence, but different by some of their nature. Laodicea was reminiscent of Rome in that it too was built on seven hills and was extremely prosperous and booming in population. Thanks to being on a trade route, Laodicea was known for large money exchanges, fine black wool, and its own minted coinage.[38]

Jesus here refers to Himself as the Amen, the "so be it" of each proclamation, the faithful and true witness (the One Who is most reliable), and the Ruler of God's creation (the One Who is Sovereign). He knows all, sees all, hears all, including their deeds, which do matter. It's interesting to note that the wording here indicates Jesus was able to tell their lukewarm attitude by their deeds. It was not a commentary on their worship, on how loud they could shout, on how fast they could dance, on how contemporary their services were, on what translation of the Bible they used, or on how, quite honestly, obnoxious they were as believers when it came to talking to non-believers. It wasn't even that they lacked deeds – because clearly, they must have had some if Jesus was assessing the church based on them. It was a matter of how the actions were done. They were not done for the faith, or not for the faith. The church at Laodicea had deeds done just to do them, just to get by, just to do them because they had to...or something like that. With an abundance of money, doing things for others came without sacrifice. They could acquire what they needed, do things, and move on, with little to no meaning. Having money, being wealthy, and having the status that comes from such identified them.

The church at Laodicea tells us clearly that income is not to define us as a church. The amount of money a church has or does not have does not indicate its level for truth. Money can't buy salvation, eternity, the presence of the Holy Spirit in our lives, the work of God, the gifts of the Spirit, any of it. This does not mean that the church does not need money, but it does mean that we should not be defined by it. As many things, as much stuff, as seemingly "prosperous" as Laodicea was, they were not rich – they were wretched, poor, pitiful, blind, and naked! They could not see their souls wasting away, eternally lost as they chased their material things, ignoring the spiritual things they needed to see to remain spiritually alive, and that they were standing before God totally nude, uncovered, in a shameful state.

How many teachings do we hear in today's church about the very issues that plagued the church at Laodicea? You can turn the television on any time, twenty-four hours a day, and find a preacher who is telling you that God wants you to have more "things." We are encouraged by so-called ministers today to exist in a state of complete discontent, always wanting more, looking for more, hoping for more, never having enough. In this chase for things, people feel they cannot afford to tithe, give, or make offerings, as they sit with their expensive phones, their latest technology, their designer outfits, their bigger houses, and their newer cars. They do the barest minimum – give just what they must, just what "looks right" – but as long as they keep receiving their material things, they think they are right with God.

Then we deal with the attitudes people have about leadership today. There are many who believe the church should represent secular governmental principles, such as democracy or election, when the church was clearly not established for that value or purpose. It was also, likewise, never intended to be controlled by those who have money, which was most likely an issue at Laodicea, based on Jesus' words to this church. Too many leaders have been guilty of allowing those who give the most to their ministries to control the direction it takes, fearing the money will dry up if the individuals who give it are in any way corrected or disciplined.

Being "lukewarm" indicates the church is doing enough to get by but not doing enough to excel. It indicates a state where people remain in the church to remain comfortable, not being challenged or pushed to move higher in Christ. Throughout history, this has been a problem of the church. The church has, as an organism, struggled to maintain its identity in a world controlled and dominated by money and materialism. Sometimes the church has successfully elevated itself above worldly values and, at other times, it has crushed beneath them. Still, there is a way in which the church conveniently adapts worldly concepts thinking it will keep the church afloat. Rather than relying on the world to keep the church going, we need to rely on God. In relying on God, the people of the church must realize their command and purpose to support the church (not just the local church but the church universal), and that they are to give of their material wealth by God's command (Leviticus 27:30-32, Deuteronomy 14:22-28, 2 Corinthians 9:7). We should receive from Christ that which is eternal, heavenly, purified for eternity, and the white garments, representative of our salvation, our baptism, our standing with Him beyond that which we can ever receive in this lifetime. We need His healing touch over our eyes to transform what we see from the temporal to the eternal, and see ourselves and our situations in eternal eyes, rather than just what we can gain in the immediate.

Jesus rebukes those He loves (Deuteronomy 4:6, Deuteronomy 8:5, Proverbs 3:12, 1 Corinthians 11:32, Hebrews 12:6-11). His words to the church at Laodicea were out of love, out of the hope and intent that they could see where they erred and turn around to see what was right. It wasn't to make them feel as if they were less than the other churches, to get them to vote differently, or to feel a certain way about political issues. He wanted them to see themselves for what they were, for what they had accepted and for how they were representing Him. We are to repent because we hear Him knocking. In that knock is our opportunity for eternity, our opportunity to walk into something that will bring forth communion, a union between the Lord and ourselves.

The ultimate overcoming is to sit on the Lord's throne with Him, signifying the right, once again, to rule along with Him in this new heavens and earth that shall come forth through His rule. In following in His footsteps and overcoming, we shall too receive that same reward.

Chapter 3 ends the epistle portion of the book of Revelation and marks the transition to powerful visions of things now and things to come. Many of these things are just beyond our sight, just beyond our realm. It is most ironic that Revelation first deals with the things that are in the immediate, the things we can see when we look at the church, both back then and even now. We can look around and see these seven churches, with their extensive issues, alive in our own congregations, in our own selves, and our own conflicts and consciences. The things that held these churches back blocked them from seeing eternity, like a tall building blocks the sun from casting its shadow upon us. We say we want more, we say we want to receive of God, then we allow the things of the world to come and consume us. Jesus is telling us through His words to the churches in Revelation how we can have what we say we seek. It is time to stop ignoring these words as applicable for us and start to receive them unto ourselves. If we want to see more, seeing the eternal, the Lord calls to us to deal with these issues, address the things that we cling to because they are a part of the world that surrounds us or that we find ourselves in, and let go of them in favor of an eternity that we can see bits and pieces of, here and there...if we will only look beyond what is right in our face (Judges 9:36, Hebrews 8:5, Hebrews 10:1, James 1:17).

Chapter Four

Key verses

- Verse 1: *After this I looked, and there before me was a door standing open in heaven. And the voice I had first heard speaking to me like a trumpet said, "Come up here, and I will show you what must take place after this."*

- Verses 6-8: *Also before the throne was what looked like a sea of glass, clear as crystal. In the center, around the throne, were four living creatures, and they were covered with eyes, in front and in back. The first living creature was like a lion, the second was like an ox, the third had a face like a man, the fourth was like a flying eagle. Each of the four living creatures had six wings and was covered with eyes all around, even under his wings. Day and night they never stop saying: "Holy, holy, holy is the Lord God Almighty, Who was, and is, and is to come."*

- Verses 10-11: *The twenty-four elders fall down before Him Who sits on the throne, and worship Him Who lives for ever and ever. They lay their crowns before the throne and say: "You are worthy, our Lord and God, to receive glory and honor and power, for You created all things, and by Your will they were created and have their being."*

Words and phrases to know

- After this: From two Greek words: *meta* which means "with, after, behind,"[1] and *tauta* which means "these."[2]

- Jasper: From the Greek word *iaspis* which means "jasper, a precious stone of various colors (for some are purple, others blue, others green, and others the color of brass)."[3]

- Carnelian: From the Greek word *sardinos* which means "a sardius, a precious stone of which there are two types, the former is called a carnelian (because flesh colored) and the latter a sard."[4]

- Rainbow: From the Greek word *iris* which means "a rainbow."[5]

- Emerald: From the Greek word *smaragdinos* which means "emerald, made of emerald."[6]

- Four and twenty elders: From three Greek words: *tessares* which means "four,"[7] *eikosi* which means "twenty,"[8] and *presbuteros* which means "elder, of age; a term of rank or office."[9]

- Sea of glass: From two Greek words: *thalassa* which means "the sea"[10] and *hualinos* which means "of glass or transparent like glass, glassy."[11]

- Crystal: From the Greek word *krustallos* which means "crystal, a kind of precious stone."[12]

- Creatures: From the Greek word *zoon* which means "a living being; an animal, brute, beast."[13]

- Eyes: From the Greek word *ophthalmos* which means "the eye; metaph. the eyes of the mind, the faculty of knowing"[14]

- Lion: From the Greek word *leon* which means "a lion; a brave and mighty hero."[15]

- Ox: From the Greek word *moschos* which means "a tender juicy shoot; offspring; a calf, a bullock, a heifer."[16]

- Face like a man: From three Greek words: *prosopon* which means "the face; the outward appearance of inanimate things,"[17] *hos* which means "as, like, even as, etc.,"[18] and *anthropos* which means "a human being, whether male or female; indefinitely, someone, a man, one; in the plural, people; joined with other words, merchantman."[19]

- Flying eagle: From two Greek words: *petomai* which means "to fly"[20] and *aetos* which means "an eagle: since eagles do not usually go in quest of carrion, this may refer to a vulture that resembles an eagle; an eagle as a standard (Roman Military)."[21]

- Wings: From the Greek word *pterux* which means "a wing: of birds."[22]

- Worthy: From the Greek word *axios* which means "weighing, having weight, having the weight of another thing of like value, worth as much; befitting, congruous, corresponding to a thing; of one who has merited anything worthy."[23]

Revelation 4:1-6a

After this I looked, and there before me was a door standing open in heaven. And the voice I had first heard speaking to me like a trumpet said, "Come up here, and I will show you what must take place after this." At once I was in the Spirit, and there before me was a throne in heaven with someone sitting on it. And the One Who sat there had the appearance of jasper and carnelian. A rainbow, resembling an emerald, encircled the throne. Surrounding the throne were twenty-four other elders. They were dressed in white and had crowns of gold on their heads. From the throne came flashes of lightning, rumblings and peals of thunder. Before the throne, seven lamps were blazing. These are the seven spirits of God. Also before the throne there was what looked like a sea of glass, clear as crystal.

(Related Bible references: Exodus 28:17, 1 Kings 22:19, 1 Chronicles 24:7-19, 1 Chronicles 25:6-31, Psalm 11:4, Ecclesiastes 4:12, Isaiah 6:1, Ezekiel 1:13, Ezekiel 1:26, Daniel 7:9, Romans 15:1, 1 Corinthians 13:12, Ephesians 4:11, Philippians 1:1, 1 Timothy 3:1-13, 1 Timothy 5:17-20, Titus 1:5-9, James 5:14, 1 Peter 5:1-5)

Nowadays I hear too many people casually mention to others that they have been "in the throne room" or "gone before the throne," like it's nothing. It is spoken of in such casual terms, like it is some sort of amusement park ride or a cartoonish-thing that seems more like clever animation than true spiritual reality. If we take away nothing from Revelation chapter 4, we need to realize just how real, how powerful, how awesome, and how life-changing such an experience is. If someone truly goes before the throne of God, they should not return the same.

The truly mystical experience should change the perspective of the individual who encounters it. It should make one desire to be more spiritual, more insightful, deeper in their thinking and approach to life. I don't believe our natural minds can truly comprehend all that the Apostle John saw, heard, smelled, touched, and tasted. I think seeing Jesus on the throne, surrounded by vibrant, jeweled colors, is beyond our imagination. The beauty which emanates from our Lord is incomparable. It is a place of complete perfection, one that commands attention and demands that you drop whatever it is and note what is to come forth from it.

Here we see eternity. Here we see diversity. Here we see clarity and color and vibrancy, all of which speak to us the power and promise of life. It is a vision for all time: occurring since the foundation of the world, happening past, present, and future as the heavenlies pay homage to the One Who reigns forever above us all. People of every era worship the Lord, pay their tribute, and honor their God without such growing tiresome or old.

The numbers of Revelation, which we have already started to speak of more than once, exist as codes by which we can know and understand greater realities without having to obviously state the direct intention. As the book of Revelation was originally a letter circulated under dangerous and threatening circumstances, so the message was considered threatening to the powers that be. Heralding visions of heaven, speech about a shift in power and authority and powers that were greater than those of earth could have easily rendered the bearer of such a letter dead without a second thought. Numbers in Revelation did not exist to divine the future or to "predict" anything. They were not to let people know what the year would hold or what to expect on a certain date. Revelation's numbers are encoded messages, things to point to other realities and let us know the things we need to know without having to outright state them.

In Revelation 4, numbers are all about pictures and images of authority, authority that, when understood properly, supersedes any and all governmental authority this world claims. We can't deny the presence of authority around the throne. The first mention of authority in heavenly realms aside from the Father and the Son is that of the twenty-four elders. These mysterious figures are not ever mentioned by name. Unlike much of Revelation, who exactly these elders are is not of particular debate. There are those who think they are angels (they are not), and some who believe they represent the entire church (they do not), but it's not one of the things that tends to be tackled when one takes on Revelation. Most of the church world seems satisfied to say we don't know who they are. This doesn't make them any less important, however. The number 12 represents governmental authority in the Kingdom, and 24 is a double of that number, representing a perfect balance of authority. I believe in understanding it as a crossover, both God's covenant of salvation with His people and the covenant of leadership with His leaders, representing the past, the present, and the future. This recalls the Levitical priesthood and the Levitical Covenant (an agreement and promise God made with leadership), recalling the Levitical priesthood was divided into twenty-four divisions (1 Chronicles 24:7-19, 1 Chronicles 25:6-31). The twenty-four divisions represented different leadership responsibilities, including worship, music, gatekeeping, sacrifices, and beyond. In the New Covenant, we know there is a five-fold ministry of apostle, prophet, evangelist, pastor and teacher (Ephesians 4:11) and three appointments of bishop, elder, and deacon (Romans 15:1, Philippians 1:1, 1 Timothy 3:1-13, 1 Timothy 5:17-20, Titus 1:5-9, James 5:14, 1 Peter 5:1-5). If we add up the five offices and three appointments, that presents eight different positions of leadership in the church today. The number eight relates to the new order of creation, the New Covenant, and eternal life in Christ, pointing us to the reality that while the imagery does connect to the Old Testament, it is also pointing us to New Covenant leadership. Not only is 24 a double to the representative of Kingdom authority, it is also three times the number of leadership authority established in the New Testament, indicating the three-fold cord (Ecclesiastes 4:12) needed to maintain a leadership strength. In ancient times, the number three represented the first of four spiritually perfect numbers (the others being seven, ten, and 12); it signifies manifestation. Twelve, when broken down and added together, also equates to three (1+2=3) and, thus, we see the number three repeatedly represented within this group. The number 24 (2+4=6) also equals six, indicating the governmental perfection also governs over man. However we break it down and despite any sort of numerical representation, the message remains the same. The 24 elders of representation represent a perfection in Kingdom government, a perfection in leadership, and God's hand upon leadership from both ancient times to modern times. The elders' white attire and crowns of gold carry an eternal purity, as gold purified in the fire, so shall their work, their legacy stand.

- In a certain sense, I believe these elders represent all who are a part of the Ephesians 4:11 ministry or the appointments who labor for the work of God. I believe their limited number speaks to the reality that not all who labor does so for the Lord. We must truly discern the heart and motives of leadership whenever we encounter a leader who claims to have a call. People truly called to Kingdom authority are different people; they are people who have been transformed into that balance between order and genuine care and concern, decency and helping people to know the love of God is bigger than just a mere musing or nice idea. True Kingdom leaders transform with their touch, their teachings, their listening heart, and their eagerness to spread the Gospel in every way.

- Attention draws away from the elders to the throne because true leaders in the Kingdom will pay attention to the throne, the power and glory that rests there. The elders surround the throne both in a protective sense, as they are the guardians of that which is holy and sacred, and it is true leadership that walks in the seven spirits, or sevenfold Spirit, of God, along with Jesus Christ in preparation for His return. Oceans, seas, and bodies of water tend to represent people, or multitudes, with the sea of glass representing those who have obtained a sense of clarity, no longer viewing through the glass dimly (1 Corinthians 13:12). Before the throne, those who overcome and seek God to the end will be able to see what they desire, having clarity of mind and understanding, no longer wondering, no longer understanding in part, but seeing and recognizing fully. This comes as we reach out to the throne and have the blessing to stand there, witnessing all this in its fullness.

<u>Revelation 4:6b-11</u>

In the center, around the throne, were four living creatures, and they were covered with eyes, in front and in back. The first living creature was like a lion, the second was like an ox, the third had a face like a man, the fourth was like a flying eagle. Each of the four living creatures had six wings and was covered with eyes all around, even under His wings. Day and night they never stop saying: "Holy, holy, holy is the Lord God Almighty, Who was, and is, and is to come." Whenever the living creatures give glory, honor and thanks to Him Who sits on the throne and Who lives for ever and ever. They lay their crowns before the throne and say: "You are worthy, our Lord and God, to receive glory and honor and power, for You created all things, and by Your will they were created and have their being."

(Related Bible references: Exodus 3:14, 1 Kings 7:25, 1 Chronicles 16:29, Psalm 47:8, Psalm 90:2, Psalm 95:6, Isaiah 6:1-3, Isaiah 52:13-53:12, Ezekiel 1:5-10, Ezekiel 1:18, Ezekiel 10:2-4, Ezekiel 10:12-20, Daniel 12:7, Hosea 5:14, Matthew 26:13, Mark 13:10, Luke 8:10, Luke 13:29, John 1:1-14, Romans 8:15, 2 Corinthians 6:14, 1 Timothy 1:17, 2 Thessalonians 1:5, Revelation 5:5)

The four living creatures surrounding the throne sound odd, even to the best of prophetic interpreters. We know that these are a reference to the same or similar beings found in Isaiah 6:1-3 and Ezekiel 10:2,4 and 20. They appear to be a rank or form of angels, often ascribed to be Cherubim, the second highest order of hierarchy in heaven. Beyond what they may be, they also hold imagery for us to teach us about the unity between the Kingdom of God on earth and the Kingdom of heaven.

- First living creature: Like a lion; the attribute of Jesus as the Lion of Judah (Hosea 5:14, Revelation 5:5), with fire, power, authority, and an intense roar. Ancient leaders were often associated with lions, known for their strength, prowess, agility, command, and force. Represents the authority of the Gospel and the authority of those who stand on Christ. Historically, the first living creature was also associated with the Gospel of Matthew and its author, given it was written for a Jewish audience.

- Second living creature: Like an ox; the attribute of strength, the ability to work, the importance of equal yoking (matching strengths) in the Kingdom. Represents the strength, working ability, and equality of the Gospel and of those who are a part of Christ's Kingdom (Matthew 26:13, Mark 13:10, 2 Corinthians 6:14). The second living creature was also associated with the Gospel of Mark and its author, given it was written to prove Jesus was the Suffering Servant (Isaiah 52:13-53:12), a role of incredible strength in Jesus' life, and was written for Christians.

- Third living creature: Like a man; being created in the image of God, reflecting the inclusion of all humanity into the Kingdom, our ability to interact with our Creator, and the Gospel in the person of Jesus Christ, both human and divine, the Word made flesh (John 1:1-14). The third living creature was also associated with the Gospel of Luke and its author, especially the powerful way in which Luke made Jesus' humanity a central theme and that this Gospel was written for Gentiles.

- Fourth living creature: Like a flying eagle; the deeply spiritual attributes of Jesus in His divinity, as well as the spirituality of the church and the spirituality of those who claim to be a part of God's Kingdom (Luke 8:10, Luke 13:29, 2 Thessalonians 1:5). Eagles soar high above the earth, soaring strong on wind currents that come from storms. The fourth living creature was also associated with the Gospel of John and its author, as it was written to prove Jesus' divinity and to give a uniquely spiritual insight into the eternal nature of the Kingdom of God.

There are four of these beings, four being a teaching number, one that represents instruction. The connection of these four beings to the four Gospels shows us its nature and purpose to teach us, and the teaching nature of the Kingdom. Their six wings each – for a total 24, mentioned once again – shows man's position within the Kingdom and mankind's ability to be transformed unto perfection through Christ, before God's throne. Six is the number of man, 24, we discussed earlier. In the place of spiritual perfection, we can ascend within God's governance and the Gospel to heights unknown and soar above to praise Him and answer issues of this world. Covered with eyes, they can see, all around; they do not miss anything that happens around the throne or anyone or any being that approaches it. For this, they never stop calling God holy; He is holy to the third power, He is holy; the Father, the Son, and the Holy Spirit are holy; and we know as they call Him Who was, and is, and is to come, they are calling upon Him as was revealed in the burning bush, the great I AM (Exodus 3:14). In the presence of such awesomeness, such power, any honors earned must be set aside, just to recognize the power of the Creator, the Redeemer, and the Sustainer.

We cannot rightly call ourselves believers if we do not acknowledge the awesome nature of God in His fullness and power. All belongs to Him, and even with such reign, He still chooses to love us, to welcome us to dwell with Him and love Him. Having this picture of the throne room affirms Who He is to us, and invites us even more to know Him, to worship before Him, and to cry, "Abba, Father!"

(Romans 8:15) as we see this picture of His power and glory, established before the foundations of the world.

The Scroll and

5 Then I saw
sealed[t] with
break the seals ar
scroll or even loo
scroll or look insi
dah, the Root of D

[6]Then I saw a I
by the four living c
its[a] of God sent ou
on the throne.[7]An
before the Lamb. Ea

Handwritten margin note: JESUS IS ALWAYS ABLE TO OVERCOME

Chapter Five

WORTHY IS THE LAMB
(REVELATION CHAPTER 5)

Key verses

- Verses 1-3: *Then I saw in the right hand of Him Who sat on the throne a scroll with writing on both sides and sealed with seven seals. And I saw a mighty angel proclaiming in a loud voice, "Who is worthy to break the seals and open the scroll?" But no one in heaven or on earth or under the earth could open the scroll or even look inside it.*

- Verse 5: *Then one of the elders said to me, "Do not weep! See the Lion of the tribe of Judah, the Root of David, has triumphed. He is able to open the scroll and its seven seals."*

- Verses 9-10: *And they sang a new song: "You are worthy to take the scroll and to open its seals, because You were slain, and with Your blood You purchased men for God from every tribe and language and people and nation. You have made them to be a Kingdom and priests to serve our God, and they will reign on the earth."*

- Verses 12-14: *In a loud voice they sang: "Worthy is the Lamb, Who was slain to receive power and wealth and wisdom and strength and honor and glory and praise!" Then I heard every creature in heaven and on earth and under the earth and on the sea, and all that is in them, singing: "To Him Who sits on the throne and to the Lamb be praise and honor and glory and power, for ever and ever!" The four living creatures said, "Amen," and the elders fell down and worshiped.*

Words and phrases to know

- Scroll: From the Greek word *biblion* which means "a small book, a scroll, a written document; a sheet on which something has been written."[1]

- Seals: From the Greek word *sphragis* which means "a seal."[2]

- Lion of the Tribe of Judah: From four Greek words: *leon* which means "a lion; a brave and mighty hero,"[3] *on* which means "being,"[4] *phule* which means "a tribe; a race, nation, people,"[5] and *Ioudas* which means "Judah or Judas = "he shall be praised;" the fourth son of Jacob; an unknown ancestor of Christ; a man surnamed the Galilean, who at the time of the census of Quirinus, excited the revolt in Galilee, Acts 5:37; a certain Jew of Damascus, Acts 9:11; a prophet surnamed Barsabas, of the church at Jerusalem, Acts 15:22,27,32; the apostle, John 14:22, who was surnamed Lebbaeus or Thaddaeus, and according to opinion wrote the Epistle of Jude; the half-brother of Jesus, Mt. 13:55; Judas Iscariot, the apostle who betrayed Jesus."[6]

- Root of David: From two Greek words: *rhiza* which means "a root; that which like a root springs from a root, a sprout, shoot; metaph. offspring, progeny,"[7] and *Dabid* which means "second king of Israel, and ancestor of Jesus Christ."[8]

- Triumphed: From the Greek word *nikao* which means "to conquer"[9]

- Lamb: From the Greek word *arnion* which means "a little lamb, a lamb."[10]

- Horns: From the Greek word *keras* which means "a horn."[11]

- Harp: From the Greek word *kithara* which means "a harp to which praises of God are sung in heaven."[12]

- Bowls: From the Greek word *phiale* which means "a broad shallow bowl, deep saucer."[13]

- Incense: From the Greek word *thumiama* which means "an aromatic substance burnt, incense."[14]

- Prayers: From the Greek word *proseuche* which means "prayer addressed to God; a place set apart or suited for the offering of prayer."[15]

- Blood: From the Greek word *haima* which means "blood; blood shed, to be shed by violence, slay, murder."[16]

- Tribe: From the Greek word *phule* which means "a tribe ; a race, nation, people."[17]

- Language: From the Greek word *glossa* which means "the tongue, a member of the body, an organ of speech; a tongue."[18]

- People: From the Greek word *laos* which means "a people, people group, tribe, nation, all those who are of the same stock and language; of a great part of the population gathered together anywhere."[19]

- Nation: From the Greek word *ethnos* which means "a multitude (whether of men or of beasts) associated or living together; a multitude of individuals of the same nature or genus; a race, nation, people group; in the OT, foreign nations not worshiping the true God, pagans, Gentiles."[20]

- Reign: From the Greek word *basileuo* which means "to be king, to exercise kingly power, to reign; metaph. to exercise the highest influence, to control."[21]

- Ten thousand: From the Greek word *murias* which means "ten thousand; an innumerable multitude, an unlimited number; innumerable hosts."[22]

- Power: From the Greek word *dunamis* which means "strength power, ability."[23]

- Wealth: From the Greek word *ploutos* which means "riches, wealth."[24]

- Wisdom: From the Greek word *sophia* which means "wisdom, broad and full of intelligence; used of the knowledge of very diverse matters."[25]

- Strength: From the Greek word *ischus* which means "ability, force, strength, might."[26]

- Honor: From the Greek word *time* which means "a valuing by which the price is fixed; honor which belongs or is shown to one."[27]

- Glory: From the Greek word *doxa* which means "opinion, judgment, view; opinion, estimate, whether good or bad concerning someone; splendor, brightness; a most glorious condition, most exalted state."[28]

- Praise: From the Greek word *eulogia* which means "praise, laudation, panegyric: of Christ or God; fine discourse, polished language; an invocation of blessing, benediction; consecration; a (concrete) blessing, benefit."[39]

- Worshiped: From the Greek word *proskuneo* which means "to kiss the hand to (towards) one, in token of reverence; among the Orientals, esp. the Persians, to fall upon the knees and touch the ground with the forehead as an expression of profound reverence; in the NT by kneeling or prostration to do homage (to one) or make obeisance, whether in order to express respect or to make supplication."[30]

Revelation 5:1-5

Then I saw in the right hand of Him Who sat on the throne a scroll with writing on both sides and sealed with seven seals. And I saw a mighty angel proclaiming in a loud voice, "Who is worthy to break the seals and open the scroll?" But no one in heaven or on earth or under the earth could open the scroll or look inside. Then one of the elders said to me, "Do not weep! See, the Lion of the tribe of Judah, the Root of David, has triumphed. He is able to open the scroll and its seven seals."

(Related Bible references: Genesis 49:9, 2 Samuel 7:12, Isaiah 11:1, Ezekiel 2:10, Isaiah 29:11, Daniel 12:9, Acts 1:7, Romans 5:11, Romans 7:14-25, Romans 15:12, 2 Corinthians 5:21, Hebrews 7:14)

Revelation 5 has one purpose, and one purpose only: to prove and expound upon the worthiness of Christ. Filled with beautiful imagery, Revelation 5 is one of the most powerful chapters in the book of Revelation, because it depicts a reality that so many of us fail to realize in our faith today. When we talk about sufficiency, feeling unworthy, or low self-esteem, we often point to the fact that "Jesus is worthy and all-sufficient," thus leading many to believe that the death of Christ was about our own self-worth and self-esteem. This is a very narrow perspective of Christ's sacrifice, on many different levels, almost reducing it to a complete misunderstanding of His atonement in the bigger picture.

Because Revelation is a book about the perfection of the saints and the perfection of the church, Revelation is a perfect place for the worthiness of Christ to be emphasized in connection with His sacrifice. Jesus Christ took on flesh but walked through His thirty-three years without committing any sin (2 Corinthians 5:21). He was the embodiment of perfection; unblemished, unstained, with the perfect opportunity to serve as the atonement for sin, once and for all (Romans 5:11).

Many today wonder about the sacrificial system and its evolution throughout the Old Testament. Some think it cruel, unfair, even an unjust system, thinking of God as insatiable and having a taste for blood. The sacrificial system of the Old Testament yes, points to Christ, but is not based on a lack of justice or on the sacrifices themselves, which were intended to teach us deeper principles and understand the consequences of sin in our lives. The Old Testament system and the principle of atonement teaches us about the essence of Revelation 5: worthiness. Sin is such a serious matter, alienating us so severely from God, we cannot, in a sinful state, worthily conquer it and "redeem" ourselves. It's a nice principle to think we'll do better next time and learn from our misgivings or missing the mark, but we all know that, time and time again, sin becomes something we do, whether we want to do it, or not (Romans 7:14-25).

Worthiness is about a state of qualification, being able and adequate to handle a situation. Jesus' sinless nature is what rendered Him worthy to stand as the reparation for our sins. It is nice to think we can improve ourselves, we can improve humanity on our own, even nicer to think we'll just "do better next time," but the reality is, we can't, we won't, and we aren't going to. This unworthiness to redeem humanity also renders us unable to stand as a judge for anyone else (Matthew 7:1-2), to stand in a position of understanding of such matters without the guidance of Christ and makes it very clear that while God does not need us, we do, indeed, desperately need Him.

The seven seals of Revelation relate, and signify, once again, a symbol of perfection. A scroll was given to proclaim a declaration or to provide information, and the contents of this seal was so vital, only perfection could open it. No one was able, worthy, or qualified to open the seal or look inside of it, save Jesus Christ, Who is spoken of as the Lion of the Tribe of Judah and the Root of David. This reaffirms Jesus' lineage while on earth, being from the tribe of Judah, the tribe to provide highest praise to God, echoing His greatness and roaring with fierceness and authority at His enemies.

The message we need to hear for ourselves in here is that we need to aspire to find our balance in Christ, not our balance in trying to adapt worldly systems to fit in Christ's atonement. Nowadays we are trying to mix our understanding of Jesus with our pop psychology and our pop cultural adaptations. The worthiness of Jesus is because, in and of ourselves, we are not worthy. In Christ, we are supposed to find balance. Jesus' worthiness is not an excuse to be arrogant, puffed up, obnoxious, or all about us. It is not the way to adapt the selfishness of this world and apply it to Christianity, because that is the opposite of the worthiness of Jesus. In Jesus' worthiness, we find our own grounding and humility. Not everything is for us, and contrary to what they may try to tell us in many Christian circles today, we do not have the right to have our hands in everything, touch everything, look at everything, or handle everything. Understanding Jesus as worthy is supposed to give us the insight into the authority He has given each one of us as believers, and that worthiness is not to have our hands all over everyone – and everything – in judgment. Jesus calls who He calls, and He equips who He equips, in exactly the way that He desires. As we look to Him and rely on Him, we find our purpose, as He transforms us into His image and likeness.

<u>Revelation 5:6-10</u>

Then I saw a Lamb, looking as if it had been slain, standing in the center of the throne, encircled by the four living creatures and the elders. He had seven horns and seven eyes, which are the seven spirits of God sent out into all the earth. He came and took the scroll from the right hand of Him Who sat on the throne. And when He had taken it, the four living creatures and the twenty-four elders fell down before the Lamb. Each one had a harp and they were holding golden bowls full of incense, which are the prayers of the saints. And they sang a new song: "You are worthy to take the scroll and to open its seals, because You were slain, and with Your blood You purchased men for God from every tribe and language and people and nation. You have made them to be a Kingdom and priests to serve our God, and they will reign on the earth."

(Related Bible references: Exodus 19:6, 2 Chronicles 29:25, Psalm 47:8, Psalm 141:2, Isaiah 6:1, Isaiah 42:10, Isaiah 53:7, Matthew 19:28, Matthew 26:28, Luke 12:32, Luke 22:29, John 1:29, Ephesians 1:20-22, 2 Timothy 2:12, Hebrews 9:12, Hebrews 12:28, 1 Peter 1:19, 1 Peter 2:9, Revelation 20:4-6)

The Lamb that was slain clearly represents Jesus in His sacrifice. Having established His worthiness, we see the way in which His sacrifice on the cross impacted heaven, as well as how it impacted us here on earth. We know from the Bible about the spiritual difference Christ's sacrifice has made in our lives, how it has changed people and how it can change us, but now, here in Revelation, we get to see it from a heavenly viewpoint.

From the heavenly perspective, we can see how integrated worthiness is with the plan of salvation. Not just anyone could enter the Holiest of places in heaven in just any state of being and in any state of holiness. Worthiness emphasizes us the essence of holiness; it is about more than just the need to be exteriorly following extensive rules and regulations. God desires that what comes before Him is transformed, and it was Jesus Who had the ability to transform. From heaven's view, salvation was a beautiful process, heralding of worthiness, one worthy of rejoicing because One Who was able had been found and was willing. The seven horns of the lamb represent a perfect, divine strength; one from which the anointing flows, as anointing oil was commonly poured from a ram's horn. His seven eyes, representing the seven spirits or seven-fold spirit, spoken of earlier, shows they are gifts that are both all-seeing and can lead to spiritual vision. As the sevenfold Spirit goes throughout the earth, they bring a unique and powerful perfection; something that perfects and edifies the church, perfects the saints, and moves us toward God's perfection in our own lives.

Identifying Jesus as the Lamb of God Who takes away the sin of the world, as the One Who is fully able and perfectly worthy to stand as our Savior, is clearly not just something we recognize this side of heaven. He was not just the High Priest Who offered the sacrifice; He was also the Lamb. He offered His very self, His very being, for our very need The elders, the living creatures, and even the angels of heaven all recognize He is worthy and has served to atone for mankind. By Jesus' blood, we are His, and none other is able to make such a claim of purchase toward our souls, and our lives. We owe all to the One Who is worthy. Just as incense rises to the skies with its fragrance and its smoke, so do our praises rise to Him, our prayers and our petitions, our hopes and our dreams, our future, and our purposes. All of us have the option to come before Him, because it is He Who is our Head, because He has made room for each and every one of us, regardless of our race, our nationality, who we are, and where we are from. We are all brought here, to be part of His Kingdom and His priests; and we shall serve Him and reign with Him (2 Timothy 2:12, Revelation 20:4-6).

Revelation 5:11-14

Then I looked and heard the voice of many angels, numbering thousands upon thousands, and ten thousand times ten thousand. They encircled the throne and the living creatures and the elders. In a loud voice they sang: "Worthy is the Lamb, Who was slain, to receive power and wealth and wisdom and strength and honor and glory and praise!" Then I heard every creature in heaven and on earth and under the earth and on the sea, and all that is in them, singing: "To Him Who sits on the throne and to the Lamb be praise and honor and glory and power, for ever and ever!"

The four living creatures said, "Amen," and the elders fell down and worshiped.

(Related Bible references: 1 Kings 22:19, Isaiah 53:7, Matthew 11:11, Matthew 18:1-5, Matthew 23:1-11, Matthew 28:18, John 1:29, John 5:23, John 10:11, John 15:13, Romans 8:18-30, Philippians 2:10, Hebrews 1:6, Hebrews 12:22, 1 John 3:16, 1 Peter 4:10, Jude 1:14)

There is no reference to the physical creation of angels in the Bible. While we know from Genesis 1:1 that "God created the heavens and the earth," we do not have a specified reference to the creation of the angels, or the establishment of their various orders and powers. Such references to their creation are not found in apocryphal or pseudepigraphic writings, either, telling us that the existence of angels is so widespread and accepted, nobody thought much about where they began or started. Being heavenly beings, it was, most likely, generally accepted that their creation occurred along with the creation of the 'heavens,' which, while they were not specifically mentioned, were also included.

What we do know about angels is that a) they are agents with free will, freely choosing to worship God (Hebrews 1:6), and b) the work of angels has been consistent throughout salvation history, and that is to serve as a messenger of sorts. The exact physical nature of angels is unknown, because they are often seen in some semblance of human form. They look somewhat human, but dwell without reproductive capabilities; they seem to be able to change forms; and despite all this, the Apostle John still knows that the beings he sees in heaven are angels. He hears their voice, their encircling of the throne, representing eternity; the life of God with no beginning and no ending, heralding the worthiness of Jesus Christ, echoing He is the one Who is truly worthy to receive all – all the power, the wealth, the wisdom, the strength, the honor, the glory, and the praise. Every creature everywhere echoes their lead, hearing their special and vital message, receiving it and reiterating it. It is a moment to worship.

We see these incredible, beyond description beings worshiping the Lamb, worshiping Him because He is worthy by His deeds and His actions. Not esteeming Himself, He sacrificed for humanity and, as we can see by this passage, for all of creation by extension (Romans 8:18-30). He did not esteem Himself too good for it, to make sacrifice for people who were and are, beneath Him in reality. Becoming the ultimate Servant of mankind, being willing to make ultimate sacrifices, is what rendered Jesus as most worthy, exclusively worthy, and worthy of our worship. This should tell us what makes us worthy of honor: service. Being willing to lay ourselves aside and do something for someone else. Being willing to not seek the palaces and worldly entitlements but being willing to make a sacrifice so someone else can have something that they could not otherwise have. All the universe, all created things, all things everywhere acknowledge godly service and godly willingness to lay down one's life for the benefit of the whole (John 10:11, John 15:13, 1 John 3:16). All of creation echoes this point of service: Our call is to be of service (Matthew 11:11, Matthew 18:1-5, Matthew 23:1-11, 1 Peter 4:10), not to be served.

The Scroll and

5 Then I saw
sealed† with
break the seals ar
scroll or even loo
scroll or look insi
dah, the Root of D

[6] Then I saw a
by the four living c
its‡ of God sent ou
on the throne.† ⁹An
before the Lamb. Ea

JESUS IS ALWAYS ABLE TO OVERCOME

G

Chapter Six

COME, NOW IS THE TIME TO BE UNSEALED
(REVELATION CHAPTER 6)

Key verses

- Verses 1-2: *I watched as the Lamb opened the first of the seven seals. Then I heard one of the four living creatures say in a voice like thunder, "Come!" I looked, and there before me was a white horse! Its rider held a bow, and he was given a crown, and he rode out as a conqueror bent on conquest.*

- Verses 4-5: *Then another horse came out, a fiery red one. Its rider was given power to take peace from the earth and to make men slay each other. To him was given a large sword. When the Lamb opened the third seal, I heard the third living creature say, "Come!" I looked and there before me was a black horse! Its rider was holding a pair of scales in his hand.*

- Verse 8: *I looked, and there before me was a pale horse! Its rider was named Death, and Hades was following close behind him. They were given power over a fourth of the earth to kill by sword, famine and plague, and by the wild beasts of the earth.*

- Verse 9: *When He opened the fifth seal, I saw under the altar the souls of those who had been slain because of the Word of God and the testimony they had maintained.*

- Verses 12-13: *I watched as He opened the sixth seal. There was a great earthquake. The sun turned black like sackcloth made of goat hair, the whole moon turned blood red, and the stars in the sky fell to earth, as late figs drop from a fig tree when shaken by a strong wind.*

- Verse 15: *Then the kings of the earth, the princes, the generals, the rich, the mighty, and every slave and every free man hid in caves and among the rocks of the mountains.*

- Verse 17: *For the great day of their wrath has come, and who can stand?*

Words and phrases to know

- Come: From the Greek word *erchomai* which means "to come; of persons; metaph. to come into being, arise, come forth, show itself, find place or influence, be established, become known, to come (fall) into or unto; to go, to follow one."[1]

- White horse: From two Greek words: *leukos* which means "light, bright, brilliant"[2] and hippos which means "a horse."[3]

- Bow: From the Greek word *toxon* which means "a bow."[4]

- Fiery red: From the Greek word *purrhos* which means "having the color of fire, red."[5]

- Slay: From the Greek word *sphazo* which means "to slay, slaughter, butcher; to put to death by violence; mortally wounded."[6]

- Black: From the Greek word *melas* which means "black; black ink."[7]

- Pair of scales: From the Greek word *zugos* which means "a yoke; a balance, pair of scales."[8]

- Quart of wheat: From two Greek words: *choinix* which means "a choenix, a dry measure, containing four cotylae or two setarii (less than our quart, one litre) (or as much as would support a man of moderate appetite for a day)"[9] and *sitos* which means "wheat, grain."[10]

- Day's wages: From the Greek word *denarion* which means "denarius = "containing ten;" A Roman silver coin in NT time. It took its name from it being equal to ten "asses", a number after 217 B.C. increased to sixteen (about 3.898 grams or .1375 oz.). It was the principal silver coin of the Roman Empire. From the parable of the laborers in the vineyard, it would seem that a denarius was then the ordinary pay for a day's wages. (Mt. 20:2-13)."[11]

- Three quarts of barley: From two Greek words: *treis* which means "three,"[12] *choinix* which means "a choenix, a dry measure, containing four cotylae or two setarii (less than our quart, one litre) (or as much as would support a man of moderate appetite for a day),"[13] and *krithe* which means "barley."[14]

- Damage: From the Greek word *adikeo* which means "absolutely; transitively to do some wrong or sin in some respect; to wrong some one, act wickedly towards him; to hurt, damage, harm."[15]

- Oil: From the Greek word *elaio* which means "olive oil."[16]

- Wine: From the Greek word *oinos* which means "wine; metaph. fiery wine of God's wrath."[17]

- Pale: From the Greek word *chloros* which means "green; yellowish pale."[18]

- Altar: From the Greek word *thusiasterion* which means "the altar for slaying and burning of victims used of, the altar of whole burnt offerings which stood in the court of the priests in the temple at Jerusalem, the altar of incense which stood in the sanctuary or the Holy Place, any other altar, metaph., the cross on which Christ suffered an expiatory death: to eat of this altar i.e. to appropriate to one's self the fruits of Christ's expiatory death."[19]

- Souls: From the Greek word *psuche* which means "breath; the soul."[20]

- Maintained: From the Greek word *echo* which means "to have, i.e. to hold; to have i.e. own, possess; to hold one's self or find one's self so and so, to be in such or such a condition; to hold one's self to a thing, to lay hold of a thing, to adhere or cling to."[21]

- Judge: From the Greek word *krino* which means "to separate, put asunder, to pick out, select, choose; to approve, esteem, to prefer; to be of opinion, deem, think, to be of opinion; to determine, resolve, decree; to judge; to rule, govern; to contend together, of warriors and combatants."[22]

- Avenge: From the Greek word *ekdikeo* which means "to vindicate one's right, do one justice; to avenge a thing."[23]

- Wait a little longer: From three Greek words: *anapauo* which means "to cause or permit one to cease from any movement or labor in order to recover and collect his strength; to give rest, refresh, to give one's self rest, take rest; to keep quiet, of calm and patient expectation,"[24] *mikros* which means "small, little,"[25] and *chronos* which means "time either long or short."[26]

- Completed: From the Greek word *pleroo* which means "to make full, to fill up, i.e. to fill to the full; to render full, i.e. to complete."[27]

- Earthquake: From the Greek word *seismos* which means "a shaking, a commotion; a tempest; an earthquake."[28]

- Sun: From the Greek word *helios* which means "the sun; the rays of the sun; the light of day."[29]

- Moon: From the Greek word *selene* which means "the moon."[30]

- Blood red: From the Greek word *haima* which means "blood; blood shed, to be shed by violence, slay, murder."[31]

- Figs: From the Greek word *olunthos* which means "an unripe fig which grows during the winter, yet does not come to maturity but falls off in the spring."[32]

- Stand: From the Greek word *histemi* which means "to cause or make to stand, to place, put, set."[33]

Revelation 6:1-8

I watched as the Lamb opened the first of the seven seals. Then I heard one of the four living creatures say in a voice like thunder, "Come!" I looked, and there before me was a white horse! Its rider held a bow, and he was given a crown, and he rode out as a conqueror bent on conquest.

When the Lamb opened the second seal, I heard the second living creature say, "Come!" Then another horse came out, a fiery red one. Its rider was given power to take peace from the earth and to make men slay each other. To him was given a large sword.

When the Lamb opened the third seal, I heard the third living creature say, "Come!" I looked, and there before me was a black horse! Its rider was holding a pair of scales in his hand. Then I heard what sounded like a voice among the four living creatures, saying, "A quart of wheat for a day's wages, and three quarts of barley for a day's wages, and do not damage the oil and the wine!"

When the Lamb opened the fourth seal, I heard the voice of the fourth living creature say, "Come!" I looked, and there before me was a pale horse! Its rider was named Death, and Hades was following close behind him. They were given power over a fourth of the earth to kill by sword, famine and plague, and by the wild beasts of the earth.

(Related Bible references: Genesis 2:2-3, Genesis 7:1-10, Exodus 12:15-19, Leviticus 13:4-21, Deuteronomy 5:14, Deuteronomy 15:1-12, Deuteronomy 16:4-15, 1 Samuel 16:10, 1 Kings 6:38, 2 Kings 5:14, Esther 2:16, Job 39:25, Psalm 12:6, Psalm 110:2, Proverbs 21:31, Isaiah 30:26, Isaiah 55:8, Jeremiah 15:2, Ezekiel 4:16, Ezekiel 5:17, Ezekiel 21:27, Amos 4:10, Matthew 7:1-6, Matthew 18:22, Matthew 24:7, Mark 13:8, Luke 21:10-11, Hebrews 4:4, Hebrews 11:3)

Revelation transitions from celebrating the glory of the throne room and the worthiness of the Lamb of God to an action that directly affects humanity and the life of humanity. This should cause us, as readers, to contemplate the message of Revelation, realizing that heaven and earth are connected. Both heaven and earth have the same Creator, the same Ruler, and are a part of the same dominion, as we learned earlier in Revelation. As the Gospel of Thomas, verse 113 points out:

For the Kingdom of Heaven is spread out over the earth, and men do not see it.[34]

One of the most powerful facets of the concept of Revelation is seeing a picture, all be it through a glass dimly. We are seeing spiritual reality, even though we can't see it with our naked eye. Revelation tells us the Kingdoms of this world "have become" the Kingdom of our Lord, and He shall reign forever." The term "have become" indicates the manifestation of its reality is progressive. God has always been supreme ruler over all. Too many assume Satan to be equal with God, just as an evil counterpart. Satan is not, in any way, shape, or form, equal with God. He is a fallen angel who knows how to twist the things of God for his own benefit, thus creating enemies of God. Just as we choose to serve God, our choices can also render us in alignment with Satan's will.

The workings and happenings of our world are not always this simple, however. There are periods where certain things happen, and they happen within the authority of the Kingdom. The reason for this is simple: the Kingdoms of this world are becoming a part of the Kingdom of God, and in that process, there is conflict. Certain things must happen for the alignment to take place, and those things aren't always fun, enjoyable, or what we would classify today as "encouraging" ...but they are necessary. We should realize that both adding to and taking away are a part of the Kingdom and are also necessary parts of faith. While many stumble or ignore the more militant-sounding aspects of Revelation (and the Bible as a whole), we cannot ignore the fact that certain things happen by divine orchestration, for reasons we may never know or understand.

This is faith. I do not believe that it is "blind faith" or God asking us to believe in things that don't make sense or are ridiculous. God is not asking us to be violent with one another or to orchestrate these things on His behalf. He is still expecting us to uphold the conduct and integrity we are called to uphold and be the people He commands us to be. What God is asking in the midst of these things is for our trust. Even though we do not always understand everything, we should know in our own humility that we are not God, and we do not have to understand all His ways or everything He does. Faith trusts that God knows what He is doing in all His ways, because His ways are not our ways (Isaiah 55:8).

Trusting in God enough to see His plan through the seven seals is extremely vital to understand just what is being unveiled here, and why it is being unveiled. The seven seals and the results therein are not included in Revelation to be vengeful. In fact, most of the commentary in Revelation is spoken in factual form, without much emotion. Revelation contains details of a mystical encounter, unveiling heaven and things on earth, not the details of a play or a reality show. The emotion and hype that is generated in fear-based interpretations of Revelation is inserted by clever preachers who want to scare people into accepting their perspectives on Revelation, thus making Revelation a big, scary, and confusing drama. Revelation does have some dramatic details, but the purpose of the book of Revelation was never to sell fictional novels or movies. It was never to scare people into believing and it was never intended to become so misinterpreted or controversial. If we step back and hear what is spoken to us through the seven seals, we can see many important parallels that reveal purposes to us and the transference from the Kingdoms of the world to the Kingdom of Christ.

The number seven is important among the seals, because there were seven of them. We have already discussed seven as the number of completion, but the reason why the number seven points to completion is important in connection with the seals. If one carefully studies the seven seals of Revelation, it is almost a recounting of creation in reverse. Seven represents completion because after six days of creation, God rested on the seventh, indicating that seven represents a cycle or purpose of completion. Repeatedly throughout the Scriptures we see the number seven used to indicate a perfection, a proclamation of "good," a proclamation of rest, because the cycle was fulfilled (Genesis 2:2-3, Genesis 7:1-

10, Exodus 12:15-19, Leviticus 13:4-21, Deuteronomy 5:14, Deuteronomy 15:1-12, Deuteronomy 16:4-15, 1 Samuel 16:10, 1 Kings 6:38, 2 Kings 5:14, Esther 2:16, Psalm 12:6, Isaiah 30:26, Matthew 18:22, Hebrews 4:4, Hebrews 11:30). In these seven seals, we see the advance of completion toward something else: the perfection of an era, a revelation, the conclusion of one thing, and the transference to another. The same pattern as we have seen in Revelation before is present again, just in a different form and to reveal something else that points us to our greater Kingdom realities.

None was worthy to even open these seals, save Christ Himself. The perfection of His nature coupled with His willingness of sacrifice allowed Him to be the One qualified to open – and, therefore, unleash – these different things upon humanity. Jesus was the One Who was prepared to usher and handle the different proclamations, as well as the results of them. We so often talk about judgments, but with judgment comes a result that one must be prepared to handle. The reason we, as people, do not have the right to be in a position of judgment (Matthew 7:1-6) is simple: we do not have the ability to handle the responsibility that comes with it. "Judge not" means exactly what it sounds like. Non-judgment demands we examine ourselves first. It does not mean that we cannot discuss matters of sin, but it does mean that we can't talk about sin without offering people an answer to sin. It means that discussion of sin has a place – but it is not the only thing we throw around and that we certainly don't throw it up in the faces of others. It does mean that we should not ever be talking about people as if we can determine their situations for them or decide the decisions they should have made. It means we listen with hearts of compassion; that we are not the ones who have to speak first, or the ones who have to have the last word. We step aside and allow the Holy Spirit to do His job, bringing people to a place where they need to be to find the fullness of God, while we leave the door open as voices of hope and promise that God really does transform lives.

This is all especially important as we consider the

results of the seven seals and their effects on humanity. These seals unravel complicated interworkings of humanity, revealing the ways in which we are often the most disobedient to God and detrimental to ourselves and others. Thus, the seven seals open with what we more commonly call the "Four Horsemen of the Apocalypse," and continue to reveal some of the most complicated and difficult aspects of the human condition – and the direction in which humanity will ultimately take itself.

The seven seals all 'go together,' if you will. They aren't isolated or detached things that randomly happen in history. In connection with a reversal of creation, each one points to and refers to specific aspects of the human

- The first seal: White horse, rider holds a bow, is given a crown, and goes out on conquest. Attacks and addresses the areas of humanity in relation to authority (Revelation 6:2).

Some have attested the first seal to be the introduction of the antichrist, but Revelation does not indicate this to us. (The word "antichrist," in fact, is found nowhere in Revelation.) The imagery of the first seal is not a spiritual power, but a political one. What we can gather from this imagery is that the individual who rides the white horse does represent a political or military power, one of a governmental line of nobility and the ability to fight in battle. He rides out as a conqueror – with an agenda to conquer individuals and nations.

This represents the first upheaval in the areas of authority. The first seal unleashes change in the area of authority and ideas people have about authority, as the rider conquers – or changes – by ideas. It represents the ultimate in paradigm shift, from one way of thinking to another. This means the shift, or conquering by authority, occurs through any way people view leadership or governance, including politics, familial relationships, and a general overthrow of individuals conquered by authority, wrong concepts of it, or general control of people through various extremes of authority (not enough or too much).

- The second seal: Fiery red horse, rider is given power to take peace from the earth and make human beings slay one another; given a large sword (Revelation 6:4).

When we think of red, we often think of strong emotions or strong icons that cause us to stop what we are doing and take notice (stop signs, love, passion, fire). In the times of Revelation, the color red had the same effect, only for different things. Red was traditionally associated in Greek culture with the god of war, Mars. The readers of Revelation would have quickly understood the fiery red nature of the horse to indicate war or aggression.

If the first seal is about conquering, the second seal is the result. When various nations, tensions, and situations arise, tension and aggression are the results. The second seal clearly refers to aggression in all its forms, which means we must not be too quick to assume it is one thing, such as war, and nothing else. Yes, it does sound like war is a part of it, but people die worldwide every day due to violence, despite its form: war, genocide, murder, domestic violence, police brutality, gang or group violence, and all forms of aggression that human beings take up against one another. Now we live in an era where people think the best way to protect themselves against violence is through violent means or ends, and we are very aware that we cannot rely on formalized organizations (such as police or government) to protect society. The absence of peace present in our world today is not all about a great, huge world war, but about the millions of smaller wars, little battles, and ways that people choose to turn on each other, every day, in many life-altering ways.

- The third seal: Black horse, rider holding a pair of scales, and the words of a voice: *A quart of wheat for a day's wages, and three quarts of barley for a day's wages, and do not damage the oil and the wine!*

(Revelation 6:5-6).

We often associate black with death today, but black is a color that does not specifically relate to death. Black can also refer to issues associated with power, formality, discipline, business, and neutrality. That is equaling, leveling, or neutrality to the secular world, the world that revolves around business and income – and presents the beginning of a universal lack that shall result. We could call the major subject of the third seal one of a leveling, of a sort of justice that does not discriminate and can affect everyone in some way, across the board. The most obvious way this happens is in the form of soaring prices, causing basic staples (as wheat, barley, oil and wine were all staples in the first century) to be so expensive, it is difficult for anyone to afford them. In an equaling of humanity, where it is not about how much we all make or how hard we work, but everyone receives the same results, many of our own concepts about reward shall be challenged...and yet taken, even further.

The leveling field could take the form of rising prices due to supply and demand, tariffs, wartime rations, scarcities, food shortages, and manufacturing issues. It could also be due to a factor that we don't know and haven't raised in an obvious sense.

- The fourth seal: Pale horse, rider named Death, Hades following behind him, and power to kill over a fourth of the earth by sword, famine, plague, and wild beasts (Revelation 6:8).

There's no question the fourth seal is clearly about death, dying, and the grave, and the effects of such upon humanity. Death is an event, Hades represents the physical grave or physical abode of the dead, and the effects when such are unleashed upon the earth. We could back up and say that from the first to the third seals, the foundation was being laid for the walk all the way up to death. We see the echo back to aggression (sword), famine (touched on in the third seal), and now plague and wild beasts, both of which would connect to excessive aggression and famine, which comes into play with abuses of power, war and violence among people, and lack of food. The more desperate and difficult circumstances become, the more people will turn on one another, and the worse conditions will become.

Revelation 6:9-11

When He opened the fifth seal, I saw under the altar the souls of those who had been slain because of the Word of God and the testimony they had maintained. They called out in a loud voice, "How long, Sovereign Lord, holy and true, until You judge the inhabitants of the earth and avenge our blood?" Then each of them was given a white robe, and they were told to wait a little longer, until the number of their fellow servants and brothers who were to be killed as they had been was completed.

(Related Bible references: Deuteronomy 32:43, Matthew 24:9, John 8:37, John 12:24, Acts 3:21, Acts 4:24, Romans 5:10, Romans 7:10, 1 Corinthians 13:11, 2 Corinthians 1:8, Galatians 6:9, 1 John 5:20)

- The fifth seal: Under the altar, the souls of the martyrs awaiting their time, dressed in white robes, are told to wait, as they await the completion of the cycle of martyrdom in the world (Revelation 6:9-11).

None of us like being told to wait. We're told in too many church circles that we should see fast and immediate results when believing in God. There are always stories of people who gave, people who did something that seems to be "good" in the eyes of the church and then received results in only a few days or weeks. We like the idea that we can see instant results with God, even if that's not a Biblical idea. The emphasis on disciplining oneself to continue in well-doing even when no results are immediately seen (Galatians 6:9) dwindles in the face of cheerleading people to think they will get immediate results if they do the same thing.

The fifth seal shows us people awaiting their time, for the situation to be avenged by the Lord Himself. It does not just show anyone but shows the individuals who were true martyrs for their faith. They find their place now under the altar, now under the place of sacrifice, as they were sacrificed for the Gospel with their own lives. The results of man's inhumanity to man, of the purveying spirit of death in the world, is to kill those who bear the light of life, the promise of eternal life for humanity.

From the beginning of the faith, Christians have always suffered persecution in the face of those who either did not understand the faith, or, more relevantly, were threatened by what the faith meant to society. While we try to use Christianity as an excuse to uphold patriarchy or outdated notions of relationships and to try and oppress people, the truth about Christianity is that it actually brought with it a spirit of liberation and change from the social systems that existed in the first century. Christianity did not just serve as a spiritual liberation front; it also changed the ways in which women viewed themselves and their choices, the way men were to treat their wives and families, the relevance of orphans and widows, upheld the right to be single, and the way in which spirituality was to affect one's life for the better, not the worse. Society has always disliked the ultimate paradigm shift present in the form of the Kingdom of God, the message that its earthly rulers are not the ultimate voices of control, nor are they the ultimate powers in the universe. If we recognize Jesus as Lord, we are saying the powers that be are temporal and failing in the face of His governance. The world may not see it as such (at least not yet, anyway), but it is a fact that when we believe, what we see in earthly government is always temporal. Rulers have never embraced this idea. In response, they think if they silence the adherents, the message will die. Two thousand years later and still going strong, we prove them wrong.

The result of such clash is martyrdom, where the earthly powers use their physical forces to attempt to stop the Kingdom by killing its people. Martyrdom proved to be a powerful force in spreading the Gospel, because we know that in death, we find life (John 12:24, Romans 5:10, Romans 7:10). These martyrs, alive in their spiritual places, awaiting the day when things shall be made right, prove to us that waiting is a part of the faith. The martyrs of every age had the right, by virtue of their sacrifice, to wonder when they would see the day when things would be made right. Under that altar were martyrs from every era in history, every point in time, going all the way back to the beginning of Christianity. If they had to wait, then certainly the rest of us can wait with patience and a good attitude when we don't get what we want immediately. The martyrs remind us that we can wait out this 'faith thing,' to the end, whatever end that end demands of us. It's not about what we get from it, but what we give.

The walk of faith demands patient waiting because there is a completion of all things that must come full circle, straight to the end (Acts 3:21, Corinthians 13:11). Whether it's our immediate situations that seem to drag on and on or the bigger cosmic picture of eternal salvation that must run its course, patience is a requirement of our faith. There is no skimping with God, no things that come about early or before their time. We must await the fullness of time, as in the case of the martyrs, there was a specific number of them that needed to sit under the altar in heaven, to sit for their testimony and their work for the Gospel, before full vengeance could come forth. This principle of completion and fullness has been seen in Revelation prior, making us even more aware that the perfection of the ages and the completion therein lies deeply in the fulfillment of times. Trying to discern the day or the hour by one sign or one headline does not work. It is about a fullness; a full circle, an entirety...and about watching God work through various times and seasons, while we await the day of full completion.

Revelation 6:12-17

I watched as He opened the sixth seal. There was a great earthquake. The sun turned black like sackcloth made of goat hair, the whole moon turned blood red, and the stars in the sky fell to earth, as late figs drop from a fig tree when shaken by a strong wind. The sky receded like a scroll, rolling up, and every mountain and island was removed from its place.

Then kings of the earth, the princes, the generals, the rich, the mighty, and every slave and every free man hid in caves and among the rocks of the mountains. They called to the mountains and the rocks, "fall on us and hide us from the face of Him Who sits on the throne and from the wrath of the Lamb! For the great day of their wrath has come, and who can stand?"

(Related Bible references: Isaiah 2:10-19, Isaiah 34:4, Isaiah 50:3, Ezekiel 33:27, Hosea 10:8, Joel 2:31, Zephaniah 1:14-18, Matthew 24:29, Luke 22:30, Acts 2:20, Romans 2:5)

- The sixth seal: Great earthquake, sun turns black, moon turns blood red, stars falling to earth; sky rolled up, every island and mountain removed from its place, and panic ensues in the earth among people (Revelation 6:12-14).

It's very easy to read the words of Revelation, in all its forms, and understand the imagery used to refer to one event, rather than seeing the bigger picture of the prophetic circle Revelation intends to show us. The sixth seal uncovers a series of disruptions in nature's order, in the natural cycles and operations of its order. This change and disruption in order shall lead everyone on the earth – from the greatest to the least – to find themselves in a state of panic. Those who are left, at this point in time, after the disruptions of every possible ecological, political, financial, and natural system, recognize something is coming.

These natural disruptions point to the reality that consequences are real. Whether felt now or earlier in time, it is all part of the same bigger picture that reminds us that nothing lasts forever, no matter how comfortable we may be with that idea. As the natural world shakes, we're reminded consequence has come...and none is qualified to stand without the grace of God.

The Scroll and

5 Then I saw
sealed[t] with
break the seals ar
scroll or even loo
scroll or look insi
dah, the Root of D
[6]Then I saw a l
by the four living cr
its[a] of God sent ou
on the throne. [7] An
before the Lamb. Ea
[incense[b] of the lamb]

(handwritten marginal note) JESUS IS ALWAYS ABLE TO OVERCOME

G

Chapter Seven

A SEALED PROMISE FULFILLED
(REVELATION CHAPTER 7)

Key verses

- Verses 3-4: *"Do not harm the land or the sea or the trees until we put a seal on the foreheads of the servants of our God." Then I heard the number of those who were sealed: 144,000 from all the tries of Israel.*

- Verse 9: *After this I looked and there before me was a great multitude that no one could count, from every nation, tribe, people and language, standing before the throne and in front of the Lamb. They were wearing white robes and were holding palm branches in their hands.*

- Verses 13-14: *Then one of the elders asked me, "These in white robes – who are they, and where did they come from?" I answered, "Sir, you know." And he said, "These are they who have come out of the great tribulation; they have washed their robes and made them white in the blood of the Lamb."*

Words and phrases to know

- Four corners of the earth: From three Greek words: *tessares* which means "four,"[1] *gonia* which means "corner,"[2] and *ge* which means "arable land; the ground, the earth as a standing place; the main land as opposed to the sea or water; the earth as a whole; a country, land enclosed within fixed boundaries, a tract of land, territory, region."[3]

- Winds: From the Greek word *anemos* which means "wind, a violent agitation and stream of air; a very strong tempestuous wind; the four principal or cardinal winds, hence the four corners of heaven."[4]

- Harm: From the Greek word *adikeo* which means "absolutely to act unjustly or wickedly, to sin, to be a criminal, to have violated the laws in some way, to do wrong, to do hurt; transitively, to do some wrong or sin in some respect, to wrong some one, act wickedly towards him, to hurt, damage, harm."[5]

- 144,000: From four Greek words: *hekaton* which means "a hundred,"[6] *tessarakonta* which means "forty,"[7] *tessares* which means "four,"[8] and *chilias* which means "a thousand, the number one thousand."[9]

- Israel: From the Greek word *Israel* which means "Israel = "he shall be a prince of God;" the name given to the patriarch Jacob (and borne by him in addition to his former name); the family or descendants of Israel, the race of Israel; Christians, the Israel of God (Gal 6:16), for not all those who draw their bodily descent from Israel are true Israelites, i.e. are those whom God pronounces to be Israelites and has chosen to salvation."[10]

- Great multitude: From two Greek words: *polus* which means "many, much, large"[11] and *ochlos* which means "a crowd; a casual collection of people."[12]

- Palm branches: From the Greek word *phoinix* which means "a palm tree, date palm."[13]

- Salvation: From the Greek word *soteria* which means "deliverance, preservation, safety, salvation; salvation as the present possession of all true Christians; future salvation, the sum of benefits and blessings which the Christians, redeemed from all earthly ills, will enjoy after the visible return of Christ from heaven in the consummated and eternal kingdom of God."[14]

- Great tribulation: From two Greek words: *megas* which means "great; predicated of rank, as belonging to persons, eminent for ability, virtue, authority, power, things esteemed highly for their importance: of great moment, of great weight, importance, a thing to be highly esteemed for its excellence: excellent; splendid, prepared on a grand scale, stately; great things"[15] and *thlipsis* which means "a pressing, pressing together, pressure; metaph. oppression, affliction, tribulation, distress, straits."[16]

- Tent: From the Greek word *skenoo* which means "to fix one's tabernacle, have one's tabernacle, abide (or live) in a tabernacle (or tent), tabernacle; to dwell."[17]

- Hunger: From the Greek word *peinao* which means "to hunger, be hungry; metaph. to crave ardently, to seek with eager desire."[18]

- Thirst: From the Greek word *dipsao* which means "to suffer thirst, suffer from thirst, figuratively, those who are said to thirst who painfully feel their want of, and eagerly long for, those things by which the soul is refreshed, supported, strengthened."[19]

- Shepherd: From the Greek word *poimaino* which means "to feed, to tend a flock, keep sheep, to rule, govern, of rulers, to furnish pasture for food, to nourish, to cherish one's body, to serve the body, to supply the requisites for the soul's need."[20]

- Springs of living water: From two Greek words: *pege* which means "fountain, spring; a well fed by a spring"[21] and *hudor* which means "water."[22]

- Wipe away: From the Greek word *exaleipho* which means "to anoint or wash in every part; to wipe off, wipe away."[23]

- Tear: From the Greek word *dakru* which means "a tear."[24]

Revelation 7:1-8

After this I saw four angels standing at the four corners of the earth, holding back the four winds of the earth to prevent any wind from blowing on the land or on the sea or on any tree. Then I saw another angel coming up from the east, having the seal of the living God. He called out in a loud voice to the four angels who had been given power to harm the land and the sea: "Do not harm the land or the sea or the trees until we put a seal on the foreheads of the servants of our God." Then I heard the number of those who were sealed: 144,000 from all the tribes of Israel.

> *From the tribe of Judah 12,000 were sealed,*
> *from the tribe of Reuben, 12,000,*
> *from the tribe of Gad 12,000,*
> *from the tribe of Asher 12,000*
> *from the tribe of Naphtali 12,000*
> *from the tribe of Manasseh 12,000*
> *from the tribe of Simeon 12,000*
> *from the tribe of Levi 12,000*
> *from the tribe of Issachar 12,000*
> *from the tribe of Zebulun 12,000*
> *from the tribe of Joseph 12,000*
> *from the tribe of Benjamin 12,000*

(Related Bible references: Genesis 49:1-51, Numbers 3:6, 1 Chronicles

5:2, Jeremiah 25:32, Ezekiel 48:4, Matthew 24:31, Matthew 25:31, John 6:27, Romans 2:29, Romans 3:22, Romans 10:12, 2 Corinthians 1:22, Galatians 3:28, Galatians 6:16, Ephesians 1:13, Ephesians 4:30, James 1:1)

The book of Revelation clearly shows the church as a complete, unified body, in keeping with its precepts of completion. Beyond just showing the church unified, Revelation clearly shows the church as eternal. For centuries, people have debated why Revelation 7 seems to be divided into two parts. The temptation exists to almost over-interpret it, reading too much into the division that seems to exist therein. It is good for us to remember the book of Revelation wasn't divided up into chapters and verses when it was first written, so the implied divisions we added to Revelation 7 are just that – implied divisions.

We could call Revelation 7 the "unity" chapter, speaking of protection for people during times of trial. It is a bold look at those who have come together by the hand of God, the sealing of His work, and become one in their call and love for the Lord. Tripping people up, the specific numbers of Revelation 7 seem to cause confusion of the ages, just as to who these "united" people are. We can't take the first part of Revelation 7 without the second, and vice versa.

The first misconception is that Revelation 7 speaks of two groups, instead of one. While I will say that it does appear to speak of a group that is within a larger group, we shouldn't be so quick to separate the two spoken of in this chapter. The Word tells us there is no longer Gentile or Jew (Romans 3:22, Romans 10:12, Galatians 3:28), which means we should be cautioned when people are quick to make the first part of Revelation 7 specifically about the modern-day Jewish community. It is important to realize modern day Judaism is a far cry from the Hebrew experience of the Bible, and is more of a cultural experience for many than it is a spiritual one. At current statistics, approximately 50% of Jews in Israel consider themselves "secular" (more of a national and cultural identity than religious) and an additional 37% of Jews consider themselves atheist or agnostic[25], which indicates to us this is not a literal reference to modern Israel. Revelation 7 first talks about

God sealing those who are His servants, and it is inclusive of servants dating back to the time of Biblical Israel. The imagery of the 144,000, 12,000 of which are from each tribe, proves to us the providence in God's plan from the very beginning to the end. God knew the diaspora would one day come into effect, where none of us knows exactly who is descended from who and those who are the physical descendants of the original Israelites are found all throughout the world, in every culture.

The use of the tribes of Israel also points to the Kingdom, or government of God, that was executed on the earth as a ruling power. God's Kingdom is among us, and has been among us, since the beginning. It shows God's authority in His plans, that prove despite humanity's best efforts to do things and fail, God has always interwoven Himself in our promises. Even the tribes that quickly faded away or were descendants of disobedient people still have the same number of people representing their tribe and still have God's hand of protection on them.

That's part of why the spiritual value in the numbers here is so relevant. 144,000 is twelve times twelve times one thousand - it is the perfection of government squared, multiplied by one thousand, indicating a large, or great number. There is perfection in leadership, and perfection in the number. However many there are – whether literal or figurative – represent the number God knew would be there, all along.

The sign God places upon them is a sign of protection, countering the mark of the beast. Not necessarily a literal face mark, it indicates these people think differently, move differently, and have a different hand guiding their lives than what may go on throughout their days. Whoever these people may be, despite where they may come from or the backgrounds they may have, they are special, for they have chosen Christ, and are servants of God.

God still protects His own, even all these years later. Revelation reveals He always has.

Revelation 7:9-17

After this I looked and there before me was a great multitude that no one could count, from every nation, tribe, people and language, standing before the throne and in front of the Lamb. They were wearing white robes and were holding palm branches in their hands. And they cried out in a loud voice:

"Salvation belongs to our God,
Who sits on the throne,
and to the Lamb."

All the angels were standing around the throne and around the elders and the four living creatures. They fell down on their faces before the throne and worshiped God, saying:

"Amen!
Praise and glory
and wisdom and thanks and honor
and power and strength
be to our God for ever and ever. Amen!"

Then one of the elders asked me, "These in white robes – who are they, and where did they come from?"

I answered, "Sir, you know."

And he said, "These are they who have come out of the great tribulation; they have washed their robes and made them white in the blood of the Lamb. Therefore,

"They are before the throne of God
and serve Him day and night in His temple;
and He Who sits on the throne
will spread His tent over them.
Never again will they hunger;
never again will they thirst.

The sun will not beat upon them,
nor any scorching heat.
For the Lamb at the center of the throne
will be their Shepherd;
He will lead them to springs of living water.
And God will wipe away every tear from their eyes."

(Related Bible references: Genesis 22:18, Leviticus 23:40, Psalm 3:8, Psalm 11:4, Psalm 117:1, Isaiah 1:18, Isaiah 2:1-2, Isaiah 25:8, Isaiah 49:10, Isaiah 60:3, Isaiah 66:18, Matthew 25:31-34, Luke 1:69, John 10:11, John 10:16, John 12:13, Acts 4:12, Hebrews 9:14, 1 John 1:7, Jude 1:25)

The unity of the saints continues into Revelation 7, now showing a great multitude. It should be mentioned that the visionary heard the word about 144,000, and is now seeing a great multitude, but John never saw a group of only 144,000 people. The 144,000 and the great multitude are one and the same, they are those from every tongue, tribe, and nation, those who represent the physical descendants of the twelve tribes, as well as those who have been covered in the Blood of Christ, having come through the spiritual Passover present in Christ, where we, the church, past, present and future, have passed from death to life. The spiritual thing that ties all of us together is Christ. Any one of us can be of a certain heritage, lineage, or belief system without Christ, and find no protection or marking on our lives. When we are in Christ, and we are truly His servants, His protection follows, marks, and keeps us from the evil of the days that is now and is to come.

In Revelation 7, the reason why this mark of God is important because we learn the church shall come out triumphant from the great tribulation, spoken of by Jesus in Matthew 24:21-29. The term "great tribulation" is used in a variety of understandings, some of which seem Biblical, some which seem extra-Biblical, and some of which just seem confusing. I do not believe the purpose of Jesus' discourse, nor of the mentions in Revelation is to make us try and "figure" it out. Rather, it is to alert us that a time of affliction, of siege and war shall come upon us, in many different ways, and shall affect people worldwide. In the case of most disasters, they center on specific areas or are localized to one place. This is why we cannot have our heads turned by every natural disaster, branding each and every one of them as a sign of "the end." We also can't be overly preoccupied with figuring out each sign, step, and facet of just what "tribulation" will specifically entail. The Bible has been specific enough to give generalities but not identify every single specific aspect of what will happen. Those who are truly of God don't need to know every little detail; that is what makes it faith. It is faith that causes those who walk upon this earth, truly protected by God, and to trust and know God is with them, and they with Him. In the face of such, the details of what are to come are really irrelevant.

Knowing the impact of salvation on the lives of so many should cause us to stand back and revere the plan of God and rejoice that we are counted worthy to be a part of it, standing in white, holding branches, and crying out to God and the Lamb. We are a part of something so much bigger than ourselves: the footsteps of our ancestors, the seeds watered by the blood of the martyrs, the promise of being made perfect and clean in white linen, standing before God unashamed, reaching the springs of living water, with every tear wiped away from our eyes. We know this promise is to come in full…but there is so much of this Kingdom alive with us right now that we fail to miss as we look for something bigger to come. Every day, in so many ways, the Spirit guides us to a better path, a better choice, a more powerful revelation, a testimony that took us from low places, and has placed us in the seats of honor by God's doing. Every time someone holds our hearts in their hands, extends themselves to us in compassion or love, we are in a good relationship (of any sort), we see a piece, a type of that ultimate time when God shall wipe away every tear from our eyes, knowing every promise is fulfilled. Every time someone extends to us in love, as true servants of the Lord, we get that much closer to seeing our past hurts and wounds close and heal, as we come to realize the Kingdom of God is much bigger, expansive, and more powerful than any of us could have ever come to imagine. Every day of our lives, we walk, bathe, and share the Living Water that satisfies, never runs dry...and brings us to the promise of eternal life in Him.

Chapter Eight

Key verses

- Verse 1: *When He opened the seventh seal, there was silence in heaven for about half an hour.*

- Verses 3-5: *Another angel, who had a golden censer, came and stood at the altar. He was given much incense to offer, with the prayers of all the saints, on the golden altar before the throne. The smoke of the incense, together with the prayers of the saints, went up before God from the angel's hand. Then the angel took the censer, filled it with fire from the altar, and hurled it on the earth; and there came peals of thunder, rumblings, flashes of lightning and an earthquake.*

- Verses 7-8: *The first angel sounded his trumpet, and there came hail and fire mixed with blood, and it was hurled down upon the earth. A third of the earth was burned up, and all the green grass was burned up. The second angel sounded his trumpet, and something like a huge mountain, all ablaze, was thrown into the sea. A third of the sea turned into blood.*

- Verse 10: *The third angel sounded his trumpet, and a great star, blazing like a torch, fell from the sky on a third of the rivers and on the springs of water.*

- Verse 12: *The fourth angel sounded his trumpet, and a third of the sun was struck, a third of the moon, and a third of the stars, so that a third of them turned dark. A third of the day was without light, and also a third of the night.*

Words and phrases to know

- Silence: From the Greek word *sige* which means "silence."[1]

- Half an hour: From the Greek word *hemiorion* which means "half an hour."[2]

- Censer: From the Greek word *libanotos* which means "the gum exuding from a frankincense tree; a censer."[3]

- Hail: From the Greek word *chalaza* which means "hail."[4]

- Fire: From the Greek word *pur* which means "fire."[5]

- Burned: From the Greek word *katakaio* which means "to burn up, consume by fire."[6]

- Mountain: From the Greek word *oros* which means "a mountain."[7]

- Thrown: From the Greek word *ballo* which means "to throw or let go of a thing without caring where it falls; to put into, insert."[8]

- Third: From the Greek word *tritos* which means "the third."[9]

- Wormwood: From the Greek word *apsinthos* which means "wormwood; the name of a star which fell into the waters and made them bitter."[10]

- Bitter: From the Greek word *pikraino* which means "to make bitter; to embitter."[11]

- Woe: From the Greek word *ouai* which means "alas, woe."[12]

Revelation 8:1

When He opened the seventh seal, there was silence in heaven for about half an hour.

(Related Bible references: Lamentations 2:10)

Revelation, being an unveiling of *karios* time in *chronos* time, means that the timeline of the book overlaps with both spiritual and natural events. We see a continuation of Revelation 6 and 7 in Revelation 8, opening as the seventh seal, the final seal indicating a completion of events, with silence in heaven for half an hour.

We know Biblical prophetic time is often spoken of in terms that we will understand but speaks of something symbolic through them. The half hour heaven speaks of here is not a literal half hour of time, but, with prophetic understanding, a period of approximately 41 and a half years. Prophetically, those reading Revelation would have understood it to parallel that of the forty years the Israelites spent in the wilderness; a period of teaching, of learning, of disciplining, and of divine intervention in ways that are intended to instruct rather than wow or awe people.

This is most appropriate as we understand the intervention of God in our world today. Silence in heaven means just that – a lack of revelation, of God's hand working the miracles that shock people, and a long and complicated test of faith for those who are down here on the earth. If we understand the things that come forth from Revelation, from the various divine interventions and educations that God provides to us, that means the silent periods, the undramatic periods, are often more poignant for education than those where we see great activities and spiritual movement among people.

Silence in heaven is not a punishment, no more than the experience of the wilderness could be classified as one. It is a moment of lapse, one by which heaven awaits to hear the response of people upon the earth, to see if they are aligning with or interacting with *karios* time. By this point, we've already seen six seals unsealed and the results therein. Are people turning toward the answer, or further away from it? Are people seeking heaven as the answer, or is more coming that's even more relevant and needed?

All throughout Revelation, we can see many things point us back to the education our ancestors in faith received throughout salvation history. The same is true here, as we see a pause in signs and wonders we desire so that we can pause and examine our faith for real, deciding if we really mean what we claim to believe about God. Heaven's pause is to await God's next steps as we see what we will do down here: will we harden our hearts (Pharaoh wasn't the only one who hardened his heart against God) as they did in the wilderness, or will we see God moving in our behalf, in practical ways because He has marked us as His own?

Revelation 8:2-5

And I saw the seven angels who stand before God, and to them were given seven trumpets.

Another angel, who had a golden censer, came and stood at the altar. He was given much incense to offer, with the prayers of all the saints, on the golden altar before the throne. The smoke of the incense, together with the prayers of the saints, went up before God from the angel's hand. Then the angel took the censer, filled it with fire from the altar, and hurled it on the earth; and there came peals of thunder, rumblings, flashes of lightning, and an earthquake.

(Related Bible references: Exodus 30:1, Psalm 97:4, Psalm 141:2, Isaiah 6:6, 1 Peter 4:7)

Trumpets were used in ancient times to get people's attention, as an alarm or notification of sorts. They were used as official blasts to bring down declarations of war, fast, kingdom proclamations, celebrations, and solemnities. The use of trumpets in Revelation is, once again, no different. The blasts of the trumpet alert those with ears to hear that something is coming, a revelation of God's perfection and His perfect will, and the perfect completion of His movements and judgments.

We know with the blasts of the trumpets that something important is coming forth. Not only is this the seventh seal, but it also has seven aspects within it. Each trumpet is played by an angel, and then we see an eighth angel appear, one who signifies a new start, a new beginning, and the anticipation of that cycle to come which begins after silence in heaven. He comes forth with incense, which represents a sweet-smelling savor, something beautiful in God's eyes, along with the prayers of the saints, which are also beautiful in God's eyes. The saints endure during the unsealings, enduring unto prayer and are in a place where they truly need to know God hears them. Watching the prayers rise as an acceptable offering, received in God's hand, lets us know He hears us, even in times of difficulty and trial. The saints are heard of God even as the world endures more trial, more of the battle of God; the fire hurled toward the earth, unleashing this time, the Kingdom, the Spirit, unto more physical disruption in the earth's shift from one paradigm to the next.

Revelation 8:6-13

Then the seven angels who had the seven trumpets prepared to sound them.

The first angel sounded his trumpet, and there came hail and fire mixed with blood, and it was hurled down upon the earth. A third of the earth was burned up, a third of the trees were burned up, and all the green grass was burned up.

The second angel sounded his trumpet, and something like a huge mountain, all ablaze, was thrown into the sea. A third of the sea turned into blood, a third of the living creatures in the sea died, and a third of the ships were destroyed.

The third angel sounded his trumpet, and a great star, blazing like a torch, fell from the sky on a third of the rivers and on the springs of water – the name of the star is Wormwood. A third of the waters turned bitter, and many people died from the waters that had become bitter.

The fourth angel sounded his trumpet, and a third of the sun was struck, a third of the moon, and a third of the stars, so that a third of them turned dark. A third of the day was without light, and also a third of the night.

As I watched, I heard an eagle that was flying in midair call out in a loud voice: "Woe! Woe! Woe to the inhabitants of the earth, because of the trumpet blasts about to be sounded by the other three angels!"

(Related Bible references: Exodus 7:1-11:10, Numbers 10:2, Deuteronomy 5:24, Deuteronomy 29:8, Psalm 65:7, Psalm 97:3, Proverbs 5:4, Isaiah 17:13, Isaiah 60:2, Jeremiah 9:15, Jeremiah 23:15, Jeremiah 51:25, Lamentations 3:15-19, Joel 2:30, Amos 5:7, Matthew 24:8, John 8:12, John 9:5, Hebrews 12:29, 1 Peter 4:9-10)

Much like the other seals, the seven different parts of the seventh seal all carry with them other meanings. Many of the components of this seventh seal are found in one form or another in the other six seals, which alerts us to the fact that things are intensifying as completion and fulfillment come forth. Just as Jesus talks about the beginning of birth pangs (Matthew 24:8), so more intensity wrapped up into one seal indicates that a completion is coming forth.

- First angel: Hail and fire mixed with blood; a third of

the earth burned up, a third of the trees were burned up, and a third of the grass was burned up (Revelation 8:7).

Most of the seventh seal relates to natural calamity or disasters, but we should recognize these are not just ordinary weather disasters. These are nature gone wrong in a way that is unexplainable, much like the plagues in Exodus were nature gone wrong in a way that had to be supernatural (Exodus 7:1-11:10). The plagues of Exodus were planned attacks, besmirching the nature and characteristics of ten of the most powerful pagan deities of Egypt[13]:

- Nile river turns to blood: Hapi (god of the Nile)
- Frogs: Heket (goddess of fertility, water, renewal)
- Gnats: Geb (god of the earth)
- Flies: Khepri (god of creation, movement of the sun, rebirth)
- Livestock: Hathor (goddess of love and protection)
- Boils: Isis (goddess of medicine and peace)
- Hail: Nut (goddess of the sky)
- Locusts: Seth (god of storms and disorder)
- Darkness: Ra (The sun god)
- Death of the firstborn: Pharaoh (The ultimate power of Egypt

It only goes to reason that the work of these seals exists to touch certain nerves, sensitive areas of human power and reasoning, upon the earth. They exist to show God is ultimate, He is stronger than human abuses and He is more powerful than any human being may think they are. Starting with the first angel, we see a third of the earth, trees, and grass, all burnt up. For far too long, humanity has used the earth for its own selfish purposes, selfishly using resources, cutting down trees, digging up grass, and spreading malice and ill will across the earth in the name of greed. Nothing lasts forever, and if we abuse it – we lose it. This is why the Bible calls us to be good stewards with all He has given to us (1 Peter 4:9-10). It shows respect to the Creator, and a wise use of dominion.

- Second angel: Huge mountain on fire, thrown into the sea; a third of the sea turned to blood, a third of the creatures in the sea died, and a third of the ships were destroyed (Revelation 8:8-9).

Waterways were a significant source of economics in ancient times. Before the development of train travel, automobile travel and air travel, most of the economic transport occurred via rivers, seas, and in port cities. It was also a great source of food for ancient cultures because it was reasonably inexpensive and readily available in coastal areas. To attack the sea was to attack the heart of commerce, both dietary and commercial. One third of commerce, dietary (related to what we eat) and commercial shall be destroyed.

- Third angel: Great star (Wormwood), blazing like a torch, fell from the sky into a third of rivers and springs of water; a third of the waters turned bitter, and many people died from bitter water (Revelation 8:10-11).

Wormwood is mentioned six times in the Old Testament (Deuteronomy 29:8, Proverbs 5:4, Jeremiah 9:15, Jeremiah 23:15, Lamentations 3:15-19, Amos 5:7) and represents bitterness, every single time it is mentioned. Many who study Revelation disagree on the literal interpretation of Wormwood's representation here, believing it could refer to an asteroid or even nuclear explosion. With Revelation often echoing back to Old Testament imagery, however, I think the answer relates in the way in which Wormwood is used prior in the Scriptures. Wormwood is always used metaphorically, to indicate difficulty, bitter pain, trial, or opposition that is hard to swallow. Water, symbolizing the ultimate life source, tells us that our waters – both physical and spiritual – shall turn bitter to us. We shall deal with contamination in our water and food sources, and we shall find our spiritual waters – our religious and spiritual systems – bitter, hard to swallow, and leading to anything but life. Such shall lead to death, both physical and spiritual.

- Fourth angel: A third of the sun was struck, a third of the moon and a third of the stars, and they turned dark; a third of the day was without light, and a third of the night (Revelation 8:12).

Darkness is also used throughout the Bible to indicate spiritual states as well as physical ones. For a third of darkness to veil the land indicates we are dealing with approximately one third of humanity that is beyond redemption in one form or another. Veiled in total darkness, they stumble and fall, unable to find their way. The physical world will mimic the spiritual condition of those who live without light, the true light of the world, Jesus (John 8:12, John 9:5), trying to survive in darkness.

This also needs to cause us to realize that even though people might claim to be Christian, claim to be holy, or claim to believe the right things, does not make it so. As the conditions of Revelation unveil that which already is in the spiritual realm – that which is already is being revealed, uncovered, and laid bare for all to see. As we continue to go deeper into the seventh seal, more is revealed – more is aware – and yes, God uncovers more for us to recognize and see as time goes forward.

The Scroll and

5 Then I saw i
sealed[t] with
break the seals an
scroll or even loo
scroll or look insi
dah, the Root of D

[6]Then I saw a L
by the four living cr
its[a] of God sent out
on the throne.[11] An
before the Lamb la
numero of the

JESUS IS ALWAYS ABLE TO OVERCOME

G

Chapter Nine

UNSEALING THE SEAL TO END ALL SEALS, PART 2 (REVELATION CHAPTER 9)

Key verses

- Verse 1: *The fifth angel sounded his trumpet, and I saw a star that had fallen from the sky to the earth. The star was given the key to the shaft of the Abyss.*

- Verse 12: *The first woe is past; two other woes are yet to come.*

- Verses 13-14: *The sixth angel sounded his trumpet, and I heard a voice coming from the horns of the golden altar that is before God. It said to the sixth angel who had the trumpet, "Release the four angels who are bound at the great river Euphrates."*

- Verses 20-21: *The rest of mankind that were not killed by these plagues still did not repent of the work of their hands; they did not stop worshiping demons, and idols of gold, silver, bronze, stone and wood – idols that cannot see or hear or walk. Nor did they repent of their murders, their magic arts, their sexual immorality or their thefts.*

Words and phrases to know

- Abyss: From the Greek word *abussos* which means "bottomless; unbounded; the abyss."[1]

- Smoke: From the Greek word *kapnos* which means "smoke."[2]

- Furnace: From the Greek word *kaminos* which means "a furnace."[3]

- Locusts: From the Greek word *akris* which means "a locust, particularly that species which especially infests oriental countries, stripping fields and trees. Numberless swarms of them almost every spring are carried by the wind from Arabia into Palestine, and having devastated that country, migrate to regions farther north, until they perish by falling into the sea. The Orientals accustomed to feed upon locusts, either raw or roasted and seasoned with salt (or prepared in other ways), and the Israelites also were permitted to eat them."[4]

- Scorpions: From the Greek word *skorpios* which means "a scorpion, the name of a little animal, somewhat resembling a lobster, which in warm regions lurk, esp. in stone walls; it has a poisonous sting in its tail."[5]

- Torture: From the Greek word *basanismos* which means "to torture, a testing by the touchstone, which is a black siliceous stone used to test the purity of gold or silver by the color of the streak produced on it by rubbing it with either metal; torment, torture."[6]

- Five months: From two Greek words: *pente* which means "five"[7] and *men* which means "a month; the time of the new moon, new moon (the first day of each month, when the new moon appeared was a festival among the Hebrews."[8]

- Women's hair: From two Greek words: *thrix* which means "the hair of the head; the hair of animals"[9] and *gune* which means "a woman of any age, whether a virgin, or married, or a widow; a wife."[10]

- Teeth: From the Greek word *odous* which means "a tooth."[11]

- Breastplates: From the Greek word *thorax* which means "the breast, the part of the body from the neck to the navel, where the ribs end; a breastplate or corset consisting of two parts and protecting the body on both sides from the neck to the middle."[12]

- Iron: From the Hebrew word *sidereos* which means "made of iron."[13]

- Abaddon: From the Hebrew word *Abaddon* which means "ruin; destruction; the place of destruction; the name of the angel-prince of the infernal regions, the minister of death and the author of havoc on the earth."[14]

- Apollyon: From the Hebrew word *Apolluon* which means "the angel of the bottomless pit, the Destroyer."[15]

- Release: From the Hebrew word *luo* which means "to loose any person (or thing) tied or fastened; to loosen, undo, dissolve, anything bound, tied, or compacted together."[16]

- Euphrates: From the Greek word *Euphrates* which means "Euphrates = "the good and abounding river;" a large, famous river which rises in the mountains of Armenia Major, flows through Assyria, Syria, Mesopotamia and the city of Babylon, and empties into the Gulf of Persia."[17]

- Sulfur: From the Greek word *theion* which means "brimstone."[18]

- Demons: From the Greek word *daimonion* which means "the divine power, deity, divinity; a spirit, a being inferior to God, superior to men; evil spirits or the messengers and ministers of the devil."[19]

Revelation 9:1-6

The fifth angel sounded his trumpet, and I saw a star that had fallen from the sky to the earth. The star was given the key to the shaft of the Abyss. When he opened the Abyss, smoke rose from it like the smoke from a gigantic furnace. The sun and sky were darkened by the smoke from the Abyss. And out of the smoke locusts came down upon the earth and were given power like that of scorpions of the earth. They were told not to harm the grass of the earth or any plant or tree, but only those people who did not have the seal of God on their foreheads. They were not given power to kill them, but only to torture them for five months. And the agony they suffered was like that of the sting of a scorpion when it strikes a man. During those days men will seek death, but will not find it; they will long to die, but death will elude them.

(Related Bible references: Joel 2:2-10, Luke 8:31, 1 Peter 4:17)

- Fifth angel: Star fallen to the earth, given the key to the shaft of the abyss; abyss opened, smoke rose from it, darkness covers the earth, and locusts given power to torture those not marked by God for five months (Revelation 9:1-11).

The seventh seal continues to unveil in its continued revelation, beginning with the fifth angel's trumpet sound. We see a different star fall this time, given a key to the shaft of the Abyss, one that represents the opening of evil, of death upon the earth. This fallen star reflects that of the devil and that of the demons, those angels that started out as worshipers, messengers, people who were agents of God, and turned aside to be agents of the devil. They are unleashed to do their work, that their end, their final termination may occur.

Just as the devil and his minions were given the opportunity to make their decision as to whom they would serve, human beings are given that same option. Those who choose to follow the enemy do not enjoy the protection of God as they are turned over to the one whom they serve who is in opposition to God. The torture such receive is not the result of an unmerciful or unloving God, but the result of the decisions and choices one makes. We follow in the image of those who lead us, and here we find the image followed unto destruction. The result was stinging, unbearable, difficult, and painful, coming face-to-face with the reality that the choice to turn around has passed and consequence must now come.

The trials spoken of here are spoken of in the terms of five months, which in prophetic time equates to 1,500 years, or an approximately 1,500-year period of trial and difficulty. The people of God are still here; but they are protected. We know judgment starts in the house of God (1 Peter 4:17), but that doesn't mean it's any easier to watch as people experience the consequences of their own actions. They still must endure through as they watch people they know: loved ones, friends, family members, even fellow church members, go through the trials and results of their own consequences.

People will seek escape, as they always do when they deal with consequences and trial. This is the ultimate answer that yes, what we do comes back and we do reap what we sow. Those who have sown destruction shall reap it and shall not escape it.

Revelation 9:7-12

The locusts looked like horses prepared for battle. On their heads they wore something like crowns of gold, and their faces resembled human faces. Their hair was like women's hair, and their teeth were like lions' teeth. They had breastplates like breastplates of iron, and the sound of their wings was like the thundering of many horses and chariots rushing into battle. They had tails and stings like scorpions, and in their tails they had power to torment people for five months. They had as king over them the angel of the Abyss, whose name in Hebrew is Abaddon, and in Greek, Apollyon.

The first woe is past; two other woes are yet to come.

(Related Bible references: Exodus 37:7-9, Numbers 7:89, 1 Kings 8:6, Psalm 18:10, Psalm 80:1, Psalm 99:1, Joel 1:6, Joel 2:4-6, John 10:10, 2 Corinthians 11:14, 1 Peter 5:8, 1 John 4:8, Hebrews 9:5, Revelation 4:6-8)

In Biblical times, locusts were used as symbols of devastation and destruction. We see them mentioned earlier in Revelation 9, used to indicate those who do the bidding work of the evil one, those who are purposed to bring destruction. Here they are used in the same manner, riding as if to a battle of destruction for the enemy, the evil one. The further nature of destruction during the same five month/1,500-year time period is to emphasize how difficult and horrible this period will be for those who incur its wrath. God is love (1 John 4:8), but Satan shows no mercy when time comes for reckoning.

What we learn about the nature of the locusts tells us about the specific ways in which demons will attack and turn on those that faithfully serve them. As with all things Revelation, symbolism is not lost, but reveals us a purpose, a warning about what to note as the time is now and is already here.

- Crowns of gold: Theologians tend to disagree on just what demons can do in terms of morphing in various forms. Demons can appear in human form, just as angels can do the same (2 Corinthians 11:14). Crowns of gold indicate authority or nobility. In the case of Revelation, most likely represents authority of a political nature. Given the context of Revelation was, in a literal sense, a commentary against the Roman Empire and prediction of its inevitable fall, there is probably a double entendre here: a reference of the empire, and specifically its emperors, as demonic in origin. Let us not forget, however, that politicians can be found everywhere: in the government, in secular institutions, and yes, even in church. Don't read this so literally that you miss the bigger picture God desires us to see.

- Human faces: If this does not prove a demon can look like a human being, I am not sure what does. I'm not the biggest advocate of as to the accuracy in movies such as *The Omen*, but the one thing such movies do point out to us is that demons can take forms that look just like anyone else, blending in with society in normal and nominative ways, undetectable to the naked eye. Demons can blend in as angels can, resembling human interests, human purposes, human actions, and human motions. For all intents and purposes, the destructive demons will look like, talk like, and resemble human beings.

- Hair like women's hair: Women's hair represents a character of attractiveness or beauty. The reference here is most likely duo fold in nature: the first is to indicate the appearance of physical attractiveness, of beings that are pleasant to look at and beings that can be charismatic and attractive in nature. There is nothing about their physical exterior that would make someone want to avoid them or ignore them.

- Teeth as lion's teeth: Lion's teeth are sharp in order to devour live prey. Such a reference warns us that they are ready to devour at any second (1 Peter 5:8), aggressive and damaging.

- Breastplates like breastplates of iron: Breastplates were used as a part of armor protection in ancient times, showing demons to be fully ready and prepared to handle battle for evil.

- Wings like the thundering of many horses and chariots, rushing into battle: As a counter to the cherubim spoken of earlier in Revelation (Revelation 4:6-8) and earlier in the Bible (Exodus 37:7-9, Numbers 7:89, 1 Kings 8:6, Psalm 18:10, Psalm 80:1, Psalm 99:1, Hebrews 9:5), the wings of demons flutter, honor, and pay tribute to Satan, the evil one.

- Tails and stings like scorpions: The tail of a scorpion is its major defense weapon. It contains venom glands and a sharp needle-like stinger that ensures any prey or enemy receives the venom. The venomous sting of a scorpion can be deadly to humans, and extraordinarily painful and dangerous in the best of circumstances. As the scorpion tail doesn't look readily dangerous to an onlooker, it catches one who is not prepared for it by surprise. This is how demons work: they look like anyone else, seem harmless enough, and appear cosmetically appealing enough, but they are ready at any time to strike their deadly blow to someone who is fully unsuspecting of their venom.

The demons follow Satan, spoken of herein two different languages as "the destroyer." There is no question how important it was that the reader understand how destructive Satan's agenda is (John 10:10). As the first woe passes – two more come, in Satan's attempt to woo – and woe – the world.

Revelation 9:13-21

The sixth angel sounded his trumpet, and I heard a voice coming from the horns of the golden altar that is before God. It said to the sixth angel who had the trumpet, "Release the four angels who are bound at the great river Euphrates." And the four angels who had been kept ready for this very hour and day and month and year were released to kill a third of mankind. The number of the mounted troops was two hundred million. I heard their number.

The horses and riders I saw in my vision looked like this: Their breastplates were fiery red, dark blue, and yellow as sulfur. The heads of the horses resembled the heads of lions, and out of their mouths came fire, smoke and sulfur. A third of mankind was killed by the three plagues of fire, smoke and sulfur that came out of their mouths. The power of the horses was in their mouths and in their tails; for their tails were like snakes, having heads with which they inflict injury.

The rest of mankind that were not killed by these plagues still did not repent of the work of their hands; they did not stop worshiping demons, and idols of gold, silver, bronze, stone and wood – idols that cannot see or hear or walk. Nor did they repent of their murders, their magic arts, their sexual immorality or their thefts.

(Related Bible references: Genesis 2:14, Exodus 20:13, Psalm 11:6, Psalm 137:1, Isaiah 44:9, Jeremiah 10:5, Galatians 5:20, Revelation 8:7-12, Revelation 9:15-18, Revelation 12:4-9)

- Sixth angel: Voice coming from the golden altar before God; four angels released bound at the river Euphrates, released to kill a third of mankind (Revelation 9:13-19).

Most anthropologists consider the Euphrates to be one of the rivers that is the original source of human life. It has, throughout history, served countless civilizations with water, travel, transportation, and life. The Euphrates is the longest river of western Asia and also one of the most important.[20] To release angels bound at this river indicates they had a certain sway and importance over all facets of humankind: physical, economic, commerce, and even, in a certain sense, spiritual life. They were released from an important fount of life to affect the lives of human beings.

We can see the work of the angels executed by men, with a number of mounted troops in the millions, a number beyond anything that we can compare or conceive with our own thoughts. The horses and riders were venomous, ready to pounce and attack, with great force, great authority, and great power. They operated as agents of Satan, whether they recognized that, as they functioned by their intense force and power. They were ready to strike, attack, move, at any moment, because they had a mission to kill one third of mankind.

Since the chapter refers to the plagues of fire, smoke, and sulfur (physically strong, pungent, and attention-getting elements), this means the events spoken of in Revelation are more widespread than just a world war or some isolated issues with mankind. The fraction one-third, or approximately 33.3%, is repeated many times in Revelation (Revelation 8:7-12, Revelation 9:15-18, Revelation 12:4-9). Three and three add up to six, indicating that the effects of whatever comes upon the 'third' will somehow have an impact upon humanity, upon the function of humanity, and the movement and commerce of humanity. The very things that keep life going shall find disruption in these times. It also means that it is just enough to make sure the entire world is touched without having to blight or kill every single person. The fraction of one-third is just enough to make sure that people know what is going on and are somehow affected by it.

You would think that being around so much calamity would cause people to step back and think about life...but that is not the case here in Revelation 9. We don't see people stopping to repent or consider the deeper realities of life, perhaps wondering what's going on and what human beings can do to stop things before they get more and more out of control. What we find instead is a plague not easily mentioned by name, but quite common: one of of entitlement, where people felt more of a justification to acting any way they pleased. They didn't miss a beat; they did not turn around and change what they were doing. There was no sight to become a better person. Instead, they worshiped demons, idols, continued to kill one another, practice all sorts of magic and witchcraft (power and control over others), walk in sexual immoralities, and steal.

Thus, the consequences...continue.

The Scroll and

5 Then I saw i
sealed[t] with
break the seals an
scroll or even loo
scroll or look insi
dah, the Root of D

[6]Then I saw a L
by the four living cr
its[a] of God sent out
on the throne [t] [t] An
before the Lamb. Ea
_____ of the ____

JESUS
IS ALWAYS
ABLE TO
OVERCOME

G

Chapter Ten

A Bittersweet Little Scroll (Revelation Chapter 10)

Key verses

- Verse 2: *He was holding a little scroll, which lay open in his hand. He planted his right foot on the sea and his left foot on the land...*

- Verse 4: *And when the seven thunders spoke, I was about to write; but I heard a voice from heaven say, "Seal up what the seven thunders have said and do not write it down."*

- Verses 9-11: *So I went to the angel and asked him to give me the little scroll. He said to me, "Take it and eat it. It will turn your stomach sour, but in your mouth it will be as sweet as honey." I took the little scroll from the angel's hand and ate it. It tasted as sweet as honey in my mouth, but when I had eaten it, my stomach turned sour. Then I was told, "You must prophesy again about many peoples, nations, languages and kings."*

Words and phrases to know

- Cloud: From the Greek word *nephele* which means "a cloud."[1]

- Thunders: From the Greek word *bronte* which means "thunder."[2]

- Swore: From the Greek word *omnuo* which means "to swear;) to affirm, promise, threaten, with an oath; in swearing to call a person or thing as witness, to invoke, swear by."[3]

- Prophets: From the Greek word *prophetes* which means "in Greek writings, an interpreter of oracles or of other hidden things; one who, moved by the Spirit of God and hence his organ or spokesman, solemnly declares to men what he has received by inspiration, especially concerning future events, and in particular such as relate to the cause and kingdom of God and to human salvation; in the religious assemblies of the Christians, they were moved by the Holy Spirit to speak, having power to instruct, comfort, encourage, rebuke, convict, and stimulate, their hearers; a poet (because poets were believed to sing under divine inspiration)."[4]

- Sour: From the Greek word *pikraino* which means "to make bitter; to embitter."[5]

- Sweet: From the Greek word *glukus* which means "sweet."[6]

- Honey: From the Greek word *meli* which means "honey."[7]

Revelation 10:1-4

Then I saw another mighty angel coming down from heaven. He was robed in a cloud, with a rainbow above his head; his face was like the sun, and his legs were like fiery pillars. He was holding a little scroll, which lay open in his hand. He planted his right foot on the sea and his left foot on the land, and he gave a loud shout like the roar of a lion. When he shouted, the voices of the seven thunders spoke. And when the seven thunders spoke, I was about to write; but I heard a voice from heaven say, "Seal up what the seven thunders have said and do not write it down."

(Related Bible references: Proverbs 20:2, Daniel 7:13, Daniel 12:4, 2 Corinthians 12:1-10, Galatians 2:9, 1 Timothy 3:15)

The seventh trumpet has yet to be sounded, but the woes have come and gone; the completion of that aspect of the unveiling is soon to arrive; and now the beginning of a new phase of Revelation's unveiling begins. We are also very close to the second half of the book, which continues to reveal, only in a closer way as we approach the great unveiling Revelation seeks to uncover for us.

The angel we now meet is mighty in power, standing both upon the sea and the land. His presence was unavoidable, brilliant in appearance and firm in his commission. The pillars he stands upon represent eternal truth, of which the church is supposed to uphold and represent (Galatians 2:9, 1 Timothy 3:15). When he shouted, everyone took notice, as the seven thunders spoke.

We have already discussed the relevance of thunder in Revelation, used to represent the authority and voice of God. Here thunder is connected to the seven thunders, representing the completion and perfection of the message that was to come forth. As with all things Revelation, what was to be spoken was not just any ordinary message. There is a difference this time, however. As the Apostle John was ready to write the revelation, he was sternly instructed not to write it down.

Given the entirety of Revelation is about an unveiling, this might sound strange to us, and especially strange to the first-century readers. Why was John going through this entire experience if he was not supposed to document all of it? What was so special about this specific unveiling that it needed to be revealed, and then sealed again?

Anyone who has a mystical experience with the Lord or any sort of deep revelation from Him knows – and understands – that not everything revealed is for this very hour, moment, time, or people. Sometimes what is seen in the mystical realm, the great unveiling, is too much for that specific era or generation to handle. This does not necessarily pertain to a whole vision, as we can see with Revelation. Up to this point, everything the apostle saw, he revealed. He wrote and he explained it, often in great and complex detail. This part of the vision, however, was not for everyone, right now, not in that moment, or that season.

We also have the dimension of personal humility when forced to "sit upon" a vision. When the Apostle Paul spoke of his great and surpassing revelation that he could not speak of, he was quick to remind everyone that he was also given a thorn in the flesh to remain humble (2 Corinthians 12:1-10). Every great mystic in history has often experienced the intensity of this life as they wrestle with human flesh and the pursuit of dying to self. We've all met the arrogant false prophet who seeks to boast about what they have seen in the flesh (whether it was genuine notwithstanding). They are quick to be proud, puffed, feeling as if God revealed something to them because they are special. The true mystic knows they are not special, but willing to receive what God is ready to show. Having to withhold part of the revelation out of obedience yields humility to the situation. The mystic must wrestle with what they have seen and examine it for themselves first, never ignoring the way in which it directly can apply to their lives. The mystic must first see the revelation through themselves, in order to understand the revelation's true purpose for the spiritual good.

Revelation 10:5-8

Then the angel I had seen standing on the sea and on the land raised his right hand to heaven. And he swore by Him Who lives for ever and ever, Who created the heavens and all that is in them, the earth and all that is in it, and the sea and all that is in it, and said, "There will be no more delay! But in the days when the seventh angel is about to sound his trumpet, the mystery of God will be accomplished, just as He announced to His servants the prophets."

Then the voice that I had heard from heaven spoke to me once more: "Go, take the scroll that lies open in the hand of the angel who is standing on the sea and on the land."

(Related Bible references: Exodus 4:16, Isaiah 28:11, Ezekiel 12:25, Habakkuk 2:3, Amos 3:7, 1 Corinthians 4:11, Ephesians 2:11-22)

As the angel stands on the land and the sea, that signifies the message he brings is for everyone. It's not just a limited message, for only a small group of people, but one that will affect the world at large and all the people in the world. No one will be exempt from its contents, and it is something vital to hear. Swearing by God Himself tells us it is something not only vital, but completely true. We can trust the message to come as being divinely inspired, something only God could reveal to us in this hour.

The angel comes to tell us that there will be no more delays. The completion, the perfection, the wholeness has come, and it shall come when the seventh angel sounds his trumpet. The complete mystery of God shall be revealed, and it shall come about just as has been prophesied! All these plagues, woes, sorrows, and issues culminate in the accomplishment of the mystery of God.

We know from the New Testament that the role of the apostle is to reveal the mysteries of God (1 Corinthians 4:1). The role of the prophets has always been to speak the mysteries of God (Exodus 4:16, Isaiah 28:11). These various mysteries, bits and pieces of types and shadows revealing God's true nature and plan for humanity, all come together to finally reveal His great mystery, the unveiling of the totality of prophecy and salvation for all humanity (Ephesians 2:11-22). Now we understand in part, but then we shall see the entire picture, clear from past to present. What the prophets have spoken, what the apostles have revealed, what the ministers of God have proclaimed shall be, in that time, understandable.

With everything understood, it is time to receive further revelation. Having received the great mystery of God, we do not need a big revelation, just a small one will do...one small enough to pack a punch for all who have ears to hear it.

Revelation 10:9-11

So I went to the angel and asked him to give me the little scroll. He said to me, "Take it and eat it. It will turn your stomach sour, but in your mouth it will be as sweet as honey." I took the little scroll from the angel's hand and ate it. It tasted as sweet as honey in my mouth, but when I had eaten it, my stomach turned sour. Then I was told, "You must prophesy again about many peoples, nations, languages and kings."

(Related Bible references: Isaiah 55:11, Jeremiah 1:10, Jeremiah 15:16, Ezekiel 2:8-3:3)

Scholars have questioned for centuries just what the little scroll contains. It is most likely a similar parallelism to Ezekiel 2:8-3:3, where Ezekiel is given a specific prophecy to deliver to the people, that was filled with lamentation and mourning, but sweet as honey to the taste. The little scroll clearly represents prophecy, the reception of prophetic word, especially given the words about the mystery of God revealed earlier in Revelation 10.

Any prophet will tell you the bittersweet nature of prophetic word. The words God reveals to the prophets have one major hope behind them, and that is the consistent hope of change. The salvation message of God reminds each and every one of us that Jesus has come so human nature can change and transform. We can become in the image and likeness as we change from glory to glory and faith to faith, but we cannot do it without the intervention of the Lord in our lives. The promise of hope: that Christ shall come again and we shall be changed is a constant type living in each and every one of us as we walk along in the promise of faith in our lives. It is sweet to deliver and speak these words, precious and glorious to herald them in one's mouth. The reality behind the major hope, however, will turn anyone's stomach. The needed change, the consequences of sin, the needed disciplines that must be implemented in order to bring about the needed change to see hope in one's life. The realities of where people are and the correction that must come turns the blessing into a sour one, one that is rejected and not embraced by too many people in this world.

The apostle is told he must prophesy anyhow. It does not matter how bitter or sweet it seems, it is word that must be delivered, word that must transform nations, peoples, kings, and languages. It crosses cultures, divides, and peoples. It must be given, because, received or not, it must be spoken and released so it will not return void (Isaiah 55:11).

The Scroll and

5 Then I saw i
sealed[t] with
break the seals an
scroll or even loo
scroll or look insi
dah, the Root of D

[6] Then I saw a L
by the four living cr
its[u] of God sent out
on the throne. [7] An
before the Lamb ha
prayers[v] of the sain

JESUS
IS ALWAYS
ABLE TO
OVERCOME

G

Chapter Eleven

A MEASURE OF A TEMPLE, TWO WITNESSES AND A SEVENTH TRUMPET (REVELATION CHAPTER 11)

Key verses

- Verse 1: *I was given a reed like a measuring rod and was told, "Go and measure the temple of God and the altar, and count the worshipers there.*

- Verses 3-4: *"And I will give power to My two witnesses, and they will prophesy for 1,260 days, clothed in sackcloth." These are the two olive trees and the two lampstands that stand before the Lord of the earth.*

- Verses 11-12: *But after the three and a half days a breath of life from God entered them, and they stood on their feet, and terror struck those who saw them. Then they heard a loud voice from heaven saying to them, "Come up here." And they went up to heaven in a cloud, while their enemies looked on.*
- Verse 14: *The second woe has passed; the third woe is coming soon.*

Words and phrases to know

- Reed: From the Greek word *kalamos* which means "a reed; a staff made of a reed, a reed staff; a measuring reed or rod; a writer's reed, a pen."[1]

- Measuring rod: From the Greek word *rhabdos* which means "a staff, a walking stick, a twig, rod, branch; a rod with which one is beaten; a staff."[2]

- Count: From the Greek word *metreo* which means "to measure, to measure out or off; to measure out, mete out to, i.e. to give by measure."[3]

- Outer court: From the Greek word *naos* which means "used of the temple at Jerusalem, but only of the sacred edifice (or sanctuary) itself, consisting of the Holy place and the Holy of Holies (in classical Greek it is used of the sanctuary or cell of the temple, where the image of gold was placed which is distinguished from the whole enclosure)."[4]

- Trample: From the Greek word *pateo* which means "to tread."[5]

- Witnesses: From the Greek word *martus* which means "a witness."[6]

- Sackcloth: From the Greek word *sakkos* which means "a sack."[7]

- Olive trees: From the Greek word *elaia* which means "an olive tree; an olive, the fruit of an olive tree."[8]

- Beast: From the Greek word *therion* which means "an animal; a wild animal, wild beast, beast; metaph. a brutal, bestial man, savage, ferocious."[9]

- Gloat: From the Greek word *chairo* which means "to rejoice, be glad; to rejoice exceedingly; to be well, thrive; in salutations, hail!; at the beginning of letters: to give one greeting, salute."[10]

- Reward: From the Greek word *misthos* which means "dues paid for work; reward: used of the fruit naturally resulting from toils and endeavours."[11]

Revelation 11:1-6

I was given a reed like a measuring rod and was told, "Go and measure the temple of God and the altar, and count the worshipers there. But exclude the outer court; do not measure it, because it has been given to the Gentiles. They will trample on the holy city for forty-two months. And I will give power to my two witnesses, and they will prophesy for 1,260 days, clothed in sackcloth." These are the two olive trees and two lampstands that stand before the Lord of the earth. If anyone tries to harm them, fire comes from their mouths and devours their enemies. This is how anyone who wants to harm them must die. These men have power to shut up the sky so that it will not rain during the time they are prophesying; and they have power to turn the waters into blood and to strike the earth with every kind of plague as often as they want.

(Related Bible references: Genesis 1:27-28, Ezekiel 40:1-49, Zechariah 4:1-14, Matthew 13:24-30, Matthew 13:36-43, Luke 21:24, 2 Corinthians 6:16, Ephesians 5:25-32)

Revelation 11 chronicles a series of events that, in some ways, seem unrelated. The Apostle John starts out measuring the temple and then ends with the triumphant reign of Christ announced, as their reign begins to overtake the world in a progressive format. The truth is that as with any Revelation, Revelation 11 has components that are all uniquely connected in a powerful way. It also brings to light an underlying purpose in the book of Revelation, which was to give place to the church in light of major prophecy. Rather than just be interpreted in the light of old covenant understanding, the prophecy of Revelation gives Old Testament prophecy New Testament insight, bringing the church into the prophetic vision.

The first – and extremely vivid vision – is John's

command to measure the temple. Revelation tells us little about it here, in contrast with Ezekiel 40:1-49, which is far more descriptive:

On April 28, during the twenty-fifth year of our captivity—fourteen years after the fall of Jerusalem—the LORD took hold of me. In a vision from God He took me to the land of Israel and set me down on a very high mountain. From there I could see toward the south what appeared to be a city. As He brought me nearer, I saw a man whose face shone like bronze standing beside a gateway entrance. He was holding in his hand a linen measuring cord and a measuring rod.

He said to me, "Son of man, watch and listen. Pay close attention to everything I show you. You have been brought here so I can show you many things. Then you will return to the people of Israel and tell them everything you have seen."

I could see a wall completely surrounding the Temple area. The man took a measuring rod that was 10 1/2 feet long and measured the wall, and the wall was 10 1/2 feet thick and 10 1/2 feet high.

Then he went over to the eastern gateway. He climbed the steps and measured the threshold of the gateway; it was 10 1/2 feet front to back. There were guard alcoves on each side built into the gateway passage. Each of these alcoves was 10 1/2 feet square, with a distance between them of 8 3/4 feet along the passage wall. The gateway's inner threshold, which led to the entry room at the inner end of the gateway passage, was 10 1/2 feet front to back. He also measured the entry room of the gateway. It was 14 feet across, with supporting columns 3 1/2 feet thick. This entry room was at the inner end of the gateway structure, facing toward the Temple.

There were three guard alcoves on each side of the gateway passage. Each had the same measurements, and the dividing walls separating them were also identical. The man measured the gateway entrance, which was 17 1/2 feet wide at the opening and 22 3/4 feet wide in the gateway passage. In front of each of the guard alcoves was a 21-inch curb. The alcoves themselves were 10 1/2 feet on each side.

Then he measured the entire width of the gateway, measuring the distance between the back walls of facing guard alcoves; this distance was 43 3/4 feet. He measured the dividing walls all along the inside of the gateway up to the entry room of the gateway; this distance was 105 feet. The full length of the gateway passage was 87 1/2 feet from one end to the other. There were recessed windows that narrowed inward through the walls of the guard alcoves and their dividing walls. There were also windows in the entry room. The surfaces of the dividing walls were decorated with carved palm trees.

Then the man brought me through the gateway into the outer courtyard of the Temple. A stone pavement ran along the walls of the courtyard, and thirty rooms were built against the walls, opening onto the pavement. This pavement flanked the gates and extended out from the walls into the courtyard the same distance as the gateway entrance. This was the lower pavement. Then the man measured across the Temple's outer courtyard between the outer and inner gateways; the distance was 175 feet.

The man measured the gateway on the north just like the one on the east. Here, too, there were three guard alcoves on each side, with dividing walls and an entry room. All the measurements matched those of the east gateway. The gateway passage was 87 1/2 feet long and 43 3/4 feet wide between the back walls of facing guard alcoves. The windows, the entry room, and the palm tree decorations were identical to those in the east gateway. There were seven steps leading up to the gateway entrance, and the entry room was at the inner end of the gateway passage. Here on the north side, just as on the east, there was another gateway leading to the Temple's inner courtyard directly opposite this outer gateway. The distance between the two gateways was 175 feet.

Then the man took me around to the south gateway and measured its various parts, and they were exactly the same as in the others. It had windows along the walls as the others did, and there was an entry room where the gateway passage opened into the outer courtyard. And like the others, the gateway passage was 87 1/2 feet long and 43 3/4 feet wide between the back walls of facing guard alcoves. This gateway also had a stairway of seven steps leading up to it, and an entry room at the inner end, and palm tree decorations along the dividing walls. And here again, directly opposite the outer gateway, was another gateway that led into the inner courtyard. The distance between the two gateways was 175 feet.

Then the man took me to the south gateway leading into the inner courtyard. He measured it, and it had the same measurements as the other gateways. Its guard alcoves, dividing walls, and entry room were the same size as those in the others. It also had windows along its walls and in the entry room. And like the others, the gateway passage was 87 1/2 feet long and 43 3/4 feet wide. (The entry rooms of the gateways leading into the inner courtyard were 14 feet across and 43 3/4 feet wide.) The entry room to the south gateway faced into the outer courtyard. It had palm tree decorations on its columns, and there were eight steps leading to its entrance.

Then he took me to the east gateway leading to the inner courtyard. He measured it, and it had the same measurements as the other gateways. Its guard alcoves, dividing walls, and entry room were the same size as those of the others, and there were windows along the walls and in the entry room. The gateway passage measured 87 1/2 feet long and 43 3⁄4 feet wide. Its entry room faced into the outer courtyard. It had palm tree decorations on its columns, and there were eight steps leading to its entrance.

Then he took me around to the north gateway leading to the inner courtyard. He measured it, and it had the same measurements as the other gateways. The guard alcoves, dividing walls, and entry room of this gateway had the same measurements as in the others and the same window arrangements. The gateway passage measured 87 1⁄2 feet long and 43 3⁄4 feet wide. Its entry room faced into the outer courtyard, and it had palm tree decorations on the columns. There were eight steps leading to its entrance.

A door led from the entry room of one of the inner gateways into a side room, where the meat for sacrifices was washed. On each side of this entry room were two tables, where the sacrificial animals were slaughtered for the burnt offerings, sin offerings, and guilt offerings. Outside the entry room, on each side of the stairs going up to the north entrance, were two more tables. So there were eight tables in all—four inside and four outside—where the sacrifices were cut up and prepared. There were also four tables of finished stone for preparation of the burnt offerings, each 31 1⁄2 inches square and 21 inches high. On these tables were placed the butchering knives and other implements for slaughtering the sacrificial animals. There were hooks, each 3 inches long, fastened all around the foyer walls. The sacrificial meat was laid on the tables.

Inside the inner courtyard were two rooms, one beside the north gateway, facing south, and the other beside the south gateway, facing north. And the man said to me, "The room beside the north inner gate is for the priests who supervise the Temple maintenance. The room beside the south inner gate is for the priests in charge of the altar—the descendants of Zadok—for they alone of all the Levites may approach the LORD to minister to Him."

Then the man measured the inner courtyard, and it was a square, 175 feet wide and 175 feet across. The altar stood in the courtyard in front of the Temple. Then he brought me to the entry room of the Temple. He measured the walls on either side of the opening to the entry room, and they were 8 3/4 feet thick. The entrance itself was 24 1/2 feet wide, and the walls on each side of the entrance were an additional 5 1/4 feet long. The entry room was 35 feet wide and 21 feet deep. There were ten steps leading up to it, with a column on each side. (NLT)

Whereas the imagery of Ezekiel is decidedly Old Covenant – it echoes and reflects the influences and ideas of people living in a time different from New Testament times – we can see there is definitely a parallel between the two that the first-century reader would have understood. For it to be here stands as an ensign of change, to point to prophetic time and prophetic promise. Many are confused by Ezekiel's vision because it doesn't appear to be possible it would be a literal, physical temple restoration built by human hands. What it does seem to be is a rendering of the church, the image of believers from the past, worshipping throughout a period of especially intense persecution. This is relevant because the revelation speaks of inclusion of the Gentiles in the temple, something that was relatively new at that period in church history and would have been scoffed or misunderstood prior to that time. The illusion to the Gentiles, however, is not in a strictly religious sense. Even though by this point in time the Gentiles (in terms of the nations) were a part of the church, the usage of the term "Gentiles" here does not mean people from all nations, but government interference from secular sources. The Apostle John was told not to measure the area of the temple where secular government would trample the temple, because it was turned over to them for a period of time: 1,260 days, or 42 months. For 1,260 days or 42 months (in prophetic time), secular authorities would interfere in the worship and operation of God's people, and those who were out there in that outer court were not individuals who were true believers.

Thus, the temple measurements reflect not just worshippers and secular government, but true worshippers separated from false ones. Even though the wheat may not be separated from the tares in a manner we can see (Matthew 13:24-30,36-43), they are separate in heaven and clearly distinguished from one another. All who have been a part of church know that those who use the church for a political gain have plagued its doorways for thousands of years, bringing into great focus the time period mentioned herein.

What exactly is the 42 months, or 1,260 days referring to in prophecy? If we look at the book of Daniel, it is spoken of as a time, a time, and half a time, or three and a half years:

This is what He said: 'The fourth beast will be a fourth kingdom on the earth which will be different from all the other kingdoms, and will devour the whole earth and trample it down and crush it. As for the ten horns, out of this kingdom ten kings will arise; and another will arise after them, and he will be different from the previous ones and will humble three kings. And he will speak against the Most High and wear down the saints of the Highest One, and he will intend to make alterations in times and in law; and they will be handed over to him for a time, times, and half a time. But the court will convene for judgment, and his dominion will be taken away, annihilated and destroyed forever. Then the sovereignty, the dominion, and the greatness of all the kingdoms under the whole heaven will be given to the people of the saints of the Highest One; His kingdom will be an everlasting kingdom, and all the empires will serve and obey Him.' (Daniel 7:23-27, NASB)

And He said, "Go your way, Daniel, for these words will be kept secret and sealed up until the end time. Many will be purged, cleansed, and refined, but the wicked will act wickedly; and none of the wicked will understand, but those who have insight will understand. And from the time that the regular sacrifice is abolished and the abomination of desolation is set up, there will be 1,290 days. (Daniel 12:9-11, NASB)

Like with most things pertaining to the book of Revelation and prophecy, very few people agree on exactly how long the three-and-a-half-year prophetic period is. The most popular theories are as follows:

- A historical period that is half of the perfection of the number seven, meaning representing the period between the first and second coming of Christ, when the church shall live perfected in a fallen world. It is the era of the New Covenant. In this instance, because it indicates half of perfection, it is an indefinite length of time, while the world experiences the 'half perfection' of the church, rather than the full perfection we shall see when Jesus returns. During this time, it is the church era, when the church must endure and persevere.

- A literal three-and-a-half-year period of time, when the antichrist will reign. This seems unlikely, given everything in Revelation is symbolic. There wouldn't be a literal three-year period surrounded by symbolic periods of time.

- A 1,260-year period of time, equating one day to a year prophetically. There are those who believe it encompasses the fall of Rome until the Reformation, the establishment of certain historical treaties with the church to the French Revolution, and still others who believe that it encompasses certain periods of time that end with the founding of a certain denominational leader's birth, their established leader, and so on.

I do agree that the 1,260-year period of time makes more sense than that of a literal three-and-a-half-year period of time. It may also refer to a very long period of time, as we can see above, rather than an exact measurement of time, one by which politics will have sway over the church. No one can deny that the church has been swayed by politics for over a thousand years, regardless of the denomination one might belong to. When exactly the 1,260-year period starts and ends, how long it may specifically be, however, seems to be up for debate. It is very obvious there are many different ways it can be interpreted. As with all things prophetic, I think everyone has something valid to bring to the table. There is a reason people see so many different events in prophecy, and that reason is because it can, in reality, refer to many different historical events. The entire history of the church: past, present, and future is encased here in the words of Revelation. Revelation proves the church was always a part of God's plan, God knew the church would, at some point in time, also be reduced to a faithful remnant, and overtaken by nations that would be hostile to it, change it, and manipulate it. People spend many hours trying to argue the finer points of the prophecies or make them fit better than another, but there is a reason we cannot do that. God wants us, as believers, to recognize that there will be a period of time when our churches will be trampled upon, used as common fodder for political gain and purposes. We are fooling ourselves if we cannot see the many ways in history that this has happened, even the ways it is happening today.

This should make believers earnestly seek the spiritual gift of discernment and watch what God has to say about people who enter the church, even when they seem all right or seem like they want to do things for the church's favor in the secular or political arenas. The Kingdom of God is not the kingdoms of this world, and no matter how much we might like to think we can make changes by swaying politicians or politics in our favor. To be in the inner place of worship means we forsake this kind of logic and accept secular authority for the position it is to have in our lives. We don't disregard the laws in place, but we stop thinking it, or politics, are going to save us.

The Two Witnesses have also become a long source of contention in the church, with various arguments over who exactly these two people are and when they will appear on the scene. The most important thing we must realize is that the Two Witnesses stand throughout the 1,260 prophetic days. However long of a period of time that refers to, the Two Witnesses must stand through it. This means the Two Witnesses may very well not refer to two literal people. The possible explanation of who exactly these "Two Witnesses" are include:

- Moses and Elijah
- Enoch and Elijah
- The Old and New Testaments
- The Apostles and Prophets
- Jews and Gentiles
- The disciples of Jesus sent out two-by-two
- A type of two-fold witness that is represented by the two olive trees and two lampstands, rather than two literal people or things
- The law and the prophets
- The Old Covenant and the New Covenant
- Leadership and followers
- The woman and her son mentioned in Revelation 12
- Love and grace
- Peace and grace
- Two people who have yet to be born who shall be of a certain role (either prophets, apostle and prophet, etc.)

Once again, I believe there is room for multiple understandings of this imagery rather than just one literal interpretation. The imagery of sackcloth and ashes represents a proclamation of humility and repentance, heralding the need for people to find God. Even in the midst of trampling and difficulty, the church's message still gets out. Are the witnesses are as important as hearing the message proclaimed? Given the imagery points back to

Zechariah 4:1-14, we know that the lampstands already point to perfection, representing heaven's perfection, as was mentioned earlier in Revelation.

Then the angel who talked with me returned and woke me up, like someone awakened from sleep. He asked me, "What do you see?"

I answered, "I see a solid gold lampstand with a bowl at the top and seven lamps on it, with seven channels to the lamps. Also there are two olive trees by it, one on the right of the bowl and the other on its left."

I asked the angel who talked with me, "What are these, my lord?"

He answered, "Do you not know what these are?"

"No, my lord," I replied.

So he said to me, "This is the word of the Lord to Zerubbabel: 'Not by might nor by power, but by my Spirit,' says the Lord Almighty.

"What are you, mighty mountain? Before Zerubbabel you will become level ground. Then he will bring out the capstone to shouts of 'God bless it! God bless it!'"

Then the word of the Lord came to me: ⁹"The hands of Zerubbabel have laid the foundation of this temple; his hands will also complete it. Then you will know that the Lord Almighty has sent me to you.

"Who dares despise the day of small things, since the seven eyes of the Lord that range throughout the earth will rejoice when they see the chosen capstone in the hand of Zerubbabel?"

Then I asked the angel, "What are these two olive trees on the right and the left of the lampstand?"

Again I asked him, "What are these two olive branches beside the two gold pipes that pour out golden oil?"

He replied, "Do you not know what these are?"

"No, my lord," I said.

So he said, "These are the two who are anointed to serve the Lord of all the earth." (Zechariah 4:1-14)

As the true church (clearly distinguished from the tares) represents God, the seven lampstands are carried by the true church, reflecting Jesus as the light of the world. The olive tree, traditionally a symbol of peace, represents the promises of God. The number two signifies agreement or covenant, and shows the unity between things, such as in marriage (Genesis 1:27-28) or as with Christ and the church (Ephesians 5:25-32).

More than anything, the Two Witnesses signify agreement or covenant. They represent the perfection of God and His peace, which come from repentance and humility. They represent the good of the church, the good of following and obeying God, and the result of a true ministry, which is one that should be noted by repentance and humility. They are people who show the church and the world the best God has to offer, and who persevere, whether their message is received, or not. It is clear that they have been given the power to purify as needed, are able to display amazing powers and miracles, and are able to control different forces of nature in order to get the message across.

Revelation 11:7-14

Now when they have finished their testimony, the beast that comes up from the abyss will attack them, and overpower and kill them. Their bodies will lie in the street of the great city, which is figuratively called Sodom, and Egypt, where also their Lord was crucified. For three and a half days men from every people, tribe, language and nation will gaze on their bodies and refuse them burial. The inhabitants of the earth will gloat over them and will celebrate by sending each other gifts, because these two prophets had tormented those who live on the earth.

But after the three and a half days a breath of life from God entered them, and they stood on their feet, and terror struck those who saw them. Then they heard a loud voice from heaven saying to them, "Come up here." And they went up to heaven in a cloud, while their enemies looked on.

At that very hour there was a severe earthquake and a tenth of the city collapsed. Seven thousand people were killed in the earthquake, and the survivors were terrified and gave glory to the God of heaven.

The second woe has passed; the third woe is coming soon.

(Related Bible references: Proverbs 24:17, Luke 13:33)

As with all ministries, the ministry of the Two Witnesses is destined to be for a period of time: the prophetic 1,260 days. When the time is up, people will rejoice over the fall of these witnesses that have sought to do nothing more than proclaim the work of God and help people find Him during difficult times. Their remains will lie desolate in the streets of Sodom and Egypt, which are used in Bible understanding to point to the world, to the places of life that reject God and reflect deplorable character. They will refuse to do the right thing, even in the demise of these individuals: be they concepts, the written Scriptures, leadership offices, literal people, or ideals.

Despite their earthly end, we can see that the Two Witnesses will receive a restoration like none other, a spiritual restoration unto heaven. This proves that despite the sufferings we encounter, God is our ultimate restorer. Even though the church, and its true agents will deal with rejection, God will restore and have the final word. He does rectify each and every wrong. The survivors were terrified, giving glory to God, because it is in the midst of these times that many will only praise or call out to God when they are in trouble or trial.

Revelation 11:15-19

The seventh angel sounded his trumpet, and there were loud voices in heaven, which said:

"The kingdom of the world has become the Kingdom of our Lord and of His Christ, and He will reign for ever and ever."

And the twenty-four elders, who were seated on their thrones before God, fell on their faces and worshiped God, saying:

"We give thanks to You, Lord God Almighty, the One Who is and Who was, because You have taken Your great power and have begun to reign. The nations were angry; and Your wrath has come. The time has come for judging the dead, and for rewarding Your servants the prophets and Your saints and those who reverence Your Name, both small and great – and for destroying those who destroy the earth."

Then God's temple in heaven was opened, and within His temple was seen the ark of His covenant. And there came flashes of lightning, rumblings, peals of thunder, and earthquake and a great hailstorm.

(Related Bible references: 1 Chronicles 29:11, Psalm 22:28, Psalm 97:1, Psalm 145:13, Daniel 2:44, Daniel 4:17, Amos 4:13)

So what does the temple measuring, two witnesses, and announcement of Jesus' reign all have in common? They all relate to a progressive overthrow of this existing world, entering a new dominion with Christ as complete and full Lord over all. In ancient times, overthrows were not immediate; they came to pass with careful and strategic planning, each battle, one step at a time. The temple is mentioned first because the church, the Kingdom of God throughout time, needs to be aware that not everyone that's with us is for us. The church needs to be taken back, with those who are true believers exalted and raised up, rejoicing despite the fact that the church is used for all sorts of political and secular gain. The Two Witnesses represent that which comes forth from the church, but ministers to the world, as well. No matter what they suffer, God will restore and align, because He adds no sorrow to His Name or His truth. Lastly, now, we see what has been going on the whole time: Jesus is aligning His people, aligning His battle, orchestrating in the spiritual realm to take back the world, to restore all things and rejoice in Who He is and the majesty of His splendor.

This is a progressive process, however. The Bible says that the kingdoms of the world 'have become,' or 'has become,' indicating it happens over a period of time. It starts with principles; with the church doing right, with the challenges the church faces and the advance of witnesses that will proclaim God's ways despite compromise around them, and with the challenges and issues already mentioned throughout in Revelation. No matter how much it may seem, Jesus has always been King and will forever be King, it is just a matter of how much power He chooses to exert, giving humanity the choice to choose Him, rather than by force. Now the rule becomes greater, and little by little, we see the realm of heaven influence the realm of the earth, the dead shall be judged, and those who have revered God shall be rewarded. Nature responds in kind, echoing the truth in heaven, and all who are honored to see the veil of heaven and earth part for the majesty of reign gain that much more inspiration, as things shall come to pass in just a little while longer.

The Scroll and

5 Then I saw i
sealed[t] with
break the seals an
scroll or even loo
scroll or look insi
dah, the Root of D

[6]Then I saw a L
by the four living cr
its[a] of God sent out
on the throne. [7]An
before the Lamb [
prayers[b] of the sain

JESUS IS ALWAYS ABLE TO OVERCOME

Chapter Twelve

A Woman Who Signaled a Coming War
(Revelation Chapter 12)

Key verses

- Verses 1-3: *A great and wondrous sign appeared in heaven: a woman clothed with the sun, with the moon under her feet and a crown of twelve stars on her head. She was pregnant and cried out in pain as she was about to give birth. Then another sign appeared in heaven: an enormous red dragon with seven heads and ten horns and seven crowns on his heads.*

- Verses 5-6: *She gave birth to a son, a male child, who will rule all the nations with an iron scepter. And her child was snatched up to God and to His throne. The woman fled into the desert to a place prepared for her by God, where she might be taken care of for 1,260 days.*

- Verse 7: *And there was war in heaven. Michael and his angels fought against the dragon, and the dragon and his angels fought back.*

- Verse 11: *They overcame him by the blood of the Lamb and by the word of their testimony; they did not love their lives so much as to shrink from death.*

- Verse 17: *Then the dragon was enraged at the woman and went off to make war against the rest of her offspring – those who obey God's commandments and hold to the testimony of Jesus.*

Words and phrases to know

- Sign: From the Greek word *semeion* which means "a sign, mark, token."[1]

- Woman: From the Greek word *gune* which means "a woman of any age, whether a virgin, or married, or a widow; a wife."[2]

- Clothed: From the Greek word *periballo* which means "to throw around, to put around."[3]

- Pregnant: From two Greek words: *en* which means "in, by, with etc."[4] and *gaster* which means "the belly; the womb; the stomach."[5]

- Dragon: From the Greek word *drakon* which means "a dragon, a great serpent, a name for Satan."[6]

- Devour: From the Greek word *katesthio* which means "to consume by eating, to eat up, devour; metaph. to devour i.e. squander, waste: substance."[7]

- Male child: From two Greek words: *arrhen* which means "a male"[8] and *huios* which means "a son; son of man; son of God."[9]

- Desert: From the Greek word *eremos* which means "solitary, lonely, desolate, uninhabited."[10]

- War: From the Greek word *polemos* which means "a war; a fight, a battle; a dispute, strife, quarrel."[11]

- Michael: From the Greek word *Michael* which means "Michael = "who is like God;" the first of the chief princes or archangels who is supposed to be the guardian angel of the Israelites."[12]

- Satan: From the Greek word *Satanas* which means "adversary (one who opposes another in purpose or act), the name given to, the prince of evil spirits, the inveterate adversary of God and Christ, he incites apostasy from God and to sin, circumventing men by his wiles, the worshippers of idols are said to be under his control, by his demons he is able to take possession of men and inflict them with diseases, by God's assistance he is overcome, on Christ's return from heaven he will be bound with chains for a thousand years, but when the thousand years are finished he will walk the earth in yet greater power, but shortly after will be given over to eternal."[13]

- Accuser: From the Greek word *kategoreo* which means "to accuse."[14]

<u>Revelation 12:1-6</u>

A great and wondrous sign appeared in heaven: a woman clothed with the sun, with the moon under her feet and a crown of twelve stars on her head. She was pregnant and cried out in pain as she was about to give birth. Then another sign appeared in heaven: an enormous red dragon with seven heads and ten horns and seven crowns on his heads. His tail swept a third of the stars out of the sky and flung them to the earth. The dragon stood in front of the woman who was about to give birth, so that he might devour her child the moment it was born. She gave birth to a son, a male child, who will rule all the nations with an iron scepter. And her child was snatched up to God and to His throne. The woman fled into the desert to a place prepared for her by God, where she might be taken care of for 1,260 days.

(Related Bible references: Genesis 3:15-16, Psalm 2:6-9, Psalm 55:7, Psalm 110:1-2, Isaiah 9:6-7, Isaiah 54:5, Isaiah 66:9, Matthew 4:1-11, Matthew 16:17-20, Galatians 4:26, Revelation 11:3)

The imagery used in Revelation 12:1-6 has been a continual source to trip people up for many years. Looking too intensely at the imagery has caused leaders to disagree, time and time again, about what its contents are trying to tell us. As a result, the most obvious point about Revelation 12 becomes the most ignored.

Before we delve into the symbolism, there are a few things about Revelation 12 that we need to notice. The first is that it completely parallels Revelation 11, just with different symbolism. In Revelation 12, we see two prominent figures used in God's plan (two witnesses), just as we see in Revelation 11, We also see the numerical figure of 1,260 days, the interaction of heaven and earth, and the presence of Satan, working against the saints. We also see protection and harassment: the protection of God and the harassment of the enemy. These parallels tell us Revelation 11 and 12 detail the same events, just in different symbolic language. This was to make sure the events were clearly understood, especially to make sure people were able to see the church in prophecy rather than simply looking at the books of the major and minor prophets and only seeing references to Israel.

Leaders, scholars, and historians disagree about just what Revelation 12 is talking about with its symbolism. Some say the woman is Israel, some say the woman is Mary, mother of Jesus; some say the woman is the church; some say the woman is a prophetess; and so on and so forth. Most agree the child is a reference to Christ and the dragon to Satan, but that's about all they agree on. Given Revelation 11 clearly speaks of the analogies of the spiritual people of God and this letter was written for the church, I believe it is obvious the woman spoken of here is the church, as the entity that brings forth Christ in this day and age, protecting and guarding Him and His Gospel through the navigational attacks and difficulties of this world.

The church is typified all throughout the Bible as being female. The general body of God's people has always been typified as female. There are multiple reasons why this is, including the analogy of a marriage relationship between

God and His people, but in the context of what we are looking at here in Revelation, it points to the reality that the church's role in the world is to proclaim eternal life. This parallels the woman's role in birthing life. Within each woman and man, born again, is the promise of life – to multiply and bring forth something deeper and greater from all they do.

In Jeremiah 31:22, we find a unique prophecy that Revelation 12 calls to mind:

How long wilt thou go about, O thou backsliding daughter? for the LORD hath created a new thing in the earth, A woman shall compass a man. (KJV)

This controversial – and seldom-preached verse – becomes more controversial in translations that seek to clarify and expand its meaning: You are an unfaithful daughter.

How long will you wander before you come home [waver]? The LORD has made [created] something new happen in the land: A woman will go seeking [or protect; or embrace; surround] a man. (EXB)

How long will you waver and hesitate [to return], O you backsliding daughter? For the Lord has created a new thing in the land [of Israel]: a female shall compass (woo, win, and protect) a man. (AMPC)

Jeremiah 31:22 relates to many different prophetic events, including the rise of female leadership. The fact that the church is typified as female and shown here as a strong, life-giving woman echoes the principle that women are, indeed, called to church leadership. The time for women to be leaders over men as well as women, as well as churches and bodies of people rather than just children, is a true reality that is here, now, because it is a part of church life. But this verse also points us to a deeper reality of the work of the church, which is to protect, embrace, surround, and compass Christ, guarding His reputation, His work, and His

Gospel with her very life.

The imagery of the church here proves the church to be the New Eve, restored from fallen nature, with her presence powerful in heaven and her dominion over the earth intact. As the New Eve, she is one with her husband, the new Adam, Christ, Who she protects during His innocent stage of infancy. It is her job to ensure He is protected, represented, and guarded. Her desire is for her husband, Christ, Who rules the nations as not just her leader, but the world's leader in Genesis 3:15-16:

I will make you and the woman
enemies to each other [place hostility/enmity between
you and the woman].
Your descendants [seed] and her descendants [seed]
will be enemies.
One of her descendants [He] will crush your head,
and you will bite [strike; bruise; crush] his heel [Rom.
16:20; Rev. 12:9]."

Then God said to the woman,
"I will cause you to have much trouble [or increase your
pain]
·when you are pregnant [in childbearing],
and when you give birth to children,
you will have great pain.
You will greatly desire [the word implies a desire to control;
4:7] your husband,
but he will rule over you." (EXB)

None of these roles of protection, leadership, or guardianship are traditionally assigned to women, at least within the boundaries of society. Society traditionally assigns the roles of guardianship to a man and the protection of the woman to the man, not the man to the woman. What we can see in this is that God's Kingdom does not comfortably follow the roles and prescriptions the world has laid out for its members. Just like the world regards women as weak, unsteady, and incapable of difficult tasks, so too the world views the church in that manner. It hasn't helped that worldly church members often reflect the values the world assigns to the church as valid. It proves, however, that God can do whatever He desires prophetically and in alignment with church vision.

It's also obvious that the church is protected from the enemy. Despite the enemy's best attempts to try and get the church, the church is protected from the enemy (and enemies that the enemy sends in). Even though the enemy may get individuals in the church to default and abandon her, the church herself shall stand, because Jesus promised even the gates of hell would not conquer her (Matthew 16:17-20). No matter how intimidating the enemy tries to be, appears, or how big he seems to be, he is not victorious over her. Her role, as the guardian and protector of Christ, shall stand firm. His rule, prophesied from the ages (Isaiah 9:6-7), shall never be shaken.

The wilderness is used often in the Scriptures to represent a place of nothingness. It is the absence of God's promise, but a place where God reveals His purpose. Sometimes to find what God wants for us, we must be in a place where we are without distraction and without difficulty. The woman being rushed to the desert for protection, in a place of preparation, one where she could focus upon God without distraction or issue and seek a deeper relationship with the Father. Even though she could no longer see Christ, she knew His presence was real, and she needed to seek even deeper to be aware of what He wanted to develop and do within her. The desert represents a place of purpose; a discovery of what to do next and what is to come.

It also represents a place of testing (Matthew 4:1-11). If the true church, the true worshippers, are trampled down upon by the nations, we must see who the true church is, as well as who the false church is. The only way this is revealed is through trial and testing. For the 1,260-year period spoken of in Revelation 11:3, the church remains in this place of purpose; doing and seeking God; and fulfilling promise, even in lacking or meager conditions. The desert places are without distraction and without extensive materialism, and yet the church was powerful in its purpose and in its plan. There was no spiritual lack, even though there may not have been many things around to point to as visible signs of earthly prosperity.

Revelation 12:7-12

And there was war in heaven. Michael and his angels fought against the dragon, and the dragon and his angels fought back. But he was not strong enough, and they lost their place in heaven. The great dragon was hurled down – that ancient serpent called the devil, or Satan, who leads the whole world astray. He was hurled to the earth, and his angels with him.

Then I heard a loud voice in heaven say:

"Now have come the salvation and the power and the authority of His Christ. For the accuser of our brothers, who accuses them before our God day and night, has been hurled down.

They overcame him by the blood of the Lamb and by the word of their testimony; they did not love their lives so much as to shrink from death.

Therefore rejoice, you heavens and you who dwell in them! But woe to the earth and the sea, because the devil has gone down to you!

He is filled with fury, because he knows that his time is short.

(Related Bible references: Job 1:7, Job 2:2, Isaiah 14:3-27, Daniel 12:1, Matthew 16:25, Romans 16:20, Ephesians 6:13, Philippians 3:20, 2 Timothy 1:8, Hebrews 2:4, Jude 1:9, Revelation 12:4)

Most Bible students would agree that the war in heaven is a recounting of Lucifer's fall from heaven (Isaiah 14:3-27). It seems odd that this incident, which happened ages ago in time, is mentioned in play following the prophecies relating to the 1,260-day period of prophetic time when the church would be in the wilderness period. We need to be aware of our adversary, the consequences of the adversary in our lives, and aware of how Satan moves. The church as the New Eve births forth a new era, a new promise, a new truth and a new reality. This doesn't change that Satan is still alive and well, working the difficulties and patients of the saints. We see an unfallen woman in Revelation 12, but the same adversary, lurking around, while she remains in her state of trial and full vision for seeking God.

The woman in Revelation 12 is the church restored, moving toward perfection in the fallen world which is clearly falling all the more as the times continue and go forward. The accuser goes to and fro (Job 1:7, Job 2:2), with one-third of heaven's angels now transformed into his minions of the demonic (Revelation 12:4). Even though this event might not have happened chronologically during the 1,260 years, its effects are widespread as the world is led astray time and time again. The accuser stands, misleading and judging, even the church. Yet there is hope, and there is promise. Those who are in Christ overcome by the blood of the Lamb and their testimony!

Within each human being, born again, is the promise of life, same as seen in the church – to multiply and bring forth something deeper and greater from all they do. When Christ is living within you, the enemy will do everything within His power to try and stop that rule. He will tempt, test, try, and send everything conceivable to try and snatch Christ away from your life. He will also try to steal what God plants within you that it may be birthed forth. With a nature to steal, kill, and destroy, he comes with a nature that will disguise, look like something else, and try to get you to think he's on your side – all in the attempt to steal your life in Christ and the product of that life away from you.

When we are under attack as members of the church, we sometimes must entrust our vision to God and move to a place of contemplation and silence. We need to be still, not abandoning what God has given us, but we need to let Him hold it to protect it while He protects us. The imagery of the woman fleeing into the wilderness fascinates me here because just as Jesus went into the wilderness to be tempted by Satan, so the woman goes into the desert to face demonic attack. In the middle of nothing, where she has no one but God to protect her, she finds divine provision. She doesn't need to run with her child to everyone she knows, hiding and cowering all along the way, but surrendering what she has to God, she receives what she needs to be safe from the enemy. She valued God above her own concepts of safety and self-preservation, totally trusting what God had for her to do.

This passage tells us we overcome by the blood of the Lamb and the word of our testimony. The woman in Revelation 12 had a testimony! She overcame as she experienced God's provision in her life. The church is the same and has the same testimony moving within herself, to this very day! Some of us are spending so much time running from the devil that we aren't standing long enough to receive God's provision unto testimony! The enemy got so mad with the woman he went and found someone else to bother. Thus, the word on today – it's time to stop running from Satan. We stand because of the blood and the testimony. Therefore, we are called to rejoice. We are citizens of heaven (Philippians 3:20), heavenly people, who the enemy can bother, but cannot touch. The angrier he gets, the more Satan knows his time is short.

The idea that the testimony of Jesus is the spirit of prophecy literally means that what He did before, for someone else, He can do again. We tell our story because it proves Jesus can do anything He desires...and He will. Regardless of Satan's pursuits, we have the victory because someone, somewhere had it before. Thus, we do what we are called to do here in the Scriptures...and stand (Ephesians 6:13).

Revelation 12:13-17

When the dragon saw that he had been hurled to the earth, he pursued the woman who had given birth to the male child. The woman was given the two wings of a great eagle, so that she might fly to the place prepared for her in the desert, where she would be taken care of for a time, times and half a time, out of the serpent's reach. Then from his mouth the serpent spewed water like a river, to overtake the woman and sweep her away with the torrent. But the earth helped the woman by opening its mouth and swallowing the river that the dragon had spewed out of his mouth. Then the dragon was enraged at the woman and went off to make war against the rest of her offspring – those who obey God's commandments and hold to the testimony of Jesus.

(Related Bible references: Genesis 3:15, Isaiah 17:12, Daniel 11:40, Luke 10:18, Luke 11:28)

The angry enemy seeks out the woman because she is the guardian of the child. The church should always expect that she will be sought out because of its love and defense of Christ. As she stood fast, she received a way of power and escape, which is what we, as believers, can expect to receive. Receiving the way of escape doesn't mean we don't have to confront things. In the wilderness periods, we must confront ourselves and the way we interact with the world. It simply means that, if we stand, Satan will not be able to harm us. In truth, the church must stand and endure for a long period of time despite the fact that relief may come. The only way we come to a point of God's intervention in our situations is if we stand through them. It's obvious that while Satan can't touch the church herself, he can touch the people who are in the church. If they do wrong, this can affect the church, and the way church is perceived. This is why it is so essential, all the while, that we follow the words of God and we obey them. Blessed are they who hear the Word of God and keep it! (Luke 11:28) That is how we make it to the end of our testimony, and ultimately, our victory.

The Scroll and

5 Then I saw i
sealed[t] with
break the seals an
scroll or even loo
scroll or look insi
dah, the Root of D

[6]Then I saw a L
by the four living cr
its[a] of God sent ou
on the throne.[7]An
before the Lamb f[a]
presence[a] of the sun

JESUS IS ALWAYS ABLE TO OVERCOME

Chapter Thirteen

A BEASTLY PLAN
(REVELATION CHAPTER 13)

Key verses

- Verse 3: *One of the heads of the beast seemed to have had a fatal wound, but the fatal wound had been healed. The whole world was astonished and followed the beast.*

- Verses 5-6: *The beast was given a mouth to utter proud words and blasphemies and to exercise his authority for forty-two months. He opened his mouth to blaspheme God, and to slander His Name and His dwelling place and those who live in heaven.*

- Verse 10: *If anyone is to go into captivity, into captivity he will go. If anyone is to be killed with the sword, with the sword he will be killed.*

- Verse 12: *He exercised all the authority of the first beast on his behalf, and made the earth and its inhabitants worship the first beast, whose fatal wound had been healed.*

- Verses 15-16: *He was given power to give breath to the image of the first beast, so that it could speak and cause all who refused to worship the image to be killed. He also forced everyone, small and great, rich and poor, free and slave, to receive a mark on is right hand or his forehead.*

- Verse 18: *This calls for wisdom. If anyone has insight, let him calculate the number of the beast, for it is man's number. His number is 666.*

Words and phrases to know

- Ten horns: From two Greek words: *deka* meaning "ten"[1] and *keras* which means "a horn."[2]

- Heads: From the Greek word *kephale* which means "the head, both of men and often of animals. Since the loss of the head destroys life, this word is used in the phrases relating to capital and extreme punishment; metaph. anything supreme, chief, prominent."[3]

- Blasphemous: From the Greek word *blasphemia* which means "slander, detraction, speech injurious, to another's good name; impious and reproachful speech injurious to divine majesty."[4]

- Wound: From the Greek word *sphazo* which means "to slay, slaughter, butcher; to put to death by violence; mortally wounded."[5]

- Astonished: From the Greek word *thaumazo* which means "to wonder, wonder at, marvel; to be wondered at, to be had in admiration."[6]

- Captivity: From the Greek word *aichmalosia* which means "captivity."[7]

- Endurance: From the Greek word *hupomone* which means "steadfastness, constancy, endurance; a patient, steadfast waiting for; a patient enduring, sustaining, perseverance."[8]

- Faithfulness: From the Greek word *pistis* which means "conviction of the truth of anything, belief; in the NT of a conviction or belief respecting man's relationship to God and divine things, generally with the included idea of trust and holy fervor born of faith and joined with it; fidelity, faithfulness."[9]

- Miraculous signs: From two Greek words: *megas* which means "great; predicated of rank, as belonging to persons, eminent for ability, virtue, authority, power; things esteemed highly for their importance: of great moment, of great weight, importance; a thing to be highly esteemed for its excellence: excellent; splendid, prepared on a grand scale, stately; great things,"[10] and *semeion* which means "a sign, mark, token."[11]

- Image: From the Greek word *eikon* which means "an image, figure, likeness."[12]

- Mark: From the Greek word *charagma* which means "a stamp, an imprinted mark; thing carved, sculpture, graven work."[13]

- Forehead: From the Greek word *metopon* which means "the space between the eyes, the forehead."[14]

- Insight: From the Greek word *nous* which means "the mind, comprising alike the faculties of perceiving and understanding and those of feeling, judging, determining."[15]

- Calculate: From the Greek word *psephizo* which means "to count with pebbles, to compute, calculate, reckon; to give one's vote by casting a pebble into the urn; to decide by voting."[16]

- 666: From the Greek term *chi xi stigma* which means "six hundred and sixty six, the meaning of which is the basis of much vain speculation."[17]

<u>Revelation 13:1-10</u>

And I saw a beast coming out of the sea. He had ten horns and seven heads, with ten crowns on his horns, and on each head a blasphemous name. The beast I saw resembled a leopard, but had feet like those of a bear and a mouth like that of a lion. The dragon gave the beast his power and his throne and great authority. One of the heads of the beast seemed to have had a fatal wound, but the fatal wound had been healed. The whole world was astonished and followed the beast. Men worshiped the dragon because he had given authority to the beast, and they also worshiped the beast and asked, "Who is like the beast? Who can make war against him?"

The beast was given a mouth to utter proud words and blasphemies and to exercise his authority for forty-two months. He opened his mouth to blaspheme God, and to slander His Name and His dwelling place and those who live in heaven. He was given power to make war against the saints and to conquer them. And he was given authority over every tribe, people, language and nation. All inhabitants of the earth will worship the beast – all whose names have not been written in the book of life belonging to the Lamb that was slain from the creation of the world.

He who has an ear, let him hear.

If anyone is to go into captivity, into captivity he will go.

If anyone is to be killed with the sword, with the sword he will be killed.

This calls for patient endurance and faithfulness on the part of the saints.

(Related Bible references: Exodus 15:1-18, Daniel 7:1-25, Luke 12:10)

Revelation 13 continues to discuss the time period of Revelation 11 and 12 and enters a few new characters in the unveiling. So far, the viewpoints of this time period have been from the perspective of the church rather than that of the world. We now see in chapter 13 a clear picture of what is going on in the world while the spiritual events of the 1,260 prophetic days march on.

Rising out from what seems to be nowhere comes this beast that seems to be impossible to fathom and literally horrific in every possible way. History has assigned this leader to be everyone from Nero to Adolf Hitler and beyond, without recognizing that these prophecies cannot be as simple as interpreting them according to the work and life of one singular leader. Surely there have been terrible leaders throughout history, who terrorized people and exercised absolute authority, with each one worse than the last. So if nobody seems to exactly fit the bill, per se, who exactly is the beast of Revelation?

Revelation 11 speaks of the Gentiles, or nations, trampling the church. The first beast of Revelation is clearly one of the ways the church is trampled upon. While many have tried to examine the beast from many different angles throughout history, there are a couple of things that we can see as characteristic of the beast.

- Ten horns, seven heads, ten crowns, with a blasphemous name: The number ten is not that relevant on its own merit but is relevant because it represents the number one plus the number zero. In this instance, it represents a singular unity, an absoluteness of authority. The seven heads and blasphemous names relate to the very nature of this being: trying to compete and usurp authority from the Most High. In paralleling Daniel chapter 7 to this chapter, the ten is parallel to ten kingdoms that will come from the beast. It is obvious that, rather than alluding to a specific person, the first beast of Revelation is analogous to an earthly kingdom (Daniel 7:23-25):

"He gave me this explanation: 'The fourth beast is a fourth kingdom that will appear on earth. It will be different from all the other kingdoms and will devour the whole earth, trampling it down and crushing it. The ten horns are ten kings who will come from this kingdom. After them another king will arise, different from the earlier ones; he will subdue three kings. He will speak against the Most High and oppress His holy people and try to change the set times and the laws. The holy people will be delivered into his hands for a time, times and half a time."

- He is like unto a leopard: He moves fast. A fast-moving presence indicates the beast comes out of nowhere, makes a big appearance on the scene, and makes moves quickly.

- Feet like a bear, mouth like a lion: Bears have stable footing, enabling them to move, grip, grasp, and stand. The beast has this stable footing, with a mouth able to roar like a lion, causing all to take notice.

- The power and authority of the beast come from the dragon: We know the dragon to be Satan. This tells us the beast operates by the power of Satan, not of God. No matter what wonders he works or the ways in which he is able to wow an audience, the beast is not operating from a divine power.

- One of the heads has a fatal wound that is healed: This can point to a wounding in the world, where the world somehow hurts or damages its work (most likely another governmental power), or it can also point to its ability to produce signs and wonders that mimic the works people consider divine. This would explain why people are so in awe of the beast and his authority.

In the book of Exodus, we find the traditional Jewish prayer, called the *Mi Chamocha* (Song of the Sea). In it, it is said, "Who is like Thee, O Lord, among the gods? Who is like Thee, Lord there is none else" (Exodus 15:1-18). For people to call out after the beast in such wonder parallels a world in blasphemy, one that sees experiments in the paranormal as those for miraculous, and in a world of confusion, where the nations trod down the church and look legitimate in the eyes of many, the beast has the perfect opportunity to infiltrate the world and its inhabitants.

In keeping with the precepts of Revelation standing to place the church in prophecy, it's important we keep Daniel's words in mind when understanding this specific piece of the puzzle:

This is what He said: 'The fourth beast will be a fourth kingdom on the earth which will be different from all the other kingdoms, and will devour the whole earth and trample it down and crush it. As for the ten horns, out of this kingdom ten kings will arise; and another will arise after them, and he will be different from the previous ones and will humble three kings. And he will speak against the Most High and wear down the saints of the Highest One, and he will intend to make alterations in times and in law; and they will be handed over to him for a time, times, and half a time. But the court will convene for judgment, and his dominion will be taken away, annihilated and destroyed forever. Then the sovereignty, the dominion, and the greatness of all the kingdoms under the whole heaven will be given to the people of the saints of the Highest One; His kingdom will be an everlasting kingdom, and all the empires will serve and obey Him.' (Daniel 7:23-27, NASB)

We know that in an immediate context, Revelation's words were a reference to the Roman government and Roman authority. The church was experiencing an intense persecution at the time, and honestly did not see a positive end to the situation. In a longer, more prophetic context, the words of Revelation relate to governmental authority that tramples upon the church, that seems insurmountable and in direct persecution to Christianity. When I speak of persecution, I am not talking about the government intervening, forcing Christians to behave like decent human beings when they don't want to. I'm not talking about someone not wanting to listen to a long-winded testimony. We are talking about persecution unto death, a time when the church would be so persecuted, the true church would be no more. This is what makes the prophecies of Revelation so interesting and unique. Even though the first-century readers of Revelation didn't see down the generations with the prophecies, the prophetic words have a way of fitting so each generation can understand things in their own context. In the time of the New Covenant, the beast would pop up, more than once, repeatedly, making life difficult for the saints. The power, or purpose of the beast, is to wear down the saints, and the point of the beast is that he has the power to do it. History has theorized so many different people to be the beast:

- The office of the papacy
- The Catholic Church
- An individual known as the antichrist (the term "antichrist" is never used in Revelation)
- The Roman government
- The French government prior to the French Revolution
- Various Middle Eastern powers
- Russia or Russian-influenced powers
- China
- The United States
- A Muslim Imam
- Various historical popes
- Megachurch pastors or leaders
- The Illuminati
- Freemasons
- A spirit of influence or control
- The media

- Sadaam Hussein
- Money
- Power
- Influential politicians
- Republicans
- Democrats

I have said many times that the prophecies pertaining to the beast seem to fit some; seem to fit in part; but all fail to fit in totality. The reason for this is because the beast is all of them, and none of them, at the same time. The underlying power, force, kingdom, demonic work is behind all of it, working, pushing, and operating through earthly vessels that are willing to be maligned and manipulated. The point is not so much who specifically the beast is, but watching and recognizing the powers behind the forces that seek to come against the church and destroy it. No matter how impressive the packaging, how impressive it seems to be that something can operate, no matter how miraculous nor powerful it may seem, the bottom line of the beast is that something behind it isn't right. Bigger is not necessarily better, and just because a nation seems powerful or influential does not mean it has its powers from God.

We learn the beast's power is influential for the 1,260 prophetic days, or 42 prophetic months. Throughout that time, his role (continually repeated through the New Covenant period) is to blaspheme God, slander God's Name, and make trouble for the saints. The church will, as she draws closer to God and remains under His place of protection, will still deal with persecution, in different places, through this long period of time. His authority is far-reaching, and influence, vast. The entire world marvels and, in one form or another, worships, seeks, and ascribes after it. Only those recorded in the book of Life will not marvel of the beast, because they know better, recognizing who he is and who is operating behind him. In those days, if captivity comes, let it come; if violence comes, it shall come; and the saints must stand, in patient endurance, awaiting the final deliverance of the ages.

Revelation 13:11-18

Then I saw another beast, coming out of the earth. He had two horns like a lamb, but he spoke like a dragon. He exercised all the authority of the first beast on his behalf, and made the earth and its inhabitants worship the first beast, whose fatal wound had been healed. And he performed great and miraculous signs, even causing fire to come down from heaven to earth in full view of men. Because of the signs he was given power to do on behalf of the first beast, he deceived the inhabitants of the earth. He ordered them to set up an image in honor of the first beast who was wounded by the sword and yet lived. He was given power to give breath to the image of the first beast, so that it could speak and cause all who refused to worship the image to be killed. He also forced everyone, small and great, rich and poor, free and slave, to receive a mark on his right hand or on his forehead, so that no one could buy or sell unless he had the mark, which is the name of the beast or the number of his name.

This calls for wisdom. If anyone has insight, let him calculate the number of the beast, for it is man's number. His number is 666.

(Related Bible references: Exodus 13:9-16, Deuteronomy 6:8, Deuteronomy 11:8, Daniel 7:8, Matthew 24:15, Mark 6:7, Luke 10:1, Hebrews 10:25, Revelation 7:4-5, Revelation 13:16-17, Revelation 14:9-11, Revelation 16:2, Revelation 19:20)

As Satan counters God's work, we see the beast does not work alone. Just as Jesus sent out His disciples in pairs (Mark 6:7, Luke 10:1), the beast is followed by a second beast. We all know that the whole concept of someone demanding the whole world bow down and worship him in a physical sense is a little far-fetched, which tells us that the work of the beast implements itself through thoughts and ideas that change the way people perceive the world around them as well as spiritual things. Just like the disciples needed each other for support and we are encouraged to assemble with other believers for support and edification (Hebrews 10:25), so too the beast has an assistant, a little or second beast, that does his bidding in the world.

Daniel tells us this beast shall come forth after the ten powers of the first beast, being different from the others, with the ability to subdue three other powers. He also comes to speak against the Most High and oppress God's people, and will change, as it says, "times and laws." We must be careful in interpretation here, because many interpret a succession from one beast to another. The renditions here seem to overlap. The power of the first beast is active in the second beast, thus we see the influence of the first beast reigning throughout time. The second beast points the world to the first, rather than pointing to himself. Also a deceiver, he executes the bidding of the first beast, making sure his beliefs and implementations are brought out spiritually, politically, and economically. He has the power to change laws, to defy God's times and God's principles, and influence the way people regard the beast and his operations.

The issue of the mark all are forced to receive in Revelation 13 is popular fodder for videos on Youtube and debates on social networking sites. It seems that the same videos with the same false information circulate year after year, causing panic and fear in people. In a literal sense, 666 was a number that alluded to Nebuchadnezzar and also one that related to Nero.[18] In order to understand the mark, we must understand the principle of Gematria, which is an ancient Assyro-Babylonian numerological system. It was done to create symbols between words and phrases, believing that there was a correlation between the numbers and the thing at hand.[19] In its literal time, it most likely referred to the Roman Emperor Nero, pointing the first-century believers to the belief that they would not live beyond that time frame. In modern times, believers believe 666 to be a handful of various propaganda scare tactics, including:

- A reference to Islam
- The code for Proctor and Gamble products used during barcode production in the 1970s, 1980s, and 1990s
- A chip that will be implanted in prisoners
- A chip implanted as a part of the health care system reforms
- A code for the SevenDust computer virus
- Aleister Crowley
- Different leaders in history
- A unified ruling power, such as the European Union
- A social mark due to various tax traditions that were customary in ancient times
- Failure of perfection
- A legally enforced Sunday worship

I believe that, if we truly look at these modern concoctions, they all pull us too far away from the true historical context of the text, and that means we miss the point of what it can mean for us today. We must also understand the ways people are differentiated in Revelation from one another. The visionary of Revelation wasn't just trying to warn people against Nero but warn the people who would read these words throughout the entire New Covenant period, however long that might be. In Revelation, there is a clear distinction between the true church of God, worshiping and honoring Him, and the world, which marvels and seeks after the beast. We see repeated references to people who were marked, either on their foreheads or in some other way (Revelation 7:4-5, Revelation 13:16-17, Revelation 14:9-11, Revelation 16:2, Revelation 19:20). We should not assume this, therefore, to be any different of a differentiation, becoming a literal thing. The revelator wanted the readers to know a time was coming when commerce would become increasingly difficult because of the differentiations between people. In the book of Deuteronomy, the people of God were told to take the words of God and bind them on their hands and their foreheads (Exodus 13:9-16,

Deuteronomy 6:8, Deuteronomy 11:8). To take the mark of a beast – of one who clearly opposes God – is to counter the work of God, and signifies being one who is opposed to God. Not being allowed to buy indicates social and economic infractions one encounters as a believer, and the inability to survive without the economy of God to protect the believer.

The number 666 also has significance beyond just a parallel to the Emperor Nero. Six was regarded as the number of man, which means that it is the magnification of six three times. It is the height of man, but yet never the attainment of seven, which indicates perfection. No matter how achieved the beast might be, he would never become God, or be equivalent to God. Six three times also equates to nine in numerological terms (6+6+6=18, 1+8=9), which is a number indicating high evolution and high understanding of various matters, especially those of the occult. Not only is the beast a power influential among men, the beast is also powerful in the occult, thus explaining the magic and abilities he has to deceive people.

Rather than look for a specific person, we need to seek out wisdom. If we seek not to follow into the conniving and manipulations of the beast, we need to be aware that his presence is alive and well in the world, even today. We need to be people who are not easily swayed, nor easily tricked, by things that look and sound great, even if the whole world sits back and marvels at them. In wisdom, we must seek discernment, which speaks to us in a powerful way. In discernment, we can avoid these ultimate deceptions.

The Scroll and

5 Then I saw
sealed[t] with
break the seals ar
scroll or even loo
scroll or look insi
dah, the Root of D

[6]Then I saw a
by the four living c
its[a] of God sent ou
on the throne.[b] [b]An
before the Lamb, ha
_____ of the _____

JESUS IS ALWAYS ABLE TO OVERCOME

G

Chapter Fourteen

THE PROMISE OF HOPE
(REVELATION CHAPTER 14)

Key verses

- Verse 1: *Then I looked, and there before me was the Lamb, standing on Mount Zion, and with Him 144,000 who had His Name and His Father's Name written on their foreheads.*

- Verses 4-5: *These are those who did not defile themselves with women, for they kept themselves pure. They follow the Lamb wherever He goes. They were purchased from among men and offered as firstfruits to God and the Lamb. No lie was found in their mouths; they are blameless.*

- Verse 7: *He said in a loud voice, "Fear God and give Him glory, because the hour of His judgment has come. Worship Him Who made the heavens, the earth, the sea and the springs of water."*

- Verses 8-10: *A second angel followed and said, "Fallen! Fallen is Babylon the Great, which made all the nations drink the maddening wine of her adulteries." A third angel followed them and said in a loud voice, "If anyone worships the beast and his image and receives his mark on the forehead or on the hand, he, too will drink of the wine of God's fury, which has been poured full strength into the cup of His wrath. He will be tormented with burning sulfur in the presence of the holy angels and of the Lamb."*

- Verse 13: *Then I heard a voice from heaven say, "Write: Blessed are the dead who die in the Lord from now on." "Yes, says the Spirit, "they will rest from their labor, for their deeds will follow them."*

- Verse 15: *Then another angel came out of the temple and called in a loud voice to Him Who was sitting on the cloud, "Take Your sickle and reap, because the time to reap has come, for the harvest of the earth is ripe."*

- Verse 18: *Still another angel, who had charge of the fire, came from the altar and called in a loud voice to Him Who had the sharp sickle, "Take your sharp sickle and gather the clusters of grapes from the earth's vine, because its grapes are ripe."*

Words and phrases to know

- Zion: From the Greek word *Sion* which means "Sion or Zion = "a parched place;" the hill on which the higher and more ancient part of Jerusalem was built; often used of the entire city of Jerusalem; since Jerusalem because the temple stood there, was called the dwelling place of God."[1]

- Harpists: From the Greek word *kitharodos* which means "a harper, one who plays the harp and accompanies it with his voice."[2]

- Defile: From the Greek word *moluno* which means "to pollute, stain, contaminate, defile."[3]

- Firstfruits: From the Greek word *aparche* which means "to offer firstlings or firstfruits; to take away the firstfruits of the productions of the earth which was offered to God. The first portion of the dough, from which sacred loaves were to be prepared. Hence term used of persons consecrated to God for all time; persons superior in excellence to others of the same class."[4]

- Blameless: From the Greek word *amomos* which means "without blemish; morally: without blemish, faultless, unblameable."[5]

- Fallen: From the Greek word *pipto* which means "to descend from a higher place to a lower; to descend from an erect to a prostrate position."[6]

- Babylon the Great: From the Greek word *Babulon* which means "Babylon = "confusion;" a very large and famous city, the residence of the Babylonian kings, situated on both banks of the Euphrates. Cyrus had formerly captured it, but Darius Hystaspis threw down its gates and walls, and Xerxes destroyed the temple of Belis. At length the city was reduced to almost solitude, the population having been drawn off by the neighboring Seleucia, built on the Tigris by Seleucus Nicanor; of the territory of Babylonia; allegorically, of Rome as the most corrupt seat of idolatry and the enemy of Christianity."[7]

- Maddening: From the Greek word *thumos* which means "anger, the natural disposition, temper, character; movement or agitation of the soul, impulse, desire, any violent emotion, but esp. anger; anger, wrath, indignation; anger exhibited in punishment, hence used for punishment itself."[8]

- Adulteries: From the Greek word *porneia* which means "illicit sexual intercourse."[9]

- Fury: From the Greek word *orge* which means "anger, the natural disposition, temper, character; movement or agitation of the soul, impulse, desire, any violent emotion, but esp. anger; anger, wrath, indignation; anger exhibited in punishment, hence used for punishment itself."[10]

- Harvest: From the Greek word *therismos* which means "harvest, the act of reaping."[11]

- Ripe: From the Greek word *xeraino* which means "to make dry, dry up, wither; to become dry, to be dry, be withered; to waste away, pine away, i.e. a withered hand."[12]

- Vine: From the Greek word *ampelos* which means "a vine."[13]

- Winepress: From the Greek word *lenos* which means "a tub or trough shaped receptacle, vat, in which grapes are trodden; the lower vat, dug in the ground, into which the must or new wine flowed from the press."[14]

Revelation 14:1-5

Then I looked, and there before me was the Lamb, standing on Mount Zion, and with Him 144,000 who had His Name and His Father's Name written on their foreheads. And I heard a sound from heaven like the roar of rushing waters and like a loud peal of thunder. The sound I heard was like that of harpists playing their harps. And they sang a new song before the throne and before the four living creatures and the elders. No one could learn the song except the 144,000, who had been redeemed from the earth. These are those who did not defile themselves with women, for they kept themselves pure. They follow the Lamb wherever He goes. They were purchased from among men and offered as firstfruits to God and the Lamb. No lie was found in their mouths; they are blameless.

(Related Bible references: Psalm 149:1, John 1:29, 1 Corinthians 6:20,

Philippians 2:12)

Revelation's tone has been serious, to say the least, for the last several chapters. In the midst of the trials and tribulations the Apostle sees, we now see a glimmer of hope, a promise that things will be better. Despite the trials, the church needs a reminder that she will survive. When it's possible to hear these words and think all is lost, we are to remember that all is not lost.

As believers reading and studying Revelation, we need to avoid the temptation to believe everything is hopeless and that everything has been predetermined in a negative slanted timeline. It's easy to read and be afraid, to listen to the myriad of voices that want to sell Revelation as a drama to sell CDs and books. The whole reason those books sell is because they pique curiosity, intrigue, and a feeling of awe and dread of the impending days. Revelation 14 proves that God doesn't want us to spend our lives terrified and afraid, focusing on every little detail and every little moment of the times. We aren't supposed to sit around, focusing on this stuff. The Lord gives us enough information to figure out what we need to figure out, to recognize things in a general sense, but expects us to go on with our lives because it is already implied we should already be doing what is right.

That's the point Revelation 14 opens with: a vision of Christ, standing on Mount Zion, a place of power, with the 144,000 who we spoke of earlier. We first met them in chapter 7, and now exactly seven chapters later, we are hearing of them again. It is not an accident that they are appearing again, representing a perfection achieved through Christ. The 144,000 symbolically represent the best of the church, those who have been truly transformed in Christ. In contrast to those who are a part of the world, receiving the mark of the beast, these who are in Christ are marked for the Lord.

It's obvious that following Christ is clearly a choice. It's not something that people do without thinking, or something we don't do without our resolve. It is not a perfect journey, and Revelation reminds us that a time will come when we are perfected in Him. Through these trial periods, through eras of tribulation and difficulty, we still have the choice to follow Christ, or walk our own way. The 144,000 are an encouragement that there is a return on our investment. While the world goes its own way, we follow the right way, the virtuous way, that proves there is no place for defilement in Him. When we fall, we start again, and we are to be encouraged as we walk this walk with fear and trembling (Philippians 2:12). We will reach that place, no matter how many times we have found ourselves unable to reach what we know we seek.

Revelation 14:6-13

Then I saw another angel flying in midair, and he had the eternal Gospel to proclaim to those who live on the earth – to every nation, tribe, language and people. He said in a loud voice, "Fear God and give Him glory, because the hour of His judgment has come. Worship Him Who made the heavens, the earth, the sea and the springs of water."

A second angel followed and said, "Fallen! Fallen is Babylon the Great, which made all the nations drink the maddening wine of her adulteries."

A third angel followed them and said in a loud voice: "If anyone worships the beast and his image and receives his mark on the forehead or on the hand, he, too, will drink of the wine of God's fury, which has been poured full strength into the cup of his wrath. He will be tormented with burning sulfur in the presence of the holy angels and of the Lamb. And the smoke of their torment rises for ever and ever. There is no rest day or night for those who worship the beast and his image, or for anyone who receives the mark of his name." This calls for patient endurance on the part of the saints who obey God's commandments and remain faithful to Jesus.

Then I heard a voice from heaven say, "Write: Blessed are the dead who die in the Lord from now on."

"Yes," says the Spirit, "they will rest from their labor, for their deeds will follow them."

(Related Bible references: Isaiah 21:9, Jeremiah 51:7-8, Matthew 10:28, Mark 12:14, Mark 13:10, Colossians 1:23, 1 Peter 4:17)

The angels that come forth all bear messages of hope, albeit in some interesting ways. The message that things will not continue as they have forever come out of the mouths of these angels, indicating that things are moving in their appointed course. The first angel brings with it the Gospel, the good news, to everyone, everywhere on the earth. He calls for people to worship the God of heaven, the One Who has created all that we see and have. Even though it has been turned over to the enemy, that does not mean God still did not create it all, and that He is still supreme over the earth. In honoring God as Creator, we are honoring Him as Lord both before and after the fall of man, and as supreme above any and all beastly activity that might occur in the world today.

The second angel heralds the fall of Babylon the Great. It is interesting that Babylon is spoken of here as being fallen already, even though the official fall of Babylon doesn't happen until later in the book of Revelation. It is clear from this passage that Babylon is already conquered, already fallen, even if it doesn't know it yet. In heaven, Babylon and all it represents (which we shall discuss later) cannot stand. We do not need to lose hope, because the systems of this world that do not align with God have already fallen in His sight. In His true mercy, God is giving everyone who is a part of them the chance to depart, to follow rightly and do what He requires, and to be a part of Him and His eternal Kingdom, that shall never fall.

The third angel proclaims a warning for those who choose to worship and follow the beast: they shall have no part in the life of the Kingdom. There are consequences for the choices we make, and the ultimate consequence for not following God and following after the beast is to receive the unpleasant wrath of God. It is quite understandable to see that, after thousands of years' worth of chances and attempts, those who still choose their own way will reap the inevitable consequences of it. The wicked shall reap their just reward, and the saints must remain patient as the time comes – and advances – for it to be in our perception of reality. Blessed are those who die in the Lord, who are now present with the Lord, for their deeds are there, with them, never to be forgotten!

Revelation 14:14-20

I looked, and there before me was a white cloud, and seated on the cloud was one "like a son of man" with a crown of gold on His head and a sharp sickle in His hand. Then another angel came out of the temple and called in a loud voice to Him Who was sitting on the cloud, "Take Your sickle and reap, because the time to reap has come, for the harvest of the earth is ripe." So He Who was seated on the cloud swung His sickle over the earth, and the earth was harvested.

Another angel came out of the temple in heaven, and he too had a sharp sickle. Still another angel, who had charge of the fire, came from the altar and called in a loud voice to Him Who had the sharp sickle, "Take your sharp sickle and gather the clusters of grapes from the earth's vine, because its grapes are ripe." The angel swung his sickle on the earth, gathered its grapes and threw them into the great winepress of God's wrath. They were trampled in the winepress outside the city, and blood flowed out of the press, rising as high as the horses' bridles for a distance of 1,600 stadia.

(Related Bible references: Deuteronomy 32:32, Jeremiah 25:33, Joel 3:12-13, Matthew 13:24-30, Matthew 13:39, Matthew 25:31, Mark 4:29)

The hope of Revelation 14 ends with a harvest, which relates with the discussions of the end of fighting and cessation of evil. It promises retribution, reiterating the announcements of the angels earlier in the chapter. As Revelation tends to be repetitive, speaking on the same events in different ways, Revelation 14 is no different. The harvest of the earth relates to the first angel's message, proclaiming the Gospel and declaring the harvest. Harvest-time is used frequently throughout Scriptures to indicate a gathering, a product of success, and a completion of matters. We should not be ignorant, however, that harvest time means a lack of work. In many instances, harvest is the beginning of work, the beginning of the production, and in this case, it is no different. The harvest is the beginning of eternity, beginning with a wheat harvest, separating the wheat from the tares (Matthew 13:24-30), separating those who are sent to trample down the church from those who are the true worshippers. The harvest of grapes relates to Babylon, those who are drinking from her cup, and the inevitable blood poured out from those who follow after Babylon and worship the beast (Joel 3:12-13). Justice is coming. In the meantime, we hold fast...and we wait.

The Scroll and

5 Then I saw i
sealed[t] with
break the seals an
scroll or even loo
scroll or look insi
dah, the Root of Da

[6]Then I saw a L
by the four living cr
its[u] of God sent out
on the throne.[v] [7]An
before the Lamb, [w] a
pr***re*[x] of the sain

**JESUS
IS ALWAYS
ABLE TO
OVERCOME**

G

Chapter Fifteen

THE COMPLETION OF GOD'S WRATH, PART 1 (REVELATION CHAPTER 15)

Key verses

- Verse 1: *I saw in heaven another great and marvelous sign: seven angels with the seven last plagues – last, because with them God's wrath is completed.*

- Verses 3-4: *And sang the song of Moses the servant of God and the song of the Lamb: "Great and marvelous are Your deeds, Lord God Almighty. Just and true are Your ways, King of the ages. Who will not fear You, O Lord, and bring glory to Your Name? For You alone are holy. All nations will come and worship before You, for Your righteous acts have been revealed."*

- Verse 8: *And the temple was filled with smoke from the glory of God and from His power, and no one could enter the temple until the seven plagues of the seven angels were completed.*

Words and phrases to know:

- Marvelous: From the Greek word *thaumastos* which means "wonderful, marvellous."[1]

- Alone: From the Greek word *monos* which means "alone (without a companion), forsaken, destitute of help, alone, only, merely."[2]

- Revealed: From the Greek word *phaneroo* which means "to make manifest or visible or known what has been hidden or unknown, to manifest, whether by words, or deeds, or in any other way."[3]

- Tabernacle of the Testimony: From two Greek words: *skene* which means "tent, tabernacle, (made of green boughs, or skins or other materials); of that well known movable temple of God after the pattern of which the temple at Jerusalem was built"[4] and *marturion* which means "testimony."[5]

- Shining: From the Greek word *lampros* which means "shining; splendid, magnificent."[6]

- Linen: From the Greek word *linon* which means "linen clothing made from flax."[7]

Revelation 15:1-8

I saw in heaven another great and marvelous sign: seven angels with the seven last plagues – last, because with them God's wrath is completed. And I saw what looked like a sea of glass mixed with fire and, standing beside the sea, those who had been victorious over the beast and his image and over the number of his name. They held harps given them by God and sang the song of Moses the servant of God and the song of the Lamb:

"Great and marvelous are Your deeds,
Lord God Almighty.
Just and true are Your ways,
King of the ages.
Who will not fear You, O Lord,
and bring glory to Your Name?
For You alone are holy.
All nations will come
and worship before You,

for Your righteous acts have been revealed."

After this I looked and in heaven the temple, that is, the tabernacle of the Testimony, was opened. Out of the temple came the seven angels with the seven plagues. They were dressed in clean, shining linen and wore golden sashes around their chests. Then one of the four living creatures gave to the seven angels seven golden bowls filled with the wrath of God, Who lives for ever and ever. And the temple was filled with smoke from the glory of God and from His power, and no one could enter the temple until the seven plagues of the seven angels were completed.

(Related Bible references: Exodus 15:1, Exodus 38:21, Leviticus 26:21, Psalm 33:8, Psalm 92:5, Psalm 111:2, Psalm 139:14, Jeremiah 3:12, John 12:28, Romans 12:19)

Revelation 15 is short, sweet, and to the point. It is a bridge chapter, meaning that it bridges the thoughts of Revelation 14 to the events that bring us to the promise of peace and security we find therein. Obviously, things don't just wrap up at the end of chapter 14 and we find the world to be a hunky-dory place. Revelation 15 reminds us more is coming, which is why we are called to persevere and believe through the difficulties that still exist. It's obvious from Revelation that the saints are called to endure, not hide, whisked away somewhere where there is no suffering or difficulty, but to stand. When we need to be in a place of protection, God will provide that. When we need to be in the place where we seek Him, God will provide that. Those places of refuge don't keep us oblivious from the problems in the world, and we should never assume nor suspect that they will.

The promise of completion is nigh: the seven last plagues indicate God's final wrath. After wrath, we shall see the promise of peace. Seeing wrath come upon the wicked, most often, doesn't feel like we think it will. The vindication we most likely think we will feel is not what comes forth, as we watch people reap the full wrath their sins and wrongdoing have incurred. It is much more of a blessing to see repentance, see people turn to the Lord and walk in His ways, than it is to watch people fall to the wayside and never know the true goodness God has for His people.

For this reason, Revelation 15 needs to remind us of the importance of prayer. While yes, it is great to know that vengeance is still the Lord's and He does repay (Romans 12:19), watching someone receive a blessing is more of an edification than watching them suffer. There are those here who will be victorious over the beast and His image; and they have a song. It is a song of overcoming, of testimony, of promise, believing in God and in His new and better day to come. It is seeing the Kingdom of heaven on earth in the Kingdom of God, in God's people who trust Him and know He will not forsake, nor abandon, them. They can sing from here to forever about the grandeur of God, His deeds, the wonderful things He has done, and the wonderful things yet to come.

The tabernacle of the testimony contains the two tablets (Exodus 38:21) of the Ten Commandments, thus representing the operation of the law unto judgment for those who are not living under God's grace in Christ. Coming forth from that judgment comes seven angels with seven plagues, prepared and ready to execute what will be the final judgment. The angels themselves present in perfection, in clean linen and gold sashes, received in seven gold bowls from the four living creatures. The glory of God was heavy, so heavy no one could see through the smoke and no one could enter into the presence of God. All stand, all wait...and watch as completion comes forth.

Chapter Sixteen

THE COMPLETION OF GOD'S WRATH, PART 2 (REVELATION CHAPTER 16)

Key verses

- Verse 1: *Then I heard a loud voice from the temple saying to the seven angels, "Go, pour out the seven bowls of God's wrath on the earth."*

- Verses 5-6: *Then I heard the angel in charge of the waters say: "You are just in these judgments, You Who are and Who were, the Holy One, because You have so judged; for they have shed the blood of Your saints and prophets, and You have given them blood to drink as they deserve."*

- Verse 15: *"Behold, I come like a thief! Blessed is he who stays awake and keeps his clothes with him, so that he may not go naked and be shamefully exposed."*

- Verses 17-18: *The seventh angel poured out his bowl into the air, and out of the temple came a loud voice from the throne, saying, "It is done!" Then there came flashes of lightning, rumblings, peals of thunder and a severe earthquake. No earthquake like it has ever occurred since man has been on earth, so tremendous was the quake.*

<u>Words and phrases to know</u>

- Ugly and painful sores: From three Greek words: *kakos* which means "of a bad nature; of a mode of thinking, feeling, acting; troublesome, injurious, pernicious, destructive, baneful,"[1] *poneros* which means "full of labors, annoyances, hardships; bad, of a bad nature or condition,"[2] and *helkos* which means "a wound, esp. a wound producing a discharge pus; a sore, an ulcer."[3]

- Scorch: From the Greek word *kaumatizo* which means "to burn with heat, to scorch; to be tortured with intense heat."[4]

- Thief: From the Greek word *kleptes* which means "an embezzler, pilferer."[5]

- Awake: From the Greek word *gregoreuo* which means "to watch; metaph. give strict attention to, be cautious, active."[6]

- Exposed: From the Greek word *aschemosune* which means "unseemliness, an unseemly deed."[7]

- Armageddon: From the Greek word *Armageddon* which means "Armageddon = "the hill or city of Megiddo;" In Rev. 16:16 the scene of the struggle of good and evil is suggested by that battle plain of Esdraelon, which was famous for two great victories, of Barak over the Canaanites, and of Gideon over the Midianites; and for two great disasters, the deaths of Saul and Josiah. Hence in Revelation a place of great slaughter, the scene of a terrible retribution upon the wicked. The RSV translates the name as Har-Magedon, i.e. the hill (as Ar is the city) of Megiddo."[8]

- Done: From the Greek word *ginomai* which means "to become, i.e. to come into existence, begin to be, receive being; to become, i.e. to come to pass, happen; to be made, finished; to become, be made."[9]

Revelation 16:1-14

Then I heard a loud voice from the temple saying to the seven angels, "Go, pour out the seven bowls of God's wrath on the earth."

The first angel went and poured out his bowl on the land, and ugly and painful sores broke out on the people who had the mark of the beast and worshiped his image.

The second angel poured out his bowl on the sea, and it turned into blood like that of a dead man, and every living thing in the sea died.

The third angel poured out his bowl on the rivers and springs of water, and they became blood. Then I heard the angel in charge of the waters say:

"You are just in these judgments, You Who are and Who were, the Holy One, because You have so judged; for they have shed the blood of Your saints and prophets, and You have given them blood to drink as they deserve.

And I heard the altar respond:

"Yes, Lord God Almighty, true and just are Your judgments."

The fourth angel poured out his bowl on the sun, and the sun was given power to scorch people with fire. They were seared by the intense heat and they cursed the Name of God, Who had control over these plagues, but they refused to repent and glorify Him.

The fifth angel poured out his bowl on the throne of the beast, and his kingdom was plunged into darkness. Men gnawed their tongues in agony and cursed the God of heaven because of their pain and sores, but they refused to repent of what they had done.

The sixth angel poured out his bowl on the great river Euphrates, and its water was dried up to prepare the way for the kings from the East. Then I saw three evil spirits that looked like frogs; they came out of the mouth of the dragon, out of the mouth of the beast and out of the mouth of the false prophet. They are spirits of demons performing miraculous signs, and they go out to the kings of the whole world, to gather them for the battle on the great day of God Almighty.

(Related Bible references: Exodus 7:1-11:10, Deuteronomy 28:35, Psalm 59:24, Psalm 78:44, Psalm 79:3, Psalm 137:1, Psalm 145:17, Isaiah 8:22, Isaiah 49:10, Isaiah 66:6, Jeremiah 50:38, Ezekiel 30:3, Ezekiel 38:16, Joel 2:1, Zephaniah 1:15, Zephaniah 3:8, Matthew 23:35, 2 Peter 3:12)

This final, general judgment poured out over all humanity calls for sobriety as we read it. It sounds an awful lot like the judgments of the past, and much like the plagues wrought against the Egyptians in the book of Exodus (Exodus 7:1-11:10). The purpose was the same: the people needed to let go of God's people, so they can worship Him. Those whom these plagues affected needed to turn and see that in this great exodus from the world, they were to also come and worship the true God, to repent and turn from their wicked ways. Every plague, every negative calamity, every crisis is an opportunity to turn rightly to God and turn away from everything that we are not supposed to do, that God has clearly outlined for us to flee from. The thing that becomes clearer and clearer is that there are some people, perhaps many people, who simply won't turn from their ways. Whether it is out of pride, vanity, pure rebellion, or anything else, Revelation proves people will be given ample time to turn away from their wicked ways and to turn toward the way in which they should go. Just as choosing to follow Jesus is a choice, the people who are in rebellion choose their rebellion. They choose to go their own way, despite the things that come against them. People wonder where God is in times of trial or disaster. He is right where He always has been. The question becomes – where are you?

As we approach the end of the complete judgment, we see the Euphrates River dries up, as it says, to prepare the way for the kings from the East. This is to prepare for what is next, symbolizing intense conflict as the nations ultimately turn on each other. In preparation, evil spirits come forth to perform various signs, to deceive people, and to insist that the occult practices of the world, those hidden, reign for as long as they can, because Satan's time is short.

Revelation 16:15-21

"Behold, I come like a thief! Blessed is he who stays awake and keeps his clothes with him, so that he may not go naked and be shamefully exposed."

Then they gathered the kings together to the place that in Hebrew is called Armageddon.

The seventh angel poured out his bowl into the air, and out of the temple came a loud voice from the throne, saying, "It is done!" Then there came flashes of lightning, rumblings, peals of thunder and a severe earthquake. No earthquake like it has ever occurred since man has been on earth, so tremendous was the quake. The great city split into three parts, and the cities of the nations collapsed. God remembered Babylon the Great and gave her the cup filled with the wine of fury of His wrath. Every island fled away and the mountains could not be found. From the sky huge hailstones of about a hundred pounds each fell upon men. And they cursed God on account of the plague of hail, because the plague was so terrible.

(Related Bible references: 2 Chronicles 35:22, Job 38:22-23, Proverbs 10;12, Isaiah 28:2, Daniel 12:1, Zechariah 12:11, Luke 21:36, Ephesians 2:2, 1 Thessalonians 5:2, Hebrews 12:26, 1 Peter 4:8, 2 Peter 3:10)

Jesus advises His people to watch, because He comes like a thief. He comes unexpected, no one knowing the day or the hour, and apprising us of this fact, even in the midst of all these events and signs. This proves, yet again, that the details of Revelation are symbolic. We can read Revelation and gain a general understanding of things, where we are, and the impact it is to have in our lives, if we read with spiritual eyes and ears and see what God is trying to tell us. Running to and fro, here and there, thinking Jesus is coming back every time there is a natural disaster, or a problem defies the principles we learn here in Revelation.

We should be living, walking, engaging, and believing as if Jesus was right here with us, because He is right here with us, in Spirit. We need to be always covered and prepared with our cover. What does this mean? It means we need to be covered by the love of God that covers a multitude of sins (Proverbs 10:12, 1 Peter 4:8). We need to walk in the protection of the Lord, in the love of God, not just as a mere idea of permissiveness, but in a discipline that extends love to the world and shows grace to our neighbors. We need to be ready, not in the sense that we stop living, but in the sense that we start loving God unto obedience.

Very simply, Revelation 16 shows that all that's happened up to this point has been an orchestration; a trial, if you will, to bring about this time, this point, that we more commonly know as Armageddon.

Armageddon is not, contrary to pop culture belief, some sort of space-alien invasion or situation where the whole world blows up. There is nothing in Scripture that indicates the world as we know it is going to explode and everyone on it is going to die. While the Scriptures do indicate the world as we know it will change, it does not indicate any of the Hollywood-style attacks we see in film will be exactly what this battle refers to. Armageddon itself is simply a gathering site of armies, a location for many different ancient battles. This tells us the battle to come is against the system of Babylon, the system represented by the world, and the system of God. Whether this is a literal battle or not (one that we can all see with our physical eyes or we will see in shades darkly this side of heaven), the point is that what needs doing will be done. Justice will be done. The evil of this world will come to an end, the cities built upon the greatness of men shall fall, and people will still stand and curse God, rather than realize sinfulness wrought it upon humanity.

I've said for many years that accountability is attractive. The common theme in Revelation is that wrongdoers curse God, they blame other people, they look outside for a source, but they never stop and blame themselves. God is calling us all to be accountable, and your accountability starts with you. Are you ready for the change that is soon to come?

The Scroll and

5 Then I saw i
sealed† with
break the seals an
scroll or even loo
scroll or look insi
dah, the Root of D

[6] Then I saw a L
by the four living cr
its⁴ of God sent out
on the throne.⁵ An
before the Lamb. Ea
prayers⁵ of the sai

JESUS IS ALWAYS ABLE TO OVERCOME

G

Chapter Seventeen

ALL EYES ON BABYLON
(REVELATION CHAPTER 17)

Key verses

- Verse 2: *"With her the kings of the earth committed adultery and the inhabitants of the earth were intoxicated with the wine of her adulteries."*

- Verses 5-6: *This title was written on her forehead: MYSTERY, BABYLON THE GREAT THE MOTHER OF PROSTITUTES AND OF THE ABOMINATIONS OF THE EARTH. I saw that the woman was drunk with the blood of the saints, the blood of those who bore testimony to Jesus.*

- Verse 8: *The beast, which you saw, once was, now is not, and will come up out of the Abyss and go to his destruction. The inhabitants of the earth whose names have not been written in the book of life from the creation of the world will be astonished when they see the beast, because he once was, now is not, and yet will come.*

- Verses 15-16: *Then the angel said to me, "The waters you saw, where the prostitute sits, are peoples, multitudes, nations and languages. The beast and the ten horns you saw will hate the prostitute. They will bring her to ruin and leave her naked; they will eat her flesh and burn her with fire."*

Words and phrases to know

- Punishment: From the Greek word *krima* which means "a decree, judgments; judgment; a matter to be judicially decided, a lawsuit, a case in court."[1]

- Prostitute: From the Greek word *porne* which means "a woman who sells her body for sexual uses; metaph. an idolatress."[2]

- Intoxicated: From the Greek word *methuo* which means "to be drunken; metaph. of one who has shed blood or murdered profusely."[3]

- Mother: From the Greek word *meter* which means "a mother; metaph. the source of something, the motherland."[4]

- Abominations: From the Greek word *bdelugma* which means "a foul thing, a detestable thing."[5]

- Hills: From the Greek word *oros* which means "a mountain."[6]

Revelation 17:1-8

One of the seven angels who had the seven bowls came and said to me, "Come, I will show you the punishment of the great prostitute, who sits on many waters. With her the kings of the earth committed adultery and the inhabitants of the earth were intoxicated with the wine of her adulteries."

Then the angel carried me away in the Spirit into a desert. There I saw a woman sitting on a scarlet beast that was covered with blasphemous names and had seven heads and ten horns. The woman was dressed in purple and scarlet, and was glittering with gold, precious stones and pearls. She held a golden cup in her hand, filled with abominable things and the filth of her adulteries. This title was written on her forehead:

*MYSTERY
BABYLON THE GREAT
THE MOTHER OF PROSTITUTES
AND OF THE ABOMINATIONS OF THE EARTH.*

O saw that the woman was drunk with the blood of the saints, the blood of those who bore testimony to Jesus.

When I saw her, I was greatly astonished. Then the angel said to me: "Why are you astonished? I will explain to you the mystery of the woman and of the beast she rides, which has seven heads and ten horns. The beast, which you saw, once was, now is not, and will come up out of the Abyss and go to his destruction. The inhabitants of the earth whose names have not been written in the book of life from the creation of the world will be astonished when they see the beast, because he once was, now is not, and yet will come.

(Related Bible references: Deuteronomy 29:17, Isaiah 54:5, Isaiah 66:3, Jeremiah 3:6-9, Jeremiah 3:14, Jeremiah 31:32, Jeremiah 51:7, Ezekiel 16:32, Ezekiel 22:2, Hosea 1:2-3, Hosea 2:2-7, Hosea 2:16, Ephesians 6:2, James 4:4)

As we get to the end of the Revelation of John, we can see things are clearly winding up. The minor things of this world, the beings that follow the main focuses, are no longer as major of a focus as those of the major ones. Increasingly, we see a shift in focus from things that affect major portions of the entire world to the things behind the different issues the world has.

We know from the Scriptures that there are spirits and powers behind what seem to be natural events (Ephesians 6:12). Yes, it is true that sometimes what we deal with is nothing more than people's flesh and their negative conduct. In a bigger sense, however, we are smack-dab in the middle of a spiritual battle, which should make us even more aware of how the powers that be manipulate individuals who do not choose to do right in their lives. Revelation's close as it starts to depict more and more the way things shall wind up tie us back to the spirits and their sources that orchestrate things in this world to function against God and make life difficult for God's people.

We are now introduced to another major player in the spiritual battle: that of the great prostitute who sits on many waters. The prostitute represents a position and place of compromise, one who comes out from many and spends her time, her life, her work in not only compromising herself, but in exploiting the weaknesses and offenses of others. It's a way of life, being an agent of stumbling in people's lives. That is how the prostitute works. Even though men and women alike may go into prostitution for any different number of reasons and may feel a variety of ways about it (not all prostitutes are victims of circumstances), the way the occupation works is by the allure and promise of temptations. This is exactly why the imagery is used here: it represents the promise of temptation and the allure of compromise.

Adultery is also used here symbolically to show forth the compromise of idolatry. In the Old Testament, the relationship between God and His people was always spoken of as a marriage (Isaiah 54:5, Jeremiah 3:14, Jeremiah 31:32, Hosea 2:2-7, Hosea 2:16) and the analogy of idolatry was always made through adultery (Jeremiah 3:6-9, Ezekiel 16:32; Hosea 1:2-3). In every regulation, dictate, and teaching on idolatry, God was trying to impress upon His people a spiritual principle. The same is true here. As she is often called, the whore of Babylon's purpose was to lead people into spiritual adultery. By the different vices she offered (spoken of as wine on purpose), the prostitute of Babylon called people to compromise their morals, their values, and their beliefs in the name of money, greed, power, lust, and worldly promise.

The woman sits in the desert on the beast, signifying their desolation. While the woman who gives birth went there to a place of safety to find what she needed, the prostitute and the beast find complete and total desolation.

Even though they might have everything which is represented by their royal attire and exterior items: all the things the world can offer and the power to manipulate people into taking what they've got in exchange for everything else, the reality is that the prostitute and the beast are empty. They don't have what people genuinely need; they can only offer what seems to be good in exchange for the self-respect, dignity, and spirituality people need. The ultimate end of this compromise is the truth that it has been all along: the mystery solved, the source of this world's compromise, Babylon the great, the mother of all prostitutes, and abominations from the earth. They have their origin, their start, their work, right in there.

Even the apostle, who had seen many things in his ministry, was astonished by what he saw. It was so overwhelming to see everything all in its form, right there in front of his eyes. Oftentimes we seek spiritual gifts or enlightenments, not realizing exactly what they are going to result in, nor seeking and understanding the great magnitude of what we wind up seeing. To see this as the influence of so many of those moments where people didn't do right, seek right, embrace the right things, or where people fell and compromised must have been a powerful sight to behold. It must also have been incredible to start to see and put together pieces of things, here and there, and see them – clearly and without hindered sight – and realize so much that the world and those in the world must go through in order to get to that place.

Revelation 17:9-18

"This calls for a mind with wisdom. The seven heads are seven hills on which the woman sits. They are also seven kings. Five have fallen, one is, the other has not yet come; but when he does come, he must remain for a little while. The beast who once was, and now is not, is an eighth king. He belongs to the seven and is going to his destruction.

The ten horns you saw are ten kings who have not yet received a kingdom, but who for one hour will receive authority as kings along with the beast. They have one purpose and will give their power and authority to the beast. They will make war against the Lamb, but the Lamb will overcome them because He is Lord of lords and King of kings – and with Him will be His called, chosen and faithful followers."

Then the angel said to me, "The waters you saw, where the prostitute sits, are peoples, multitudes, nations and languages. The beast and ten horns you saw will hate the prostitute. They will bring her to ruin and leave her naked; they will eat her flesh and burn her with fire. For God has put it into their hearts to accomplish his purpose by agreeing to give the beast their power to rule, until God's words are fulfilled. The woman you saw is the great city that rules over the kings of the earth."

(Related Bible references: Jeremiah 51:11-12, Jeremiah 51:25, Daniel 7:24, Daniel 8:20-23, Zephaniah 2:13, Matthew 16:17-20, Matthew 24:15)

Revelation makes two references to things calling for wisdom: the first is the meaning and allusion behind the number 666, and the second is the imagery as relates to the prostitute. Both were allusions, clearly, to the Roman Empire and the other nations that it spawned and that followed it, and that is the reason the words called for wisdom. The writer of Revelation desired the first-century readers to hear loud and clear that their immediate occupiers and persecutors were going to face their downfall. In an immediate context, they were correct: Rome did fall and was replaced by other nations. Still, the question remains as to who exactly Babylon can be or refer to today, and since Rome has long come and gone, trying to get this prophecy to fit in other ways has proven tricky. There are many who try to imply the Roman Catholic Church is the whore of Babylon, or in some other way, connected to these prophecies. There are obviously many other ways people have interpreted these prophecies, including various governments, powers, world figures, denominations, and leaders, and the longer we go on, the more ways people try to force the prophecy to fit. As I mentioned earlier in the prophecies, it's all of it, it's none of it, at the same time. While we can't question the Roman Catholic Church has been the purveyor of horrible persecutions and political questionability throughout history, there have also been many individuals who, throughout that same sorted history, did incredible things in service of the Lord and their fellow man. There are also lots of people who have been guilty of the same things the Catholic Church has done throughout history, with no connection to it, whatsoever. This also indicates that if the Catholic Church were to be the whore of Babylon, every church that has ever had any tie to it – whether directly or indirectly, from a denomination that split with it – is also, by extension, that same whoredom. This would make every spiritual entity we call "church" a part of the problem rather than the solution, and we know that cannot fit God's promise for the church to withstand even the gates of hell (Matthew 16:17-20). Can the Catholic Church fit the prophecy of the whore of Babylon in some ways? Sure, the same way all the other institutions, individuals, and people seem to fit in the same exact way. That means that Revelation's words must be warning us of something else, something different, something that we need to pay more attention to as believers.

That "something else" is the ultimate compromise asked by the world. To get by in the world, function in the world, and interact in the world, compromise is a necessary component. Whether it's one moral compromise or many, the price we pay to belong is the same. In the Bible, Babylon is used to allude to the concept of the world, all it owns and all it holds dear, especially worldly values.

We talk about the "world" in vague, leading terms anytime something seems contrary to someone's concept about God. We talk about music, about attire, about language, about concepts, about money, about thoughts, about all these different things, but we forget that, just like with what I said about the Catholic Church above, there are exceptions in every situation to the rule. Worldly Babylon doesn't just purvey one specific message; it calls out to people to compromise with the temptations that will make one's current circumstances, hopes, pains, and difficulties melt away into something else. It takes people who hurt, people who just don't really care, and people who are confused and offers them the world if they will but give up their soul. It doesn't work through the obvious ways we think. It might work through religion. It might work through politics. We all know it works through drugs, alcohol, sex, money, promotions, and power. But the way that the "world" gets people to compromise comes in different forms to play on each person's flesh as it is able.

This is why the Scriptures tell us, over and over again, to be so careful about controlling our desires and controlling our emotions. When we don't have ourselves right, we are more open to the temptations the world offers us. At the time, it might even seem like a solution to something rather than the idolatrous trap it really is. The world operates by the right sway at the right time, offering up the right thing in that moment, and causing the compromise. This means that the whore of Babylon is every worldly temptation that comes our way, right at the right moment, and the right (or perhaps, opportune) time. It isn't just one thing...it can be anything...and it often becomes everything.

The prostitute sits over many nations and peoples, because she influences everyone. Her influence is vast and wide and doesn't just come for people in a certain station or belief system in life. The world can touch us, no matter where we are in it, what we believe or think, or what we have. And, just like the world leaves us when it's done with us, so the beast leaves the prostitute destitute, burned, destroyed, and beaten. With compromise destroyed, we see God's ultimate plan play out, even with the beast being used to bring about God's purposes. This proves, once and for all, God is truly sovereign, even in the midst of those running about, to and fro, choosing everything except Him in their lives. No matter how evil the beast might have been, all that comes forth is, indeed, necessary to bring judgment and vindication to a compromised world. Worldly compromise only rules until God says it's done.

The Scroll and

5 Then I saw i
sealed[t] with
break the seals an
scroll or even lool
scroll or look insic
dah, the Root of D

[6]Then I saw a L
by the four living cr
its[a] of God sent out
on the throne.[,] [8]And
before the Lamb [...]
[...] of the [...]

JESUS
IS ALWAYS
ABLE TO
OVERCOME

Chapter Eighteen

BABYLON FALLS
(REVELATION CHAPTER 18)

Key verses

- Verses 4-5: *Then I heard another voice from heaven say: "Come out of her, my people, so that you will not share in her sins, so that you will not receive any of her plagues; for her sins are piled up to heaven, and God has remembered her crimes."*

- Verses 9-10: *When the kings of the earth who committed adultery with her and shared her luxury see the smoke of her burning, they will weep and mourn over her. Terrified at her torment, they will stand far off and cry: "Woe! Woe, O great city, O Babylon, city of power! In one hour your doom has come!"*

- Verses 11-13: *The merchants of the earth will weep and mourn over her because no one buys their cargoes any more - cargoes of gold, silver, precious stones and pearls; fine linen, purple, silk and scarlet cloth; every sort of citron wood, and articles of every kind made of ivory, costly wood, bronze, iron and marble; cargoes of cinnamon and spice, of incense, myrrh and frankincense, of wine and olive oil, of fine flour and wheat; cattle and sheep; horses and carriages; and bodies and souls of men.*

- Verses 20-21: *Rejoice over her, O heaven! Rejoice, saints and apostles and prophets! God has judged her for the way she treated you." Then a mighty angel picked up a boulder the size of a large millstone and threw it into the sea, and said: "With such violence the great city of Babylon will be thrown down, never to be found again."*

Words and phrases to know

- Bird: From the Greek word *orneon* which means "a bird."[1]

- Merchants: From the Greek word *emporos* which means "one on a journey, whether by sea or by land, esp. for trade; a merchant as opposed to a retailer or petty tradesman."[2]

- Excessive luxuries: From the Greek word *strenos* which means "excessive strength which longs to break forth, over strength; luxury; eager desire."[3]

- Share: From the Greek word *sugkoinoneo* which means "to become a partaker together with others, or to have fellowship with a thing."[4]

- Sins: From the Greek word *hamartia* which means "to be without a share in; to miss the mark; to err, be mistaken; to miss or wander from the path of uprightness and honor, to do or go wrong; to wander from the law of God, violate God's law, sin; that which is done wrong, sin, an offence, a violation of the divine law in thought or in act; collectively, the complex or aggregate of sins committed either by a single person or by many."[5]

- Double: From the Greek word *diploo* which means "to double."[6]

- Queen: From the Greek word *basilissa* which means "queen."[7]

- Widow: From the Greek word *chera* which means "a widow; metaph. a city stripped of its inhabitants and riches is represented under the figure of a widow."[8]

- Mourn: From the Greek word *penthos* which means "mourning."[9]

- Cargoes: From the Greek word *gomos* which means "a lading or freight of a ship, cargo, merchandise conveyed in a ship; any merchandise."[10]

- Silver: From the Greek word *arguros* which means "silver."[11]

- Precious stones: From two Greek words: *timios* which means "properly, valuable as having recognized value in the eyes of the beholder"[12] and *lithos* which means "a stone."[13]

- Pearls: From the Greek word *margarites* which means "a pearl; a proverb, i.e. a word of great value."[14]

- Purple: From the Greek word *porphura* which means "the purple fish, a species of shell fish or mussel; a fabric colored with purple dye, a garment made from purple cloth."[15]

- Silk: From the Greek word *serikos* which means "made of silk; silk, i.e. the fabric, silken garments."[16]

- Scarlet: From the Greek word *kokkinos* which means "crimson, scarlet colored. A kernel, the grain or berry of the "ilex coccifera"; these berries are the clusters of the eggs of a female insect, the "kermes" (resembling the cochineal), and when collected and pulverized produces a red which was used in dyeing (Pliny); scarlet cloth or clothing."[17]

- Citron: From the Greek word *thuinos* which means "the citrus, an odoriferous North African tree used as incense, prized by the ancient Greeks and Romans on account of the beauty of its wood for various ornamental purposes."[18]

- Ivory: From the Greek word *elephantinos* which means "of ivory."[19]

- Marble: From the Greek word *marmaros* which means "a stone, a rock; marble."[20]

- Cinnamon: From the Greek word *kinamomon* which means "cinnamon was a well-known aromatic substance, the rind of "Laurus cinnamonum" called "Korunda-gauhah" in Ceylon."[21]

- Spice: From the Greek word *thumiama* which means "an aromatic substance burnt, incense."[22]

- Incense: From the Greek word *libanos* which means "the frankincense tree; the perfume, frankincense."[23]

- Myrrh: From the Greek word *muron* which means "ointment."[24]

- Fine flour: From the Greek word *semidalis* which means "the finest wheat flour."[25]

- Sheep: From the Greek word *probaton* which means "any four footed, tame animal accustomed to graze, small cattle (opp. to large cattle, horses, etc.), most commonly a sheep or a goat."[26]

- Slaves: From the Greek word *soma* which means "the body both of men or animals; the bodies of plants and of stars (heavenly bodies); is used of a (large or small) number of men closely united into one society, or family as it were; a social, ethical, mystical body; that which casts a shadow as distinguished from the shadow itself."[27]

- Souls of men: From two Greek words: *psuche* which means "breath; the soul"[28] and *anthropos* which means "a human being, whether male or female; indefinitely, someone, a man, one; in the plural, people; joined with other words, merchantman."[29]

- Fruit: From the Greek word *opora* which means "the season which succeeds summer, from the rising of Sirius to that of Arcturus, i.e. from late summer, early autumn, our dog days; ripe fruits (of trees)."[30]

- Rejoice: From the Greek word *euphraino* which means "to gladden, make joyful."[31]

- Millstone: From the Greek word *mulos* which means "a mill stone; a mill, the noise made by a mill."[32]

- Violence: From the Greek word *ballo* which means "to throw or let go of a thing without caring where it; to put into, insert."[33]

Revelation 18:1-8

After this I saw another angel coming down from heaven. He had great authority, and the earth was illuminated by his splendor. With a mighty voice he shouted:

"Fallen! Fallen is Babylon the Great!
She has become a home for demons
and a haunt for every evil spirit,
a haunt for every unclean and detestable bird.
For all the nations have drunk
the maddening wine of her adulteries.
The kings of the earth committed adultery with her,

*and the merchants of the earth grew rich from her
excessive luxuries."*

Then I heard another voice from heaven say:

*"Come out of her, my people,
so that you will not share in her sins,
so that you will not receive any of her plagues;
for her sins are piled up to heaven,
and God has remembered her crimes.
Give back to her as she has given;
pay her back double for what she has done.
Mix her a double portion from her own cup.
Give her as much torture and grief
as the glory and luxury she gave herself.
In her heart she boasts,
'I sit as a queen;
I am not a widow,
and I will never mourn.'
Therefore in one day her plagues will overtake her;
death, mourning and famine.
She will be consumed by fire,
for mighty is the Lord God Who judges her."*

(Related Bible references: Psalm 119:113, Psalm 137:8 Isaiah 21:9, Isaiah
47:1-5, Isaiah 52:11, Jeremiah 50:1-8, Jeremiah 51:1-64, Zechariah 2:7,
John 17:15-16, Romans 12:2, Galatians 6:7, 1 John 2:15, James 4:8, 2 Peter
3:8)

The major end to the devastating encounters of sin upon
this world is the fall of Babylon. The seat of vices,
temptations, commerce, politics and controls for thousands
upon thousands of years, the great and mighty worldly
system comes to an end. It's obvious nobody will see it
coming. With all the dramatic events that have been
unfolding for quite awhile, you would think the fall of
Babylon will be some sort of event that people would realize
was ahead.

Because the events of Revelation happen over a period
of many years, life will go on for people much in the form it

always does and always has. People forget about their traumas and offenses, and because the period of Babylon's fall doesn't happen all at once, but over a period of time, people only marvel in hindsight. We are warned to pay attention and stand alert because these things will go down around us, even as we walk through our everyday lives and as we go about our ordinary works.

This means when Babylon falls, the world itself will find itself in a position of chaos. The luxuries people traded in for compromises will find their quick and fleeting ending and will be no more. People will have to deal with that result, even though the one day she falls in equates to approximately 1,000 years in the sight of the Lord (2 Peter 3:8). This means the fall of Babylon will take about 1,000 years – or, if we look at the entire scope of Revelation, at least 1,260 years. The middle and later parts of the chapter focus on the last part of that, the last hour – which equates to about eighty-three years. A society that was built for thousands of years, standing strong and firm, now falls apart in a fraction of the time it took to build it.

What we are told to do, the warning we receive, is to come out of Babylon, those who are the Lord's people. The Apostle's warning wasn't to stop having lives and jobs, live off the grid, leave the world all together, or act crazy while we are still here. It does mean that we are called to be people of the Kingdom of God and live our lives by those principles and precepts as we walk day in and day out, in the world but not of the world. For thousands of years, believers have debated what it means to be in the world, but not of it (John 17:15-16, Romans 12:2, 1 John 2:15). It seems that with each new advancement, there is someone waiting in the wings to herald it as evil and herald it as "of the world." Is this really what Jesus was trying to tell us? Revelation clearly tells us, no. It encourages the believer to be exactly what God has called them to be, with patience and careful observation, watching and discerning the days, but staying true to exactly what God has asked the believer to do. There is no confusion if we remain single-minded of heart and remain stable in our ways (Psalm 119:113, James

4:8). The sins of Babylon will pile up, we will watch people we know and knew compromise (even those we thought would never do so) and see that God has had a plan, firm and in place, right to the end. Babylon will fall and receive double for the deception and infliction that has been inflicted, sowing exactly what she has reaped (Galatians 6:7).

Let us also not fail to see the imagery present in this chapter. Babylon is typified as female: a prostitute, a compromiser, a manipulator, a contriver. The church is also typified as female: a bride, a standard, virtuous, and holy. Babylon is the counter to everything the church is about, representing the opposite standards. Rather than being consumed by the fire of the Holy Spirit, Babylon is consumed by the fire of judgment.

This is important because even though it may seem that Revelation takes on a lot of extremes, it is still God's desire that we, as His people, find balance in our lives. We should never be so obsessed with one thing or one way that we lose sight of what God wants to teach us and show us in the bigger picture. Revelation is an illustration of the "bigger picture," displaying to us many events that will happen over a course of several thousand years. Even though it only seems like it happens in moments, it happens much longer than that in literal time. Throughout every person's life, there will be the pull between Babylon and the Bride, between the world and the church, because both call to us. That is why we must never forget the element of choice in our sins, in our work, in our wrongdoings, and in what we are doing right, as well. God is bringing Babylon to a swift end, as the current paradigm we know shifts into a new one. Change is hard. Birth pangs are intense. Change has its moments where we all want to go back and do things differently. Babylon, however, will fall...where the church will not.

Revelation 18:9-24

"When the kings of the earth who committed adultery with her and shared her luxury see the smoke of her burning, they will weep and mourn over her. Terrified at her torment, they will stand far off and cry:

'Woe! Woe, O great city,
O Babylon, city of power!
In one hour your doom has come!'

"The merchants of the earth will weep and mourn over her because no one buys their cargoes any more – cargoes of gold, silver, precious stones and pearls; fine linen, purple, silk and scarlet cloth; every sort of citron wood, and articles of every kind made of ivory, costly wood, bronze, iron and marble; cargoes of cinnamon and spice, of incense, myrrh and frankincense, of wine and olive oil, of fine flour and wheat; cattle and sheep; horses and carriages; and bodies and souls of men.
  "They will say, 'The fruit you longed for is gone from you. All your riches and splendor have vanished, never to be recovered.' The merchants who sold these things and gained their wealth from her will stand far off, terrified at her torment. They will weep and mourn and cry out:

'Woe! Woe, O great city,
dressed in fine linen, purple and scarlet,
and glittering with gold, precious stones and pearls!
In one hour such great wealth has been brought to ruin!'

"Every sea captain, and all who travel by ship, the sailors, and all who earn their living from the sea, will stand far off. When they see the smoke of her burning, they will exclaim, 'Was there ever a city like this great city?' They will throw dust on their heads, and with weeping and mourning cry out"

'Woe! Woe, O great city,

where all who had ships on the sea
became rich through her wealth!
In one hour she has been brought to ruin!

Rejoice over her, O heaven!
Rejoice, saints and apostles and prophets!
God has judged her
for the way she treated you.'

Then a mighty angel picked up a boulder the size of a
large millstone and threw it into the sea, and said:

"With such violence
the great city of Babylon will be thrown down,
never to be found again."
The music of harpists and musicians,
flue players and trumpeters,
will never be heard in you again.
No workman of any trade
will ever be found in you again.
The sound of a millstone
will never be heard in you again.
The light of a lamp
will never shine in you again.
The voice of bridegroom and bride
will never be heard in you again.
Your merchants were the world's great men.
By your magic spell all the nations were led astray.
In her was found the blood of prophets and of the saints,
and of all who have been killed on the earth.'"

(Related Bible references: Proverbs 11:4, Ecclesiastes 5:10, Jeremiah 50:46, Jeremiah 51:1-64, Ezekiel 26:17, Ezekiel 27:12-36, Daniel 4:30, Matthew 18:6, Romans 12:19, 1 Timothy 6:10)

With Babylon goes the merchants of the world. This is no accident, because it is these luxuries that lead to prestige and power are things the entire world seeks after, hoping to be top dog and top in financial power. The various lists of goods all relate to natural resources, all of which people have obtained through illegal, dishonest, poaching, stealing, and thieving. They are also objects used to fashion false idols and to make burnt and food offerings to them. In the pursuit of the love of money (1 Timothy 6:10), people loving the things of the world have pierced themselves with all sorts of sorrows. The ultimate end of Babylon is the ultimate end of everything Babylon represents, and in that moment, woe, woe unto all those who have loved things more than people and contents and items more than God. Woe, because in one moment, they will realize it is all for naught.

The reason the Bible encourages us to focus on the spiritual rather than the material is because material things will not pass from this world into the next. Heavenly beings are decked out in gorgeous array, all throughout Revelation...and, ironically enough, it's the same array that the world tries to dress itself in, to the point of lusting after that image. here is nothing wrong with looking good, dressing good, liking pearls or jewelry, or in being fashionable and attractive. There is nothing wrong with liking things or wanting to have nice things. There is something wrong with those things having you, dominating your life, controlling your every move. If you can't live and be happy without things, then those things possess you.

In what will seem like one moment, the love of money will be over. The things that held people bound, that they put their faith in, will be done. The seize of violence will surrender in the presence of the Lord, and Babylon shall fall...all at once, one thing at a time. The music shall stop, the rejoicing over everything that is wrong and questionable shall end, the boasting and gloating over the saints, over wrongdoing, ever every evil thing, shall end. There shall be a pause, and a silence as God's people realize they have been avenged, just as God promised they would be.

The Scroll and

5 Then I saw i,
sealed[t] with
break the seals an
scroll or even loo
scroll or look insi
dah, the Root of Da

[6]Then I saw a L
by the four living cr
its[u] of God sent out
on the throne.[v] An
before the Lamb. Ea
prepared at the sam

Handwritten margin note: JESUS IS ALWAYS ABLE TO OVERCOME

Chapter Nineteen

THE FINAL RIDE
(REVELATION CHAPTER 19)

Key verses

- Verses 1-2: *After this I heard what sounded like the roar of a great multitude in heaven shouting: "Hallelujah! Salvation and glory and power belong to our God, for true and just are His judgments. He has condemned the great prostitute who corrupted the earth by her adulteries. He has avenged on her the blood of His servants."*

- Verses 9-10: *Then the angel said to me, "Write: 'Blessed are those who are invited to the wedding supper of the Lamb!'" And he added, "These are the true words of God." At this I fell at his feet to worship him. But he said to me, "Do not do it! I am a fellow servant with you and with your brothers who hold to the testimony of Jesus. Worship God! For the testimony of Jesus is the spirit of prophecy."*

- Verse 16: *On His robe and on His thigh He has this name written: KING OF KINGS AND LORD OF LORDS.*

- Verses 19-21: *Then I saw the beast and the kings of the earth and their armies gathered together to make war against the rider on the horse and his army. But the beast was captured, and with him the false prophet who had performed the miraculous signs on his behalf. With these signs he had deluded those who had received the mark of the beast and worshiped his image. The two of them were thrown alive into the fiery lake of burning sulfur. The rest of them were killed with the sword that came out of the mouth of the rider on the horse, and all the birds gorged themselves on their flesh.*

Words and phrases to know

- Hallelujah: From the Greek word *hallelouia* which means "praise ye the Lord, Hallelujah."[1]

- Wedding: From the Greek word *gamos* which means "a wedding or marriage festival, a wedding banquet, a wedding feast; marriage, matrimony."[2]

- Bride: From the Greek word *gune* which means "a woman of any age, whether a virgin, or married, or a widow; a wife."[3]

- Invited: From the Greek word *kaleo* which means "to call; to call i.e. to name, by name."[4]

- Supper: From the Greek word *deipnon* which means "supper, especially a formal meal usually held at the evening; food taken at evening."[5]

- Word of God: From two Greek words: *logos* which means of speech; its use as respect to the MIND alone; In John, denotes the essential Word of God, Jesus Christ, the personal wisdom and power in union with God, his minister in creation and government of the universe, the cause of all the world's life both physical and ethical, which for the procurement of man's salvation put on human nature in the person of Jesus the Messiah, the second person in the Godhead, and shone forth conspicuously from His words and deeds,"[6] and *theos* which means "a god or goddess, a general name of deities or divinities; the Godhead; whatever can in any respect be likened unto God, or resemble him in any way."[7]

Revelation 19:1-10

After this I heard what sounded like the roar of a great multitude in heaven shouting:

"Hallelujah!
Salvation and glory and power belong to our God,
for true and just are His judgments.
He has condemned the great prostitute
who corrupted the earth by her adulteries.
He has avenged on her the blood of His servants."

And again they shouted:

"Hallelujah!
The smoke from her goes up for ever and ever."

The twenty-four elders and the four living creatures fell down and worshiped God, Who was seated on the throne. And they cried:

"Amen, Hallelujah!"

Then a voice came from the throne, saying:

"Praise our God,
all you His servants,
you who fear Him,
both small and great!"

Then I heard what sounded like a great multitude, like the roar of rushing waters and like loud peals of thunder, shouting:

"Hallelujah!
For our Lord God Almighty reigns.

Let us rejoice and be glad
and give Him glory!
For the wedding of the Lamb has come,
and His bride has made herself ready.
Fine linen, bright and clean,
was given her to wear."

(Fine linen stands for the righteous acts of the saints."

*Then the angel said to me, "Write: 'Blessed are those who
are invited to the wedding supper of the Lamb!'" And he
added, "These are the true words of God."*

*At this I fell at his feet to worship him. But he said to
me, "Do not do it! I am a fellow servant with you and with
your brothers who hold to the testimony of Jesus.
Worship God! For the testimony of Jesus is the spirit of
prophecy."*

(Related Bible references: Deuteronomy 32:4, Deuteronomy 32:43,
Psalm 19:9, Psalm 79:10, Psalm 97:1, Psalm 106:48, Psalm 113:1, Psalm
115:13, Psalm 134:1, Psalm 135:1, Psalm 150:6, Psalm 117:1, Isaiah 6;1,
Daniel 7:9-10, 1 Peter 1:17)

Revelation 19 has served as an inspiration for many hymns,
praise and worship songs, and spiritual poetic writings
because it opens with a great song of praise to God.
Throughout the ages and the long history of struggle and
difficulty that the saints have encountered, God kept His
promise. When we read the words of Revelation 19, we hear
that God will be faithful to us to the very end. There is no
reason to grow dismal or hopeless with God, because in the
long run, He will handle every matter that needs to be
handled.

If God can take care of every dirty business deed, every
wayward commercial dealing, every false spiritual system,
and every lie uttered from the beginning of time until the
very end of the period Revelation speaks about, then God
can take care of you and all of your needs, too. No matter
what anyone may teach about Revelation, it proves that God
is faithful and will be faithful to the end with us, faithful in

the long-run and faithful right up until the end. We are called to this wedding feast of the Lamb, because the closer we get to this time when all shall fall, the closer it comes to our ultimate and complete union with Jesus Christ. As discouraging as this world often is, the more things that come along, the closer we are to that wedding supper with Christ.

We also must constantly check our own selves, our own motives, and yes, our own idolatries. The one who brings the good news is not the one we should worship. It's easy to be in awe of God's servants, because God has greatly blessed them with gifts and abilities to bring the message to the world. This angel brought good news; in fact, he brought more than just good news with him...he brought an entire vision, an entire mystical experience that the Apostle John had the opportunity to witness and write about. Even in the instance of this incredible experience, the Apostle was told not to fall down and worship this angel. If an apostle of the Lord can be so overcome that they desire to worship the messenger, it can happen to any one of us. No matter what one may be called to in the Kingdom of God, we are all brothers and sisters in the Lord before the Father. May we always keep our eyes on the work of Jesus, the Author and Finisher of our faith, and while we hold admiration and respect for our messengers, never pass the pass that point with them. Let us worship God, because the testimony of Jesus – what He has done for us, through us, in us, for us, and with us – is the very spirit of prophecy. Jesus is the heart of the prophetic, and the center of prophetic history. It does not mean that God has nothing else to say prophetically, but it does mean that Jesus is the very heart of all we do, every good message we bring, every good action, and every hope of the future as we prepare for our wedding banquet with Him.

Revelation 19:11-21

I saw heaven standing open and there before me was a white horse, whose rider is called Faithful and True. With justice He judges and makes war. His eyes are like blazing fire, and on His head are many crowns. He has a Name written on Him that no one knows but He Himself. He is dressed in a robe dipped in blood, and His Name is the Word of God. The armies of heaven were following Him, riding on white horses and dressed in fine linen, white and clean. Out of His mouth comes a sharp sword with which to strike down the nations. "He will rule them with an iron scepter." He treads the winepress of the fury of the wrath of God Almighty. On His robe and on His thigh He has this name written:

KING OF KINGS AND LORD OF LORDS.

And I saw an angel standing in the sun, who cried in a loud voice to all the birds flying in midair, "Come, gather together for the great supper of God, so that you may eat the flesh of kings, generals, and mighty men, of horses and their riders, and the flesh of all people, free and slave, small and great."

Then I saw the beast and the kings of the earth and their armies gathered together to make war against the rider on the horse and His army. But the beast was captured, and with him the false prophet who had performed the miraculous signs on his behalf. With these signs he had deluded those who had received the mark of the beast and worshiped his image. The two of them were thrown alive into the fiery lake of burning sulfur. The rest of them were killed with the sword that came out of the mouth of the rider on the horse, and all the birds gorged themselves on their flesh.

(Related Bible references: Isaiah 11:4, Jeremiah 25:30, Ezekiel 39:1-29, John 1:1-18, Philippians 2:10, 2 Thessalonians 2:8, Hebrews 1:8-9, 1 John 1:1, Revelation 6:1-8)

Earlier in Revelation, we saw other riders:

- Rider on a white horse, with a bow and crown, going out to conquer and conquer (Revelation 6:1-2)

- Rider on a fiery red horse, there to take peace from the earth and make people slay each other (Revelation 6:3-4)

- Rider on a black horse, holding a pair of scales and bringing an impending famine (Revelation 6:5-6)

- Rider on a pale horse, named death, with Hades behind him, given the power to kill a fourth of the earth by sword, famine, plague, and the wild beasts of the earth (Revelation 6:7-8)

All these riders brought specific and terrible things upon the earth. Now, here at the end of Revelation, we see a final ride, with Jesus at the helm, prepared and ready to conquer anything left lingering after the fall of Babylon. He is Faithful and True because He has proven Himself to be that to His people. He is the King of all Kings and the Lord of all Lords and has kept His each and every promise. He is the ultimate Overcomer, and He has overcome on behalf of those who have trusted and believed in Him. As He rides into battle displaying His warrior tattoo, Jesus is ready to, once and for all, complete the battle that finishes it all.

The call goes forth to come to this great supper, that people might be free and move into the greatest phase of human existence known since life prior to the fall of mankind. Jesus shall set us free from every trace of the beast, the false prophet, the effects of sin and death, which shall fall into the eternal pit, the smoke of which shall ascend forever and ever. There shall be no more delusions, no more pain, and no trace of the world that dominated for so long.

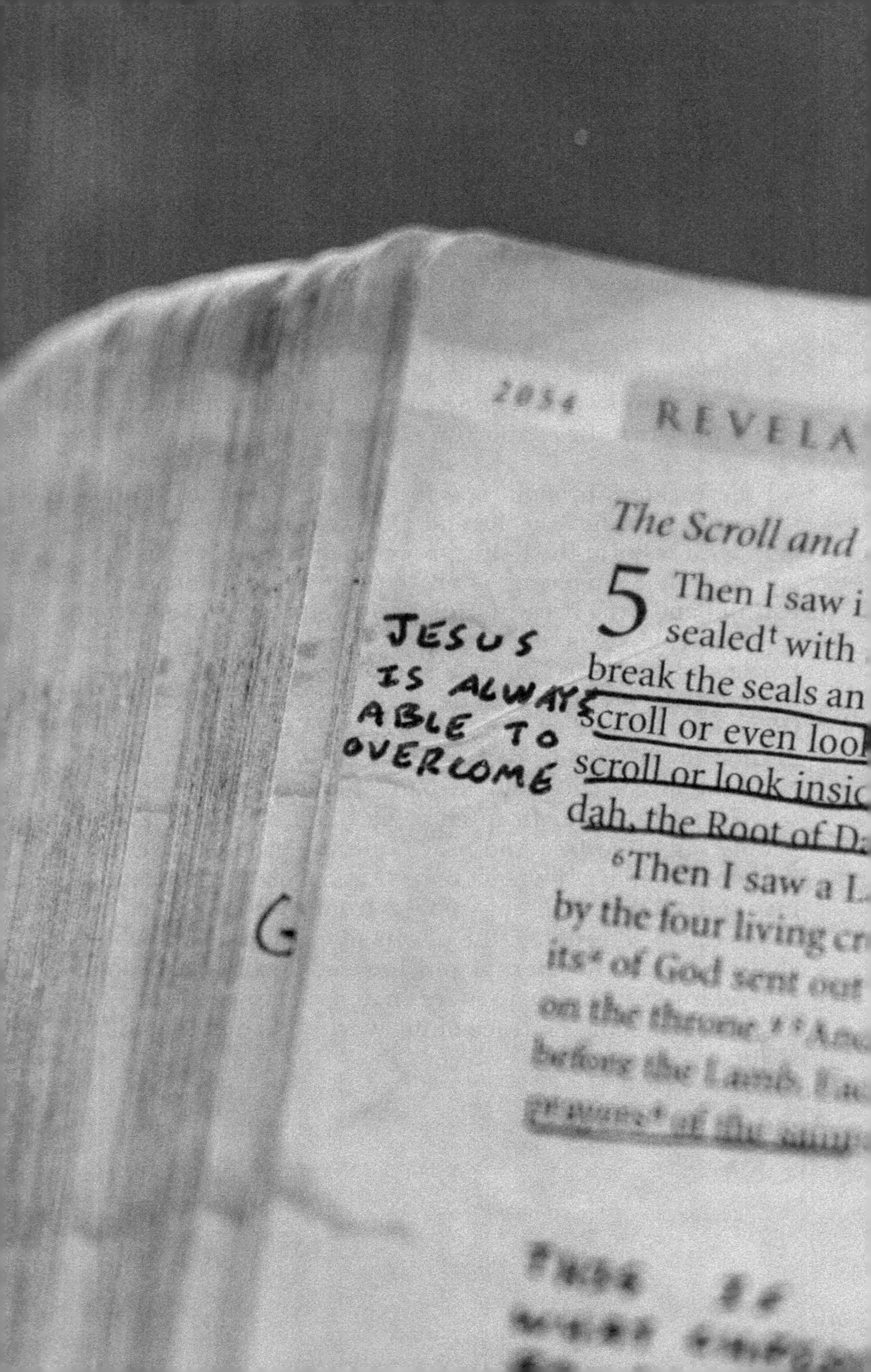

The Scroll and

5 Then I saw i
sealed[t] with
break the seals an
scroll or even look
scroll or look insid
dah, the Root of D

[6] Then I saw a L
by the four living cr
its[u] of God sent out
on the throne. [7] And
before the Lamb. Eac
prayers[v] of the saint

(handwritten margin note): JESUS IS ALWAYS ABLE TO OVERCOME

(handwritten margin note): G

Chapter Twenty

Key verses

- Verses 2-3: *He seized the dragon, that ancient serpent, who is the devil, or Satan, and bound him for a thousand years. He threw him into the Abyss, and locked and sealed it over him, to keep him from deceiving the nations anymore until the thousand years were ended. After that, he must be set free for a short time.*

- Verse 6: *Blessed and holy are those who have part in the first resurrection. The second death has no power over them, but they will be priests of God and of Christ and will reign with Him for a thousand years.*

- Verse 10: *And the devil, who deceived them, was thrown into the lake of burning sulfur, where the beast and the false prophet had been thrown. They will be tormented day and night for ever and ever.*

- Verses 12-13: *And I saw the dead, great and small, standing before the throne, and books were opened. Another book was opened, which is the book of life. The dead were judged according to what they had done as recorded in the books. The sea gave up the dead that were in it, and death and Hades gave up the dead that were in them, and each person was judged according to what he had done.*

- Bound: From the Greek word *deo* which means "to bind tie, fasten."[1]

- Thousand years: From two Greek words: *chilioi* which means "a thousand"[2] and *etos* which means "year."[3]

- Resurrection: From the Greek word *anastasis* which means "a raising up, rising (e.g. from a seat); a rising from the dead."[4]

- Gog: From the Greek word *Gog* which means "Gog = "mountain;" the king of the land of Magog who will come from the north and attack the land of Israel."[5]

- Magog: From the Greek word *Magog* which means "Magog = "overtopping: covering;" a land north of Israel from which the King of Gog will come to attack Israel."[6]

Revelation 20:1-10

And I saw an angel coming down out of heaven, having the key to the Abyss and holding in his hand a great chain. He seized the dragon, that ancient serpent, who is the devil, or Satan, and bound him for a thousand years. He threw him into the Abyss, and locked and sealed it over him, to keep him from deceiving the nations anymore until the thousand years were ended. After that, he must be set free for a short time.

I saw thrones on which were seated those who had been given authority to judge. And I saw the souls of those who had been beheaded because of their testimony for Jesus and because of the Word of God. They had not worshiped the beast or his image and had not received his mark on their foreheads or their hands. They came to life and reigned with Christ a thousand years. (The rest of the dead did not come to life until the thousand years were ended.) This is the first resurrection. Blessed and holy are those who have part in the first resurrection. The second death has no power over them, but they will be priests of God and of Christ and will reign with Him for a thousand years.

When the thousand years are over, Satan will be released from his prison and will go out to deceive the nations in the four corners of the earth – Gog and Magog – to gather them for battle. In number they are like the sand on the seashore. They marched across the breadth of the earth and surrounded the camp of God's people, the city He loves. But fire came down from heaven and devoured them. And the devil, who deceived them, was thrown into the lake of burning sulfur, where the beast and the false prophet had been thrown. They will be tormented day and night for ever and ever.

(Related Bible references: Ezekiel 38:2, Ezekiel 48:35, Zechariah 3:1, Matthew 19:28, Matthew 25:46, Luke 22:30, John 5:28, Acts 24:15, 1 Corinthians 6:2, 1 Corinthians 15:23, 1 Corinthians 15:52-54, 1 Thessalonians 4:16, 2 Timothy 2:12)

The exact details of Revelation get even murkier than before as we enter the final three chapters of this vitally important book. I think we deal with complications in understanding and visualizing these final three chapters because they deal with a realm and a world that most of us do not understand this side of heaven. With the fall of the beast, the false prophet, the whore of Babylon, Babylon itself, and the merchants and individuals attached to these things, it becomes more and more obvious that the full splendor and glory of the Kingdom of God are coming into a real-time reality that many have not considered in their lifetimes. It is a promise that was as far off to the first-century believers, with imagery that was beyond their wildest imaginations. For a people that came out of various nations, experienced the tyranny of governmental oppression at all times, watched their friends and leaders escorted to violent and brutal deaths, and had no idea how the Kingdom of God was going to continue as an entity down the ages, the idea of Satan's ultimate demise and the Kingdom of God manifesting full-time was unfathomable, yet beautiful. There was a comfort in knowing God was still sovereign and Satan would not win.

Revelation has been full of symbolism and symbolic time periods. It ends as it began, talking about a long duration of time by which incredible things would unfold. This long period of time is spoken of as "the millennium," or a thousand-year time frame after Christ's second coming, after the long battles and conflicts, by which the saints rule with Christ and the resurrection of the dead who are not in Christ has yet to occur. I don't believe that this will be a literal one-thousand-year period, if for no other reason than everything else in Revelation has been symbolic, pointing us to other things and other ideals. The time of Revelation is as symbolic as the rest of it. The use of a thousand years here symbolizes our long walk into eternity, and the millennial period as just the beginning of all of eternity, and all the many thousands of years, millennia, and eons that we will spend with the Lord, blessed of Him. We start this period with a training session, where the saints rule with Christ, preparing to judge the world (1 Corinthians 6:2). As the firstfruits of the resurrection, we are the first who shall stand, resurrected from the dead or living without death, walking in a period without the confines of the enemy because we have chosen to follow and live with Christ forever. They shall stand and never be touched by the second death, and they, in all things, have refused to worship the beast, no matter what has gone on in their lives and where their lives have taken them.

The "nations" spoken of in this chapter are unknown. We know from the fall of Babylon and the death of so many that the world as we know it now will not exist in those days. It does say Satan will be released for a period of time after this initial phase of eternity for a short time. That unspecific 'short time' is to give all individuals, even those who are now in this new world, one final chance to make sure the choice they are making is for God, of their own free will, and not by force.

Who exactly "Gog and Magog" refer to is unclear. Given we are reading about a time frame far into the future where the world will be different, we really don't know who they are talking about. What we do know from the book of Ezekiel is that Gog and Magog are used as an image of coming against the people of God (Ezekiel 38:2), but in the end, God will establish that which is new and dwell forever with the people that are His. That is why Gog and Magog are mentioned here, because they represent a spiritual demonism that seeks to destroy God's people, leaving the way for a further restoration of all things spiritual. This battle will go nowhere, because God will stop this fight before it even starts, paving the way for eternity to continue without blemish or trial and with Satan and his minions firmly confined to hell, for a period of complete eternity.

<u>Revelation 20:11-15</u>

Then I saw a great white throne and Him Who was seated on it. Earth and sky fled from His presence, and there was no place for them. And I saw the dead, great and small, standing before the throne, and books were opened. Another book was opened, which is the book of life. The dead were judged according to what they had done as recorded in the books. The sea gave up the dead that were in it, and death and Hades gave up the dead that were in them, and each person was judged according to what he had done. Then death and Hades were thrown into the lake of fire. The lake of fire is the second death. If anyone's name was not found written in the book of life, he was thrown into the lake of fire.

(Related Bible references: Exodus 32:33, Psalm 69:28, Daniel 12:1, John 5:29, Hebrews 12:22-23, 2 Peter 3:7)

Following this period, the judgment of all those who died not knowing the Lord commences with anticipation and excitement. Those who have spent their prior eternal years learning about the things of God and judging the saints now also join in to judge the world. Each person will be judged according to their deeds, what they have or have not done. With the end of this, all death, the grave, and all associated it were thrown into the lake of fire, the second death, from which none shall come forth from. Those who were not in the Lamb, those who were not in the book of life, in the registry of those who seek God and life, will join death and hell in the lake of fire, for all of eternity. This is not an easy prospect, nor a fun one, nor a casual musing. We must take seriously the ways of God, and the promises of life, and seek them out for ourselves. Eternity is now, as much as it will be later. Let's prepare for eternal life today, in each and every choice we seek to make.

Chapter Twenty-One

THE NEW JERUSALEM REPLACES THE OLD BABYLON
(REVELATION CHAPTER 21)

<u>Key verses</u>

- Verses 1-4: *Then I saw a new heaven and a new earth, for the first heaven and the first earth had passed away, and there was no longer any sea. I saw the Holy City, the new Jerusalem, coming down out of heaven from God, prepared as a bride beautifully dressed for her husband. And I heard a loud voice from the throne saying, "Now the dwelling of God is with men, and He will live with them. They will be His people, and God Himself will be with them and be their God. He will wipe every tear from their eyes. There will be no more death or mourning or crying or pain, for the old order of things has passed away."*

- Verse 6: *He said to me: "It is done. I am the Alpha and the Omega, the Beginning and the End. To him who is thirsty I will give to drink without cost from the spring of the water of life."*

- Verses 10-12: *And he carried me away in the Spirit to a mountain great and high, and showed me the Holy City, Jerusalem, coming down out of heaven from God. It shone with the glory of God, and its brilliance was like that of a very precious jewel, like a jasper, clear as crystal. It had a great, high wall with twelve gates, and with twelve angels at the gates. On the gates were written the names of the twelve tribes of Israel.*

- Verses 22-23: *I did not see a temple in the city, because the Lord God Almighty and the Lamb are its temple. The city does not need the sun or the moon to shine on it, for the glory of God gives it light, and the Lamb is its lamp.*

- Verse 27: *Nothing impure will ever enter it, nor will anyone who does what is shameful or deceitful, but only those whose names are written in the Lamb's book of life.*

Words and phrases to know

- Holy City: From two Greek words: *hagios* which means "most holy thing, a saint"[1] and *polis* which means "a city."[2]

- Husband: From the Greek word *aner* which means "with reference to sex, of a male, of a husband, of a betrothed or future husband; with reference to age, and to distinguish an adult man from a boy; any male; used generically of a group of both men and women."[3]

- Cowardly: From the Greek word *deilos* which means "cowardly, fearful."[4]

- Unbelieving: From the Greek word *apistos* which means "unfaithful, faithless, (not to be trusted, perfidious); incredible; unbelieving, incredulous."[5]

- Vile: From the Greek word *bdelusso* which means "to render foul, to cause to be abhorred; abominable; to turn one's self away from on account of the stench; metaph. to abhor, detest."[6]

- Murderers: From the Greek word *phoneus* which means "murderer, a homicide."[7]

- Sexually immoral: From the Greek word *pornos* which means "a man who prostitutes his body to another's lust for hire; a male prostitute; a man who indulges in unlawful sexual intercourse, a fornicator."[8]

- Magic arts: From the Greek word *pharmakeus* which means "one who prepares or uses magical remedies; sorcerer."[9]

- Idolaters: From the Greek word *eidololatres* which means "a worshipper of false gods, a idolater; a covetous man as a worshipper of Mammon."[10]

- Liars: From the Greek word *pseudes* which means "lying, deceitful, false."[11]

- Square: From the Greek word *tetragonos* which means "quadrangular, square."[12]

- Sapphire: From the Greek word *sappheiros* which means "sapphire, a precious stone."[13]

- Chalcedony: From the Greek word *chalkedon* which means "chalcedony is a precious stone of misty grey color, clouded with blue, yellow, or purple."[14]

- Sardonyx: From the Greek word *sardonux* which means "a sardonyx, a precious stone marked by the red colors of the carnelian (sard) and the white of the onyx."[15]

- Chrysolite: From the Greek word *chrusolithos* which means "chrysolite is a precious stone of golden colour."[16]

- Beryl: From the Greek word *berullos* which means "beryl, a precious stone of a pale green colour."[17]

- Topaz: From the Greek word *topazion* which means "topaz, a greenish yellow precious stone (our chrysolite)."[18]

- Chysoprase: From the Greek word *chrusoprasos* which means "chrysoprasus is a stone of green color, inclined to that of gold, from whence it has its name; for this is agate in the breast plate, which was Naphtali's stone. (Gill)."[19]

- Jacinth: From the Greek word *huakinthos* which means "hyacinth, the name of a flower, also of a precious stone of the same color, a dark blue verging on black."[20]

- Amethyst: From the Greek word *amethustos* which means "amethyst, a precious stone of a violet and purple colour."[21]

- Gates: From the Greek word *pulon* which means "a large gate: of a palace; the front part of a house, into which one enters through the gate, porch."[22]

Revelation 21:1-5

Then I saw a new heaven and a new earth, for the first heaven and the first earth had passed away, and there was no longer any sea. I saw the Holy City, the New Jerusalem, coming down out of heaven from God, prepared as a bride beautifully dressed for her husband. And I heard a loud voice from the throne saying, "Now the dwelling of God is with men, and He will live with them. They will be His people, and God Himself will be with them and be their God. He will wipe every tear from their eyes.

There will be no more death or mourning or crying or pain, for the old order of things has passed away."

He Who was seated on the throne said, "I am making everything new!" Then He said, "Write this down, for these words are trustworthy and true."

(Related Bible references: Genesis 3:8, 2 Chronicles 18:18, Isaiah 35:10, Isaiah 42:9, Isaiah 52:1, Isaiah 65:19, Lamentations 5:21, Ezekiel 36:26, Ezekiel 37:27, Ezekiel 43:7, Ezekiel 48:35, John 3:29, 1 Corinthians 15:26, 2 Peter 3:13)

The fall of Babylon ends the world's system of operation. This means that as God has taken back the earth, His governmental implementation must fall into place and begin its full, visible, undeniable rule. The heavens and the earth become new, visibly changed and different from that which we already know. Just as the people of the earth undergo a healing process, so too the world must go through one. It must be healed and transformed from the abuses and consequences of sin, ravaging through and destroying it for so many years. In beginning a new era, the first earth passes away, and the veil between earth and heaven is no more. There will not be as much of a distinction between the earthly and the heavenly, and the two will be one in a singular form, changing the way in which people regard and interact with the divine.

There is a holy city, a new Jerusalem, coming down from heaven to earth, to stand as the capital for God's Kingdom government. The current city of Jerusalem has been a sore spot for political gains for thousands of years, with no clear answer in sight. In fighting over the current city, the world is missing the point that there shall be a new city, with the current one passing away, no more relevant, and no more thought of. It is God's desire that we are a future people who do not allow modern politics to blind our thoughts and that we continue to seek and await the perfection of God's government. Jerusalem as a peaceful city has never existed this side of heaven, and it will take the true Jerusalem to come down forth from heaven, to reveal unto us the truth of the city of peace and the perfection of government we seek.

We know that God is with us, but the way we will have God with us is beyond our comprehension. We will be able to walk with God, as Adam and Eve walked with God, in the cool of the day (Genesis 3:8). He will wipe away every tear from our eyes, and we will sorrow and mourn no more. All things that cause pain and dissatisfaction will cease, and we will finally have God in our lives in a way that we long for and believe for but have not experienced...not quite yet.

Even though this time is yet to come, we still can see types and shadows of it now, in our everyday lives. Making all things new doesn't just mean the things will be new, but that we will see them differently. Whenever we are in circumstances where we can experience love, good relationships, great spiritual insights, or yes, revelations, we are seeing a picture of eternity. We are experiencing a type of that which is to come, walking it out, and remembering less and less the hurts we experienced. Healing is a transformative touch when we see it in action, and here, we are seeing and experiencing God's love for us in a healing moment, in moments of love that change our lives, and moments of purpose that soothe the soul.

<u>Revelation 21:6-14</u>

He said to me: "It is done. I am the Alpha and the Omega, the Beginning and the End. To him who is thirsty I will give to drink without cost from the spring of the water of life. He who overcomes will inherit all this, and I will be his God and he will be my son. But the cowardly, the unbelieving, the vile, the murderers, the sexually immoral, those who practice magic arts, the idolaters and all liars – their place will be in the fiery lake of burning sulfur. This is the second death."

One of the seven angels who had the seven bowls full of the seven last plagues came and said to me, "Come, I will show you the bride, the wife of the Lamb." And he carried me away in the Spirit to a mountain great and high, and showed me the Holy City, Jerusalem, coming down out of heaven from God. It shone with the glory of God, and its brilliance was like that of a very precious jewel, like a jasper, clear as crystal. It had a great, high wall with twelve gates, and with twelve angels at the gates. On the gates were written the names of the twelve tribes of Israel. There were three gates on the east, three on the north, three on the south and three on the west. The wall of the city had twelve foundations, and on them were the names of the twelve apostles of the Lamb.

(Related Bible references: Psalm 36:9, Psalm 45:9, Isaiah 2:2, Isaiah 55:1, Micah 4:1, John 4:10-14, John 4:24, John 7:38, Acts 5:3, 1 Corinthians 6:9, 1 Corinthians 15:28, Galatians 5:20, Ephesians 5:5, Hebrews 10:26, 1 John 3:15)

God gives all people the opportunity to come and to know Him and to partake of this beautiful and wonderful future. To anyone that thirsts – longs for, seeks after, or desires eternity – there is the water of life, the water that shall cause people to never thirst again (Isaiah 55:1, John 4:10-14, John 7:38). The true worshipers of God worship Him in Spirit and in truth (John 4:24), and He gives us the ability to follow Him, to do right unto the end, to persevere. We can be the sons of God, turned toward the Father and graced with His Kingdom. There is a list of those who will never find their place in the Kingdom if they find themselves in eternity without repentance, and it is interesting to look at this list, because the list in many ways contradicts the teaching of many today. We like the idea of a weak-willed, impressionable church that follows after every vague and undiscerning wind of doctrine. Yet the following will not inherit God's Kingdom:

- Cowardly: A cowardly person is one who knows what is right, but they don't do what is right out of fear. The fear can be fear of being noticed, imitated, or simply making a choice. Cowardly people cannot inherit the Kingdom because they know the Kingdom is right but refuse to follow it because of what following the Kingdom will mean.

- Unbelieving: Unbelieving has a strong connotation to it, but in the context of Revelation, it is applied to someone who does not believe in Jesus as Savior in the way they must to follow Him as a follower of the Lamb. It is very clear that those who follow Christ are the ones who will inherit eternal life. "Unbeliever" can also apply to someone who did believe but has abandoned faith, or who knows the truth about belief, but refuses to follow the principles of belief.

- Vile: To be vile is to be completely despicable, without moral or character. It is often used to indicate the worst of the worst, someone who is so without moral fiber that they are not in any way ashamed of their ways. Vile people are without repentance, and to be without repentance means one cannot be a part of the Kingdom.

- Murderers: We know murderers to be people who kill other people with deliberate intent. A murderer is not someone who takes life by accidental means. This indicates a murderer is an individual without regard for life. Those who prowl with murder in their heart: seeking to destroy lives and reputations, ministries and relationships, and who massacre other people with no regard for God or what is right cannot be a part of the Kingdom.

- Sexually immoral: Sexual immorality is defined in a broad sense as any sort of sexual activity expressly forbidden by God's guidelines. The problem with this general definition is that the different guidelines and regulations have changed throughout the Bible, often representing cultural standards and norms. This means God is trying to teach us something through teaching on sexual immorality, and that is a level of faithfulness, fidelity, and protectiveness within each and every one of us. In Biblical context, sex outside of divine limits was usually related to idolatry. Those who deliberately seek to defy God's boundaries for sexuality cannot inherit the Kingdom, because they do not espouse the faithfulness, fidelity, and self-respect needed to stand in God's presence.

- Practicing magic arts: To practice a magic art is beyond just casting a spell or playing with magic. One who practices magic arts is a practitioner to the point where they are well-versed enough to use magic to handle any and everything they seek to do in life and teach it to others. Magic operates by spiritual manipulation, which is akin to rebellion. Spiritual rebellion renders a person far from God, and they cannot be a part of this new thing He is doing because they will not be able to obey Him with an upright heart.

- Idolaters: The Bible spends a lot of time defining and discussing idolatry. In short, idolatry is placing anything, anyone, or any ideal above that of God. Idolaters aren't obedient unto the end, thus not able to stand in God's Kingdom.

- Liars: Liars don't tell or live the truth. Truth is essential to the Kingdom; thus, liars aren't coming into the Kingdom.

This seems like a disconnected and strange list of prohibitions, but it really is not. All these issues impede Kingdom understanding and Kingdom work. They inhibit the desired and necessary flow of teaching, righteousness, and worship that must infiltrate the Kingdom into eternity. These characteristics, which we find at the root of many human issues and problems today, do not signify the right understanding of life. They are not people that are redeemable, because they refuse to repent.

Moving from who won't be there, John then sees a vision of who will be there: the church watching on as the New Jerusalem descends, the seat of where God's Kingdom shall be headquartered. Peace, wise instruction, and life shall truly come from this New Jerusalem. It shall be beautiful, gated so no impure thing can enter, and have the foundations of old, of the foundations of the Old Covenant (the Twelve Tribes of Israel) and the New (the twelve Apostles of the Lamb).

<u>Revelation 21:15-27</u>

The angel who talked with me had a measuring rod of gold to measure the city, its gates and its walls. The city was laid out like a square, as long as it was wide. He measured the city with the rod and found it to be 12,000 stadia in length, and as wide and high as it is long. He measured its wall and it was 144 cubits thick, by man's measurement, which the angel was using. The wall was made of jasper, and the city of pure gold, as pure as glass. The foundations of the city walls were decorated with every kind of precious stone. The first foundation was jasper, the second sapphire, the third chalcedony, the fourth emerald, the fifth sardonyx, the sixth carnelian, the seventh chrysolite, the eighth beryl, the ninth topaz, the tenth chrysoprase, the eleventh jacinth, and the twelfth amethyst. The twelve gates were twelve pearls, each gate made of a single pearl. The great street of the city was of pure gold, like transparent glass.

I did not see a temple in the city, because the Lord God Almighty and the Lamb are its temple. The city does not need the sun or the moon to shine on it, for the glory of God gives its light, and the Lamb is its lamp. The nations will walk by its light, and the kings of the earth will bring their splendor into it. On no day will its gates ever be shut, for there will be no night there. The glory and honor of the nations will be brought into it. Nothing impure will ever enter it, nor will anyone who does what is shameful or deceitful, but only those whose names are written in the Lamb's book of life.

(Related Bible references: Song of Solomon 5:14, Isaiah 54:11-12, Isaiah

60:19, Ezekiel 28:13, Ezekiel 40:1-5, Ezekiel 47:1-23, Acts 7:49)

The incredible description of the New Jerusalem mirrors the heavenly visions seen earlier in Revelation. It also echoes Ezekiel's vision where the temple is restored (Ezekiel 47:1-23). The major difference between Revelation and Ezekiel's vision is that John's vision goes further, to elaborate why there is no need for a physical temple anymore. Amidst the beautiful colors, streets paved with gold and the pearly gates are the Lamb of God and the Lord God Almighty, not needing endless sacrifices or even the sun or a lamp. God's glory, His honor and might shall light the way to the promise, where nothing impure can come forth, no shameful thing can show its face, and those who are in the Lamb's book of life can finally live aright, in the way they know God desires, without interference from the enemy.

The Scroll and

5 Then I saw i
sealed[t] with
break the seals an
scroll or even look
scroll or look insi
dah, the Root of Da

[6]Then I saw a L
by the four living cr
its[a] of God sent out
on the throne.[11] And
before the Lamb. Ea
creatures[a] of the

JESUS IS ALWAYS ABLE TO OVERCOME

Chapter Twenty-Two

Key verses

- Verses 3-5: *No longer will there be any curse. The throne of God and of the Lamb will be in the city, and His servants will serve Him. They will see His face, and His name will be on their foreheads. There will be no more night. They will not need the light of a lamp or the light of the sun, for the Lord God will give them light. And they will reign for ever and ever.*

- Verse 7: *"Behold, I am coming soon! Blessed is he who keeps the words of the prophecy in this book."*

- Verses 10-11: *Then he told me, "Do not seal up the words of the prophecy of this book, because the time is near. Let him who does wrong continue to do wrong; let him who is vile continue to be vile; let him who does right continue to do right; and let him who is holy continue to be holy."*

- Verse 17: *The Spirit and the bride say, "Come!" And let him who hears say, "Come!" Whoever is thirsty, let him come; and whoever wishes, let him take the free gift of the water of life.*

- Verse 20: *He Who testifies to these things says, "Yes, I am coming soon."*

Words and phrases to know

- River: From the Greek word *potamos* which means "a stream, a river;) a torrent; floods."[1]

- Water: From the Greek word *hudor* which means "water."[2]

- Leaves: From the Greek word *phullon* which means "a leaf."[3]

- Healing: From the Greek word *therapeia* which means "service, rendered by any one to another; special medical service, curing, healing; by meteon. household, i.e., body of attendants, servants, domestics."[4]

- Near: From the Greek word *eggus* which means "near, of place and position; of time."[5]

- Soon: From the Greek word *tachu* which means "quickly, speedily (without delay)."[6]

- Wrong: From the Greek word *adikeo* which means "absolutely to act unjustly or wickedly, to sin, to be a criminal, to have violated the laws in some way, to do wrong, to do hurt; transitively, to do some wrong or sin in some respect, to wrong some one, act wickedly towards him, to hurt, damage, harm."[7]

- Vile: From the Greek word *rhupoo* which means "to make filthy, defile, soil; to be filthy (morally)."[8]

- Right: From the Greek word *dikaios* which means "righteous, observing divine laws."[9]

- Wash: From the Greek word *pluno* which means "to wash."[10]

- Robes: From the Greek word *stole* which means "equipment, apparel."[11]

<u>Revelation 22:1-6</u>

Then the angel showed me the river of the water of life, as clear as crystal, flowing from the throne of God and of the Lamb down the middle of the great street of the city. On each side of the river stood the tree of life, bearing twelve crops of fruit, yielding its fruit every month. And the leaves of the tree are for the healing of the nations. No longer will there be any curse. The throne of God and of the Lamb will be in the city, and His servants will serve Him. They will see His face, and His Name will be on their foreheads. There will be no more night. They will not need the light of a lamp or the light of the sun, for the Lord God will give them light. And they will reign for ever and ever.

The angel said to me, "These words are trustworthy and true. The Lord, the God of the spirits of the prophets, sent His angel to show His servants the things that must soon take place."

(Related Bible references: Psalm 9:7, Psalm 17:15, Isaiah 60:19, Ezekiel 47:1-23, Daniel 7:18, Zechariah 14:11, Matthew 4:14, Matthew 5:8, John 3:19, John 8:12, John 9:5, Titus 1:2, 1 John 1:5)

There are those who tell me they don't like reading the Bible, but they will read the book of Revelation. This doesn't make sense to me, as Revelation is the entire Bible. It is the revelation of history, of things past, present, and future, all concurrent in eternity. It takes us through the course of history in only twenty-two chapters. It ends, much as it began, praising and exalting the majesty of God. The water of life, flowing from the throne of God and the Lamb, echoes Ezekiel's prophecy:

In my vision, the man brought me back to the entrance of the Temple. There I saw a stream flowing east from beneath the door of the Temple and passing to the right of the altar on its south side. The man brought me outside the wall through the north gateway and led me around to the eastern entrance. There I could see the water flowing out through the south side of the east gateway.

Measuring as he went, he took me along the stream for 1,750 feet and then led me across. The water was up to my ankles. He measured off another 1,750 feet and led me across again. This time the water was up to my knees. After another 1,750 feet, it was up to my waist. Then he measured another 1,750 feet, and the river was too deep to walk across. It was deep enough to swim in, but too deep to walk through.

He asked me, "Have you been watching, son of man?" Then he led me back along the riverbank. When I returned, I was surprised by the sight of many trees growing on both sides of the river. Then he said to me, "This river flows east through the desert into the valley of the Dead Sea. The waters of this stream will make the salty waters of the Dead Sea fresh and pure. There will be swarms of living things wherever the water of this river flows. Fish will abound in the Dead Sea, for its waters will become fresh. Life will flourish wherever this water flows. Fishermen will stand along the shores of the Dead Sea. All the way from En-gedi to En-eglaim, the shores will be covered with nets drying in the sun. Fish of every kind will fill the Dead Sea, just as they fill the Mediterranean. But the marshes and swamps will not be purified; they will still be salty. Fruit trees of all kinds will grow along both sides of the river. The leaves of these trees will never turn brown and fall, and there will always be fruit on their branches. There will be a new crop every month, for they are watered by the river flowing from the Temple. The fruit will be for food and the leaves for healing."

This is what the Sovereign LORD says: "Divide the land in this way for the twelve tribes of Israel: The descendants of Joseph will be given two shares of land. Otherwise each tribe will receive an equal share. I took a solemn oath and swore that I would give this land to your ancestors, and it will now come to you as your possession.

"These are the boundaries of the land: The northern border will run from the Mediterranean toward Hethlon, then on through Lebo-hamath to Zedad; then it will run to Berothah and Sibraim which are on the border between Damascus and Hamath, and finally to Hazer-hatticon, on the border of Hauran. So the northern border will run from the Mediterranean to Hazar-enan, on the border between Hamath to the north and Damascus to the south.

"The eastern border starts at a point between Hauran and Damascus and runs south along the Jordan River between Israel and Gilead, past the Dead Sea and as far south as Tamar. This will be the eastern border.

"The southern border will go west from Tamar to the waters of Meribah at Kadesh and then follow the course of the Brook of Egypt to the Mediterranean. This will be the southern border.

"On the west side, the Mediterranean itself will be your border from the southern border to the point where the northern border begins, opposite Lebo-hamath.

"Divide the land within these boundaries among the tribes of Israel. Distribute the land as an allotment for yourselves and for the foreigners who have joined you and are raising their families among you. They will be like native-born Israelites to you and will receive an allotment among the tribes. These foreigners are to be given land within the territory of the tribe with whom they now live. I, the Sovereign LORD, have spoken!* (Ezekiel 47:1-23, NLT).

Water is used to signify all sorts of things in the Bible, including the Word of God, the Scriptures, and the Holy Spirit. It also signifies the essence of giving life, purification, spiritual refreshment and nourishment. It is obvious that deep into eternity, the world will still receive healing. It will still be receiving God's powerful balm of healing, along with the fruitful productivity that is needed to transform and bring hope. We see the world back to its state of Eden, heaven and earth as one, with a transformed atmosphere as well as transformed people. No longer is there a curse or sin, no longer is their pain or offense, no longer are there even sun or lamps. The light of the world (Matthew 4:14, John 3:19, John 8:12, John 9:5) will live with us and transform us.

It is a trustworthy promise that these things shall come about. Even though we may not understand every single detail of them right now, this side of the transformation, we can know and trust that God shall restore all things. If He can restore the entire world, He can restore each and every one of us...right where we are, right now. We can trust that we can walk with and dwell with Him, all the way throughout eternity and beyond.

Revelation 22:7-21

"Behold, I am coming soon! Blessed is he who keeps the words of the prophecy in this book."

I, John, am the one who heard and saw these things. And when I had heard and seen them, I fell down to worship at the feet of the angel who had been showing them to me. But he said to me, "Do not do it! I am a fellow servant with you and with your brothers the prophets and of all who keep the words of this book. Worship God!"

Then he told me, "Do not seal up the words of the prophecy of this book, because the time is near. Let him who does wrong continue to do wrong; let him who is vile continue to be vile; let him who does right continue to do right; let him who is holy continue to be holy."

"Behold, I am coming soon! My reward is with me, and I will give to everyone according to what he has done. I am the Alpha and the Omega, the First and the Last, the Beginning and the End.

"Blessed are those who wash their robes, that they may have the right to the tree of life and may go through the gates into the city. Outside are the dogs, those who practice magic arts, the sexually immoral, the murderers, the idolaters and everyone who loves and practices falsehood.

"I, Jesus, have sent My angel to give you this testimony for the churches. I am the Root and the Offspring of David, and the bright Morning Star."

The Spirit and the bride say, "Come!" And let him who hears say, "Come!" Whoever is thirsty, let him come; and whoever wishes, let him take the free gift of the water of life.

I warn everyone who hears the words of the prophecy of this book: If anyone adds anything to them, God will add to him the plagues described in this book. And if anyone takes words away from this book of prophecy, God will take away from him his share in the tree of life and in the holy city, which are described in this book.

He who testifies to these things says, "Yes, I am coming soon."

Amen. Come, Lord Jesus.

The grace of the Lord Jesus be with God's people. Amen.

(Related Bible references: Numbers 24:17, Psalm 29:2, Psalm 62:12, Isaiah 11:1-10, Isaiah 40:10, Isaiah 44:6, Isaiah 55:1-2, Jeremiah 23:5, Jeremiah 33:15, Daniel 12:10, Joel 2:28, John 4:14, John 7:37, John 13:17, Romans 2:6, Romans 5:1, Romans 13:11, 2 Corinthians 11:4, Galatians 5:20, Philippians 3:16, Colossians 3:9, Hebrews 11:6, 1 Peter 1:15, 1 John 4:7, Jude 1:10)

It's obvious that God's "soon" and our "soon" are not the same. Two thousand years ago, the believers of the first century believed "soon" would come to pass in their lifetime. Now, down through the ages, we know "soon" is closer than it was in the hour we first believed (Romans 13:11). Whether "soon" is tomorrow or "soon" is not for another thousand years should matter not in our faithfulness and devotion to Him. His reward comes with Him, and He is the beginning and the end. Jesus should be at the beginning of all we do, and right there, in the very end, right in accord with each and every prophecy we've received. It is He Who gave us these words, specifically for us, His churches. Even though we like to run around and try and inflict bits and pieces of them on the world unto conviction, it's clear that He has given us these words for our conviction, our repentance, our encouragement, and ultimately, our understanding. It is Jesus' desire that we would turn away from every action that will keep us out of the Kingdom and turn unto Him in a greater and more profound way, hear His testimony and His prophecy, and hear the Spirit call out to us, that we will be at the wedding supper of the Lamb. The water He offers is free; the banquet is free (Isaiah 55:1-2); and whoever wishes has the same freedom to come and receive in abundance, blessing of that abundant life.

Jesus does not encourage the prophecy of Revelation to be hidden. It is something that, throughout the ages, we are encouraged to return to, in every generation, and understand that we might receive hope. It speaks for itself, even though people have tried to put words in its mouth and make it speak things it often does not say. Those who do not want to keep the words of this book are not going to receive them in fancier packaging, by pressure or coercion, or by what we often call "hard preaching." It doesn't come about by fire and brimstone mentality. If anything, Revelation's words – if someone is wrong, let him be wrong – if he is vile, let him be vile – if he does right, let him do right – if he is holy, let him be holy – sums up the truth of the believer's life in a balanced way. We learn in Revelation that we are not responsible for other people's actions. We cannot make people do the right thing; even God doesn't force people to do the right thing. What we need to do is attend to ourselves. Leaders need to attend to their churches. Each of us needs to change the world, do what we can, each in the way we are able to and right where we are, with what we have.

Let us hear the Spirit calling. Let us see the whole of history, all that we can see now and all we can't, in Revelation's words to us. Even though we can't see it all with our physical eyes right now, it now is already real, in heaven, in the spirit realm. It is awaiting the right time to manifest this side of heaven, as the times, the days unfold. Let us hear the preparations each of us can make, and the changes and differences we can take, to show people the Kingdom of God is a reality right now that will be soon, someday visible to them all with their naked eyes. Let's uphold the words of the prophecy, not adding drama to them, nor taking away from their contents, but by living and being the message.

With that, amen, come, Lord Jesus. We are Your church, and we are waiting, as with each revelation You reveal more and more to us of all that is seen and unseen.

The Scroll and

5 Then I saw i
sealed[t] with
break the seals an
scroll or even loo
scroll or look insid
dah, the Root of Da

[6]Then I saw a La
by the four living cr
its[a] of God sent out
on the throne. [7]And
before the Lamb. Eac
[prayers][a] of the sain

JESUS IS ALWAYS ABLE TO OVERCOME

References

Opening Quotation

[1] "Hosanna." Hillsong United Lyrics.
http://www.azlyrics.com/lyrics/hillsongunited/hosanna.html.
Accessed June 4, 2015.

Introduction

"Book Of Revelation."
http://en.wikipedia.org/wiki/Book_of_Revelation. Accessed
January 23, 2015.

"John The Apostle."
http://en.wikipedia.org/wiki/John_the_Apostle. Accessed January
23, 2015.

Chapter 1

[1] Strong's Exhaustive Concordance of the Bible, #602
[2] Ibid., #1401
[3] Ibid., #32
[4] Ibid., #2491
[5] Ibid., #3056
[6] Ibid., # 3141
[7] Ibid., #3107
[8] Ibid., #314
[9] Ibid., #4394
[10] Ibid., #191
[11] Ibid., #5083
[12] Ibid., # 1125
[13] Ibid., # 2540
[14] Ibid., # 1451
[15] Ibid., #2033
[16] Ibid., #1577
[17] Ibid., #4151
[18] Ibid., #4103

[19] Ibid., #3144
[20] Ibid., #4416
[21] Ibid.,#3498
[22] Ibid., #935
[23] Ibid., #2409
[24] Ibid., #1
[25] Ibid., #5598
[26] Ibid., #5456
[27] Ibid., #4536
[28] Ibid., #991
[29] Ibid., #975
[30] Ibid., #5552
[31] Ibid., #3087
[32] Ibid., #2223
[33] Ibid., #5474
[34] Ibid., #792
[35] Ibid., #1366
[36] Ibid., #4501
[37] Ibid., #2246
[38] Ibid., #4413
[39] Ibid., #2078
[40] Ibid., #2807
[41] Ibid., #2288
[42] Ibid., #86
[43] Ibid., #3466
[44] Ibid., #602
[45] http://bibleandscience.com/bible/books/genesis/genesis1_beginning.htm. Accessed on January 25, 2015.
[46] Strong's Exhaustive Concordance of the Bible, #4853
[47] http://blogs.ancientfaith.com/orthogals/2014/12/03/the-sacred-and-the-secular/. Accessed on January 25, 2015.

Chapter 2

[1] Strong's Exhaustive Concordance of the Bible, #2179
[2] Ibid., #5281
[3] Ibid., #2556
[4] Ibid., #863
[5] Ibid., #26
[6] Ibid., #3340
[7] Ibid., #3531
[8] Ibid., #3586
[9] Ibid., #2222

[10] Ibid., #3857
[11] Ibid., #4668
[12] Ibid., #2347
[13] Ibid., #4432
[14] Ibid., #2453
[15] Ibid., #4864
[16] Ibid., #4567
[17] Ibid., #3958
[18] Ibid., #5438
[19] Ibid., #3985
[20] Ibid., #4735
[21] Ibid., #4010
[22] Ibid., #493
[23] Ibid., #1322
[24] Ibid., #903
[25] Ibid., #904
[26] Ibid., #1494
[27] Ibid., #4203
[28] Ibid., #3528
[29] Ibid., #2928
[30] Ibid., #3131
[31] Ibid., #3022
[32] Ibid., #5586
[33] Ibid., #3686
[34] Ibid., #2363
[35] Ibid., #1439
[36] Ibid., #2403
[37] Ibid., #4105
[38] Ibid., #2902
[39] Ibid., #1849
[40] Ibid., #4407
[41] Ibid., #792
[42] Ibid., #4668
[43] Ibid., #4010
[44] "Pergamum." http://www.bibleplaces.com/pergamum.htm. Accessed January 31, 2015.
[45] "Revelation Simplified." http://breadoflifeministriesassoc.blogspot.com/2015_04_01_arch ive.html. Accessed January 31, 2015.

Chapter 3

[1] Strong's Exhaustive Concordance of the Bible, #4554

[2] Ibid., #2198
[3] Ibid., #4741
[4] Ibid., #4137
[5] Ibid., #3435
[6] Ibid., #976
[7] Ibid., #2222
[8] Ibid., #5359
[9] Ibid., #40
[10] Ibid., #1411
[11] Ibid., #5610
[12] Ibid., #3986
[13] Ibid., #5035
[14] Ibid., #4769
[15] Ibid., #3485
[16] Ibid., #2537
[17] Ibid., #2419
[18] Ibid., #3772
[19] Ibid., #281
[20] Ibid., #2994
[21] Ibid., #5593
[22] Ibid., #2200
[23] Ibid., #5513
[24] Ibid., #4145
[25] Ibid., #5005
[26] Ibid., #1652
[27] Ibid., #4434
[28] Ibid., #5185
[29] Ibid., #1131
[30] Ibid., #1651
[31] Ibid., #3811
[32] Ibid., #2374
[33] Ibid., #2925
[34] Ibid., #172
[35] Ibid., #4554
[36] Ibid., #5359
[37] "Philadelphia: The Seven Churches of Revelation."
http://www.biblestudy.org/biblepic/churches-of-revelation-philadelphia.html. Accessed February 2, 2015.
[38] "The Church at Laodicea." http://wwcconline.org/links/7-churches/laodicea/. Accessed on February 2, 2015.

Chapter 4

[1] Strong's Exhaustive Concordance of the Bible, #3326
[2] Ibid., #5023
[3] Ibid., #2393
[4] Ibid., #4555
[5] Ibid., #2463
[6] Ibid., #4664
[7] Ibid., #5064
[8] Ibid., #1501
[9] Ibid., #4245
[10] Ibid., #2281
[11] Ibid., #5193
[12] Ibid., #2930
[13] Ibid., #2226
[14] Ibid., #3788
[15] Ibid., #3023
[16] Ibid., #3448
[17] Ibid., #4383
[18] Ibid., #5613
[19] Ibid., #444
[20] Ibid., #4072
[21] Ibid., #105
[22] Ibid., #4420
[23] Ibid., #514

Chapter 5

[1] Strong's Exhaustive Concordance of the Bible, #975
[2] Ibid., #4973
[3] Ibid., #3023
[4] Ibid., #4973
[5] Ibid., #5443
[6] Ibid., #2455
[7] Ibid., #4491
[8] Ibid., #1138
[9] Ibid., #3528
[10] Ibid., #721
[11] Ibid., #2768
[12] Ibid., #2788
[13] Ibid., #5357

[14] Ibid., #2368
[15] Ibid., #4335
[16] Ibid., #129
[17] Ibid., #5443
[18] Ibid., #1100
[19] Ibid., #2992
[20] Ibid., #1484
[21] Ibid., #936
[22] Ibid., #3461
[23] Ibid., #1411
[24] Ibid., #4149
[25] Ibid., #4678
[26] Ibid., #2479
[27] Ibid., #5092
[28] Ibid., #1391
[29] Ibid., #2129
[30] Ibid., #4352

Chapter 6

[1] Strong's Exhaustive Concordance of the Bible, #2064
[2] Ibid., # 3022
[3] Ibid., # 2462
[4] Ibid., #5115
[5] Ibid., #4450
[6] Ibid., #4969
[7] Ibid., 3189
[8] Ibid., #2218
[9] Ibid., #5518
[10] Ibid., #4621
[11] Ibid., #1220
[12] Ibid., #5140
[13] Ibid., #5518
[14] Ibid., #2915
[15] Ibid., #91
[16] Ibid., #1637
[17] Ibid., #3631
[18] Ibid., #5515
[19] Ibid., #2379
[20] Ibid., #5590

[21] Ibid., #2192
[22] Ibid., #2919
[23] Ibid., #1556
[24] Ibid., #373
[25] Ibid., #3398
[26] Ibid., #5550
[27] Ibid., #4137
[28] Ibid., #4578
[29] Ibid., #2246
[30] Ibid., #4582
[31] Ibid., #129
[32] Ibid., #3653
[33] Ibid., #2476
[34] Lambdin, Thomas O., from the Coptic Fragment. "Gospel of Thomas, The." http://www.sacred-texts.com/chr/thomas.htm. Available in the Public Domain. Accessed on February 3, 2015

Chapter 7

[1] Strong's Exhaustive Concordance of the Bible, #5064
[2] Ibid., #1137
[3] Ibid., #1093
[4] Ibid., #417
[5] Ibid., #91
[6] Ibid., #1540
[7] Ibid., #5062
[8] Ibid., #5064
[9] Ibid., #5505
[10] Ibid., #2474
[11] Ibid., #4183
[12] Ibid., #3793
[13] Ibid., #5404
[14] Ibid., #4991
[15] Ibid., #3173
[16] Ibid., #2347
[17] Ibid., #4637
[18] Ibid., #3983
[19] Ibid., #1372
[20] Ibid., #4165
[21] Ibid., #4077
[22] Ibid., #5204
[23] Ibid., #1813
[24] Ibid., #1144

[25] "Demographics of Atheism."
http://en.wikipedia.org/wiki/Demographics_of_atheism.
Accessed February 10, 2015.

Chapter 8

[1] Strong's Exhaustive Concordance of the Bible, #4602
[2] Ibid., #2256
[3] Ibid., #3031
[4] Ibid., #5464
[5] Ibid., #4442
[6] Ibid., #2618
[7] Ibid., #3735
[8] Ibid., #906
[9] Ibid., #5154
[10] Ibid., #894
[11] Ibid., #4087
[12] Ibid., #3759
[13] Marino, Lee Ann B. Notes and Assignments For: Exodus Typology And History. Raleigh, North Carolina: Apostolic University Press, January 2014.

Chapter 9

[1] Strong's Exhaustive Concordance of the Bible, #12
[2] Ibid., #2586
[3] Ibid., #2575
[4] Ibid., #200
[5] Ibid., #4651
[6] Ibid., #929
[7] Ibid., #4002
[8] Ibid., #3376
[9] Ibid., #2359
[10] Ibid., #1135
[11] Ibid., #3599
[12] Ibid., #2382
[13] Ibid., #4603
[14] Ibid., #3
[15] Ibid., #623
[16] Ibid., #3089
[17] Ibid., #2166
[18] Ibid., #2303
[19] Ibid., #1140

[20] "Euphrates." http://en.wikipedia.org/wiki/Euphrates. Accessed March 4, 2015.

Chapter 10

[1] Strong's Exhaustive Concordance of the Bible, #3507
[2] Ibid., #1027
[3] Ibid., #3660
[4] Ibid., #4396
[5] Ibid., #4087
[6] Ibid., #1099
[7] Ibid., #3192

Chapter 11

[1] Strong's Exhaustive Concordance of the Bible, #2563
[2] Ibid., #4464
[3] Ibid., #3354
[4] Ibid., #3485
[5] Ibid., #3961
[6] Ibid., #3144
[7] Ibid., #4526
[8] Ibid., #1636
[9] Ibid., #2342
[10] Ibid., #5463
[11] Ibid., #3408

Chapter 12

[1] Strong's Exhaustive Concordance of the Bible, #4592
[2] Ibid., #1135
[3] Ibid., #4016
[4] Ibid., #1722
[5] Ibid., #1064
[6] Ibid., #1404
[7] Ibid., #2719
[8] Ibid., #730
[9] Ibid., #5207
[10] Ibid., #2048
[11] Ibid., #4171
[12] Ibid., #3413
[13] Ibid., #4567
[14] Ibid., #2723

Chapter 13

[1] Strong's Exhaustive Concordance of the Bible, #1176
[2] Ibid., #2768
[3] Ibid., #2776
[4] Ibid., #988
[5] Ibid., #4969
[6] Ibid., #2296
[7] Ibid., #161
[8] Ibid., #5281
[9] Ibid., #4102
[10] Ibid., #3173
[11] Ibid., #4592
[12] Ibid., #1504
[13] Ibid., #5480
[14] Ibid., #3359
[15] Ibid., #3563
[16] Ibid., #5585
[17] Ibid., #5516
[18] "666 (number)." http://en.wikipedia.org/wiki/666_%28number%29. Accessed on March 15, 2015.
[19] "Gematria." http://en.wikipedia.org/wiki/Gematria. Accessed on March 15, 2015.

Chapter 14

[1] Strong's Exhaustive Concordance of the Bible, #4622
[2] Ibid., #2790
[3] Ibid., #3435
[4] Ibid., #536
[5] Ibid., #299
[6] Ibid., #4098
[7] Ibid., #897
[8] Ibid., #2372
[9] Ibid., #4202
[10] Ibid., #3709
[11] Ibid., #2326
[12] Ibid., #3583
[13] Ibid., #288
[14] Ibid., #3025

Chapter 15

[1] Strong's Exhaustive Concordance of the Bible, #2298
[2] Ibid., #3441
[3] Ibid., #319
[4] Ibid., #4633
[5] Ibid., #3142
[6] Ibid., #2986
[7] Ibid., #3043

Chapter 16

[1] Strong's Exhaustive Concordance of the Bible, #2556
[2] Ibid., #4190
[3] Ibid., #1668
[4] Ibid., #2739
[5] Ibid., #2812
[6] Ibid., #1127
[7] Ibid., #808
[8] Ibid., #717
[9] Ibid., #1096

Chapter 17

[1] Strong's Exhaustive Concordance of the Bible, #2917
[2] Ibid., #4204
[3] Ibid., #3184
[4] Ibid., #3384
[5] Ibid., #946
[6] Ibid., #3735

Chapter 18

[1] Strong's Exhaustive Concordance of the Bible, #3732
[2] Ibid., #1713
[3] Ibid., #4764
[4] Ibid., #4790
[5] Ibid., #266
[6] Ibid., #1363
[7] Ibid., #938
[8] Ibid., #5503
[9] Ibid., #3997
[10] Ibid., #1117

[11] Ibid., #696
[12] Ibid., #5093
[13] Ibid., #3037
[14] Ibid., #3135
[15] Ibid., #4209
[16] Ibid., #4596
[17] Ibid., #2847
[18] Ibid., #2367
[19] Ibid., #1661
[20] Ibid., #3139
[21] Ibid., #2792
[22] Ibid., #2368
[23] Ibid., #3030
[24] Ibid., #3464
[25] Ibid., #4585
[26] Ibid., #4263
[27] Ibid., #4983
[28] Ibid., #5590
[29] Ibid., #444
[30] Ibid., #3703
[31] Ibid., #2165
[32] Ibid., #3458
[33] Ibid., #906

Chapter 19

[1] Strong's Exhaustive Concordance of the Bible, #239
[2] Ibid., #1062
[3] Ibid., #1135
[4] Ibid., #2564
[5] Ibid., #1173
[6] Ibid., #3056
[7] Ibid., #2316

Chapter 20

[1] Strong's Exhaustive Concordance of the Bible, #1210
[2] Ibid., #5507
[3] Ibid., #2094
[4] Ibid., #386
[5] Ibid., #1136
[6] Ibid., #3098

Chapter 21

[1] Strong's Exhaustive Concordance of the Bible, #40
[2] Ibid., #4172
[3] Ibid., #435
[4] Ibid., #1169
[5] Ibid., #571
[6] Ibid., #948
[7] 5406
[8] Ibid., #4205
[9] Ibid., #5332
[10] Ibid., #1496
[11] Ibid., #5571
[12] Ibid., #5068
[13] Ibid., #4552
[14] Ibid., #5472
[15] Ibid., #4557
[16] Ibid., #5555
[17] Ibid., #969
[18] Ibid., #5116
[19] Ibid., #5556
[20] Ibid., #5192
[21] Ibid., #271
[22] Ibid., #4440

Chapter 22

[1] Strong's Exhaustive Concordance of the Bible, #4215
[2] Ibid., #5204
[3] Ibid., #5444
[4] Ibid., #2322
[5] Ibid., #5035
[6] Ibid., #1451
[7] Ibid., #91
[8] Ibid., #4510
[9] Ibid., #342
[10] Ibid., #4150
[11] Ibid., #4749

The Scroll and

5 Then I saw i
sealed† with
break the seals an
scroll or even lool
scroll or look insi
dah, the Root of Da

[6]Then I saw a La
by the four living cr
its* of God sent out
on the throne.†*And
before the Lamb. Ea
atures* of the anim

JESUS IS ALWAYS ABLE TO OVERCOME

About The Author

DR. LEE ANN B. MARINO, PH.D., D.MIN., D.D.

Dr. Lee Ann B. Marino, Ph.D., D.Min., D.D. (she/her) is "everyone's favorite theologian" leading Gen X, Millennials, and Gen Z with expertise in leadership training, queer and feminist theology, general religion, and apostolic theology. She has served in ministry since 1998 and was ordained as a pastor in 2002 and an apostle in 2010. She founded what is now Sanctuary Apostolic Fellowship Empowerment (SAFE) Ministries in 2004. Under her ministry heading Dr. Marino is founder and Overseer of Sanctuary International Fellowship Tabernacle (SIFT) (the original home of National Coming Out Sunday) and The Sanctuary Network, and Chancellor of Apostolic Covenant Theological Seminary (ACTS).

Affectionately nicknamed "the Spitfire," Dr. Marino has spent over two decades as an "apostle, preacher, and teacher" (2 Timothy 1:11), exercising her personal mandate to become "all things to all people" (1 Corinthians 9:22). Her embrace of spiritual issues (both technical and intimate) has found its home among both seekers and believers, those who desire spiritual answers to today's issues.

Dr. Marino has preached throughout the United States, Puerto Rico, and Europe in hundreds of religious services and experiences throughout the years. A history maker in her own right, she has spent over two decades in advocacy, education, and work for and within minority spiritual communities (including African American, Hispanic, and LGBTQ+). She has also served as the first woman on all-male synods, councils, and panels, as well as the first preacher or speaker welcomed of a different race, sexual orientation, or identity among diverse communities. Today, Dr. Marino's work extends to over 150 countries as she hosts the popular *Kingdom Now* podcast, which is in the top 20 percentile of all podcasts worldwide. She is also the author of over 35 books and the popular Patheos column, *Leadership on Fire.* To date, she has had five bestselling titles within their subject matter: *Understanding Demonology, Spiritual Warfare, Healing, and Deliverance: A Manual for the Christian Minister; Ministry School Boot Camp: Training for Helps Ministries, Appointments, and Beyond; Discovering Intimacy: A Journey Through the Song of Solomon; Fruit of the Vine: Study and Commentary on the Fruit of the Spirit;* and *Ministering to LGBTQ+ (and Those Who Love Them): A Primer for Queer Theology* (and its accompanying workbook).

As a public icon and social media influencer, Dr. Marino advocates healthy body image (curvy/full-figured), representation as a demisexual/aromantic, and albinism awareness as a model. Known to those she works with, she is a spiritual mom, teacher, leader, professor, confidant, and friend. She continues to transform, receiving new teaching, revelation, and insight in this thing we call "ministry." Through years of spiritual growth and maturity, Dr. Marino stands as herself, here to present what God has given to her for any who have an ear to hear.

For more information, visit her website at kingdompowernow.org.